LEIBNIZ & CLARKE

LEIBNIZ & CLARKE

A Study of Their Correspondence

Ezio Vailati

New York   Oxford   •   Oxford University Press   1997

Oxford University Press

Oxford   New York

Athens   Auckland   Bangkok   Bogota   Bombay   Buenos Aires
Calcutta   Cape Town   Dar es Salaam   Delhi   Florence   Hong Kong
Istanbul   Karachi   Kuala Lumpur   Madras   Madrid   Melbourne
Mexico City   Nairobi   Paris   Singapore   Taipei   Tokyo   Toronto   Warsaw

and associated companies in
Berlin   Ibadan

Copyright © 1997 by Ezio Vailati

Published by Oxford University Press, Inc.
198 Madison Avenue, New York, New York 10016

Oxford is a registered trademark of Oxford University Press

Library of Congress Cataloging-in-Publication Data
Vailati, Ezio.
Leibniz and Clarke : a study of their correspondence
/ Ezio Vailati.
p. cm.
Includes bibliographical references and index.
ISBN 0-19-511399-3
1. Leibniz, Gottfried Wilhelm, Freiherr von, 1646–1716.
2. Clarke, Samuel, 1675–1729.   3. Leibniz, Gottfried Wilhelm,
Freiherr von, 1646–1716—Correspondence.   4. Clarke, Samuel,
1675–1729. Collection of papers which passed between the late Mr.
Leibniz and Dr. Clarke in the years 1715 and 1716.   5. Clarke,
Samuel, 1675–1729—Correspondence.   6. Natural theology—History of
doctrines—18th century.   7. Metaphysics—History—18th century.
8. Physics—History—18th century.   I. Title.
B2598.V25 1997
193—dc21   96-45589

1   3   5   7   9   8   6   4   2

Printed in the United States of America
on acid-free paper

To my parents
ANNA AND FERMO

and to my wife
JULIE WARD

PREFACE

This book is about the philosophical exchange that occurred in the years 1715–16 between Leibniz, the great German philosopher, and Clarke, the greatest English theologian of his generation and the most gifted philosophical exponent of Newtonianism. It was a famous and heated debate that took place against the background of the quarrel between Leibniz and Newton on the invention of calculus and other mathematical and physical issues. It covered many topics, theological (e.g., divine immensity and eternity, and divine knowledge of the world), metaphysical (e.g., space and time, and the extension of the soul), and physical (e.g., motive force and gravitation). However, its focus was natural religion, to which Leibniz and Clarke, like so many of their contemporaries, connected theology, physics, and metaphysics.

Both Leibniz and Clarke were concerned with the advance of naturalism and worried that the corrosion of natural religion would bring about the downfall of morality. Both devised systems encompassing philosophical, theological, and physical views that attempted to counter naturalism and reinforce natural religion. However, they not only deeply disagreed on how to answer the naturalist threat, but ended up by seeing in each other's views the germs of naturalism itself. This book tries to disentangle the various strands of the debate and illustrate this internecine fight within the antinaturalist camp.

I could not have written this work had I not had access to higher education. My gratitude goes to those Italians whose economic and political struggles made college education widely available in time for me to take advantage of it. I pursued my Ph.D. at the University of California at San Diego, and to that institution and to the people of California I owe special thanks. This book was started during the tenure of an Andrew W. Mellon fellowship at Cornell University in 1990–91 and finished during the tenure of an NEH fellowship in 1996. I am grateful to the Andrew W. Mellon Foundation, to the Sage School of Philosophy at Cornell, and to the National Endowment for the Humanities for allowing me to pursue my research. In my work I have incurred debts to various people. My interest in Clarke was awakened by John Perry, who with Bill Uzgalis and Trip McCrossin, organized a Clarke reading group at Stanford. Allen Wood read many of the chapters and provided prompt, clear, and helpful comments. Nicholas Jolley read the full manuscript and gave valuable suggestions. Julie Ward has been a judicious critic, and my colleagues at Southern Illinois University at Edwardsville have helped me in many ways. I should also like to thank two anonymous referees for their criticisms.

Parts of chapters 2 and 5 draw on material from "Clarke's Extended Soul," *Journal of the History of Philosophy* 31 (1993): 387–403, and "Leibniz and Clarke on Miracles," *Journal of the History of Philosophy* 33 (1995): 563–92. I am grateful to the editor and publisher for permission to reprint.

Finally, I want to thank the staff at Oxford University Press, and especially Cynthia Read, Jessica Ryan, and Michele McEnroe, for their expert assistance.

CONTENTS

ABBREVIATIONS

A   *Leibniz, Sämtliche Schriften und Briefe. Heraugegeben von der Deutschen Akademie der Wissenschaften zu Berlin.* Darmstadt and Berlin: Berlin Academy, 1923–, followed by series, volume, and page.

C   Couturat, L., ed. *Opuscules et Fragments inédits de Leibniz.* Paris: Presses Universitaires de France, 1903. Reprint, Hildesheim: G. Olms, 1966, followed by page.

CI   Clarke's letter to Leibniz, followed by letter number and section.

GM   Gerhardt, C. I., ed. *Die Mathematischen Schriften von G. W. Leibniz.* Berlin, 1875–90. Reprint, Hildesheim: G. Olms, 1963, followed by volume and page.

GP   Gerhard, C. I., ed. *Die Philosophischen Schriften von G. W. Leibniz.* Berlin: 1875–90. Reprint, Hildesheim: G. Olms, 1961, followed by volume and page.

Grua   Grua, G., ed. *G.W. Leibniz. Textes Inédits.* Paris: Presses Universitaires de France. Reprint, New York: Garland Publishing, 1985, followed by page.

KLC   Klopp, O., ed. *Die Werke von Leibniz*. Reihe I, Bd. XI (*Correspondenz mit Caroline*) Hanover, 1864–84. Reprint, Hildesheim: G. Olms, 1973, followed by page.

L   Loemker, L., ed. and trans. *G. W. Leibniz: Philosophical Papers and Letters*. 2d ed. Dordrecht: D. Reidel, 1976, followed by page.

Lz   Leibniz's letter to Clarke, followed by letter number and section.

NC   Turnbull, H. W., J. F. Scott, A. R. Hall, and L. Tilling, eds. *The Correspondence of Isaac Newton*. Cambridge: Cambridge University Press, 1959–77, followed by volume and page.

NE   Remnant, P., and J. Bennett, ed. and trans. *G. W. Leibniz: New Essays on Human Understanding*. Cambridge: Cambridge University Press, 1981, followed by book, chapter, and section.

NO   Newton, I. *Optice: sive de Reflexionibus, Refractionibus & Coloribus Lucis libri tres*. Translated by S. Clarke. London, 1706, followed by page.

NP   Newton, I. *Isaac Newton's Philosophiae Naturalis Principia Mathematica. The Third Edition (1726) with Variant Readings*. Edited by A. Koyré and I. B. Cohen. Cambridge, Mass: Harvard University Press, 1972, followed by book, section, proposition and page.

R   Robinet, A., ed. *Correspondance Leibniz-Clarke presentée d'apres les manuscripts originaux des bibliothéques de Hanovre et de Londres*. Paris: Presses Universitaires de France, 1957, followed by page.

W   Clarke, S. *The Works*. 1738. Reprint, New York: Garland Publishing, 1978, followed by volume and page.

WB   Clarke, S. *A Demonstration of the Being and Attributes of God*. In W II, 521–77, followed by page.

WN   Clarke, S. *A Discourse Concerning the Unchangeable Obligations of Natural Religion and the Truth and Certainty of Christian Revelation*. In W II, 580–733, followed by page.

LEIBNIZ & CLARKE

INTRODUCTION

The correspondence between Leibniz and Clarke (1715–16), in which they pitted their views against each other through the mediation of Caroline, Princess of Wales, was probably the most famous and influential philosophical exchange of the eighteenth century.[1] It covered many central metaphysical and theological topics, such as divine immensity and eternity, the relation of God to the world, the soul and its relation to the body, free will, space and time, and the nature of miracles. It also discussed more strictly scientific issues, such as the nature of matter, the existence of atoms and the void, the size of the universe, and the nature of motive force, which were then often given both a philosophical and a scientific treatment.

News of the exchange between Leibniz and Clarke spread quickly through Leibniz's letters to some of his correspondents (including the mathematician and physicist Johann Bernoulli, the philosopher Christian Wolff, and savants such as Rémond and Bourguet), and through the reviews of its various editions in leading journals like the *Acta Eruditorum* (1717), the *Nouvelles de la République des Lettres* (1718), the *Journal des Savants* (1721). Parts of it were discussed by important eighteenth-century figures including, among others, McLaurin, Voltaire, and Euler, and it probably influenced Kant's analysis of the Antinomies.[2] Even some contemporary discussions of some of the topics it dealt with not only refer to, but also tackle some its arguments, once stripped of their theological clothing.[3] However, in spite of the theoretical and historical significance of the correspondence, no full length monograph on it exists, although there are a few articles on some of its aspects. This neglect is unfortunate because Clarke and Leibniz were systematic philosophers whose views can only be appreciated in the context of others discussed in the correspondence or elsewhere.

One of the main reasons for such surprising neglect, I suspect, arises from the combination of two factors: the notorious obscurity of Newton's theological and metaphysical views, and the historical judgment that Clarke was little more than Newton's mouthpiece, and that consequently, the Leibniz-Clarke correspondence was really the Leibniz-Newton correspondence. However, while Newton's views are certainly obscure, this historical judgment should be challenged for two reasons.

First, the documentary evidence about Newton's role in the correspondence is scant at best. There are neither drafts of Clarke's letters to Leibniz by Newton nor letters between Clarke and Newton that might help in assessing the latter's role in the correspondence. Since Clarke was Newton's parish priest at St. James's, Piccadilly, they were neighbors, which rendered epistolary exchanges unlikely.[4] Indeed, as the editors of Newton's correspondence note, "Samuel Clarke nowhere figures even indirectly in Newton's correspondence" (NC VI, xxx).

We know that Newton played some indirect role in the correspondence. There is a copy in Newton's hand of the postscript on atoms and void to Clarke's fourth letter, and almost certainly Clarke consulted some of his papers in drafting the physical arguments that make up much of the notes to his fifth letter; but whether Newton played a direct role, and if so what its extent and depth were, is unclear at best. To be sure, since Caroline thought that Clarke's answers were "not written without the advice of the *Chevalier* Newton," it is probable that Clarke and Newton discussed some of the answers to Leibniz (To Leibniz, 10 January 1716: KLC 71). However, Newton seemed to have little conceptual interest in Leibniz's metaphysical attacks, which he saw as mere "railery" irrelevant to the real bone of contention between them (To Conti, 26 February 1716: NC VI, 285, 460 n. 8).[5] It is, therefore, unlikely that he stood behind Clarke's shoulders as the letters were drafted, as it were.[6]

Second, and more important, viewing Clarke as little more than Newton's mouthpiece does him injustice. To be sure, Clarke's views were said by Whiston to coincide with Newton's, and there is no doubt that Newton's influence on Clarke was great.[7] However, all the philosophical positions and most of the arguments Clarke aired in the correspondence had appeared in his 1705–6 Boyle Lectures, in previous epistolary exchanges with Collins (1707–8) and Butler (1714–5), and in philosophical sermons. Clarke had not only sufficient competence in physics to translate Newton's *Optikcs* into Latin in 1706, but also, and more important, he was the most gifted Newtonian philosopher of his generation, described by Voltaire, who met him, as "a veritable thinking machine."[8] A reading of his works shows that Clarke was a clear and systematic thinker capable of holding his ground against Leibniz. In this respect, his philosophical relation to Newton was, at most, analogous to the relation between Johann Bernoulli and Leibniz, not to that between, say, Keill and Newton. One can, indeed one should, view the correspondence essentially as a confrontation between Leibniz and Clarke, the most important philosophical exponent of Newtonianism.

Clarke's basic philosophical interests were theological and, to a lesser degree, metaphysical; epistemology seems to have held little attraction for him. His philosophical vocabulary and basic ontology were influenced by Descartes: the world contains two types of substance, mind and matter. We humans are a combination of mind and body and, like our creator, endowed with a contra-causal free will whose existence we can ascertain introspectively. Although he conceded to Locke that the substratum of things is unknown and agreed with More, against Descartes, that the soul is extended and is not present to the body merely by operation, he claimed that the attributes of matter are demonstrably incompatible with consciousness, and that therefore not even God can endow matter with it (W III, 730, 763 ff., 841). Clarke's disagreement with Descartes, however, went beyond the topic of the soul, involving a mixture of interconnected metaphysical and theological objections. He held that the Cartesian views that matter is infinite and eternal (Clarke thought that by making extension the essence of matter Descartes had de facto identified space with matter), that the behavior of all bodies can be explained mechanically, that final causes ought to be expunged from physics, and that the divine will, intelligence, and providence are removed from the "governement of the world," had been deleterious to religion (To Butler, 8 April 1714: W II, 750).

The origins of the Leibniz-Clarke correspondence lay in the confrontation between Leibniz and Newton, which by 1715 involved science and philosophy, not to mention bruised egos. The genesis of Newton's suspicions that Leibniz had plagiarized his work is unclear. In October 1693 he could still write Leibniz a friendly letter, and in spite of early turbulence between the Newtonians Fatio and Cheyne and Leibniz, the official inception of the dispute was in 1710 with Keill's (wrong) accusation in the 1708 *Philosophical Transactions* (which came out in 1710) that Leibniz had plagiarized Newton's work on calculus (NC III, 285–86). What moved Keill to such a deliberate provocation is unclear, but Hall has argued that probably he was reacting to the frequent criticisms of attractive forces by Leibnizians in the *Acta Eruditorum*, on which Leibniz had considerable influence.[9]

Leibniz had always been opposed to attractive forces and felt free privately to criticize Newton's centripetal forces in his correspondence with Huygens (October 1690. NC III, 80). He also saw a dangerous link between Newtonian attraction and mortalism, the view that the soul is naturally mortal, or even outright materialism, as he clearly indicated in the (unpublished) *New Essays* and related correspondence critical of Locke.[10] At last, in 1710, he openly criticized Newtonian gravitation in the *Theodicy* as involving action at a distance (Preliminary Discourse § 19: GP VI, 61–62).

When Leibniz became aware of Keill's charges, he tried to get redress from the Royal Society, which in turn asked Keill to state his account of the affair, and in May 1711 communicated his letter to Leibniz. Being dissatisfied with it, Leibniz appealed again to the Royal Society, which appointed a committee that at the beginning of 1713 issued a report, the *Commercium Epistolicum*, written by none other than Newton himself, in effect condemning Leibniz. In the meantime, Leibniz had renewed his attacks against Newtonian gravity in an open letter to Hartsoeker printed in 1712 (GP III, 516–21). Although Newton prepared a draft for a direct answer, the reply came in Cotes's preface to the second (1713) edition of *Principia*: those who challenge Newtonian forces must clearly explain what is wrong with them; as for the plenists (read Leibniz), they should make sure to avoid Spinozistic materialism (NC V, 298–300; NP, editor's preface, 33).

Leibniz's anonymous answer to the Royal Society's report was the so-called *Charta volans*, published at the end of 1713 by Wolff in the *Journal littéraire* in The Hague, in which he charged Newton with having little mastery of the calculus, perhaps because the calculus of fluxions had been developed in imitation of his own, providing as evidence an error in *Principia*, book 2, proposition 10. (The error had been pointed out to him by Johann Bernoulli, who had required anonymity and had mistakenly attributed it to Newton's mishandling of higher differentials). Keill's riposte in the same journal in the autumn of the following year was based on material written by Newton and (wrongly) attacked Leibniz's *Tentamen Anagogicum*, a paper on planetary motion, as being absurd and involving basic mistakes in the handling of higher differentials. (This time, however, Newton's animosity against Leibniz was justified: his suspicion that Leibniz had plagiarized sections of the *Principia* was correct).[11] In spite of pressures from Wolff, Leibniz chose not to reply to Keill, whom he considered a rude country-bumpkin. Even an indirect further exchange in the Spring of 1716 between Leibniz and Newton prompted by Caroline (through Conti's mediation) failed to end the dispute.[12]

On the scientific front, Leibniz had been put on the defensive. The Royal Society, albeit unfairly, had in effect sided with Newton on the priority dispute about calculus, and Leibniz's failure to answer Keill's recent attacks did not help him. But more important, Leibniz was probably aware that his physical work, interesting as it was, paled with respect to Newton's. It was in this context that Leibniz's piqued sense of honor gave rise to the exchange with Clarke.

For some time, Leibniz had wanted to leave Hanover and move to a city like Paris or London rich with intellectual life (To Burnett, 17 March 1696: GP III, 175). He must then have been pleased at Caroline's desire that he accompany her to London in October 1714. Unfortunately, in spite of having some of his mail delivered there, perhaps because of ill health he was unable to go.[13] However, in late October or early November 1714, he wrote to Caroline and Minister von Bernstorff of his intention of bringing near completion a major part of his history of the House of Brunswick. At the same time, he requested help in convincing the king to give him "the honor and the pension" of Historian of Great Britain, a reasonable request, he noted, since he often had to touch on the history of England (KLC 20). Both Caroline and von Bernstorff pursued Leibniz's cause and told him that once the king could see with his own eyes a part of the history of the House of Brunswick, it would not be difficult to obtain what he wanted (KLC 34, 36).

Leibniz was not pleased with such conditional replies and told Caroline that what pushed him to obtain the position was "in good part a point of honor. I would not like to concede anything to a certain opponent which the English have put in my mind. Perhaps Your Royal Highness knows that it is the *Chevalier* Newton, who has a pension from the King because of his oversight of the Mint which the King has assigned to him" (KLC 37–38). Leibniz continued by trying to link the calculus controversy to the political and dy-

nastical events of the last years: it was started when the relations
between the British and Hanoverian courts were not cordial, by some
Messieurs rigides, contextually identified as Newtonians, who being
little favorable to Hanover pushed it to such an extent that it could
be taken to resemble more a controversy between England and Germany than between Newton and Leibniz.[14] Hence, giving Leibniz
the same honors attributed to Newton would be a good way to honor
Hanover and Germany.

Leibniz continued by attacking Newton's gravitation, again ma-
liciously taken to be action at a distance, as unintelligible but accepted by *ces Messieurs* who seemed to agree with Locke (whom
Caroline had just read and criticized), in holding that everything is
corporeal, matter can think, and other similar views corrosive of
religion. Newton was a man of very great merit, but he dealt unfairly
with Leibniz: "il est mon rival—Leibniz self-righteously commented—c'est tout dire" (KLC 38–40). A few months later, these
same accusations were repeated and amplified in the letter to Caroline, that she showed to Clarke, the court chaplain and a man of
great reputation who had been recommended to her by the bishop
of Lincoln as the best person to translate the *Theodicy* into English
(Lz I; Caroline to Leibniz, 15 November 1715: KLC 49–50). Clarke's
reply started the Leibniz-Clarke correspondence. On the defensive
on the scientific front, Leibniz had decided to renew his attacks on
the metaphysical and theological front by reproposing and aug-
menting his criticisms expressed in the *Theodicy*.[15]

The correspondence to a large extent overcame its rather unpromising origin. In spite of the great number of issues discussed,
both Leibniz and Clarke perceived their exchange as revolving
around natural religion, a topic of great concern to them. Both
thought that natural religion was under attack by naturalism (the
view that nature constitutes a self-sufficient system of which we are
but a part), which had been revived by Hobbes and, especially, Spinoza. Both came to its defense by appealing to philosophy and science alike. Nevertheless, their exchange culminated in open and
often pointed opposition springing from a disagreement on how to
deal with naturalism. Of course, both denied that nature is a self-
sufficient system encompassing humans, but they disagreed on the
grounds for such a denial.

Clarke's attack against naturalism revolved around four connected points. First, matter is spatio-temporally finite, and being endowed only with the *vis inertiae* it has no power of self-motion (WN
697). Second, God is substantially present in nature (or better, nature

is literally in God, since space and time are divine attributes) and constantly exercises his power by applying attractive (e.g., gravitational) and repulsive forces to bodies (W II, 792). With the exception of the law of inertia, which describes the essentially passive nature of matter, strictly speaking the laws of nature (e.g., Newton's inverse law) do not describe the behavior of matter, which is just dead mass constantly pushed around, but modalities of operation of the divine power; as for Occasionalism, they prescribe the actions of the divine will rather than describe those of bodies (WN 601, 697–98). Third, nature and its laws are radically contingent. God, endowed with a libertarian contra-causal will, chose to create the world and operate in it by a reasonable but uncaused fiat (WB 552–53, 565). Fourth, although the soul is extended and interacts with the body, it is necessarily immaterial because matter, being constituted of *partes extra partes*, cannot possibly think even by divine intervention (W III, 730, 763). The first three points guaranteed that nature is not a self-sufficient system, so much so that without direct and constant divine physical intervention planets would fly away from their orbits, atoms would break into their components, and the machinery of the world would literally grind to a halt; the fourth guaranteed that the soul is not a part of nature. The first two points were mainly grounded in Newtonian physics; the second two mainly in Clarke's metaphysics.

Leibniz, by contrast, having (rather unclearly) reduced matter to a "well-founded phenomenon," had no qualms in attributing to bodies a motive power arising from the activity of their component monads (*De Causa Gravitatis*: GM VI, 202; *Specimen Dynamicum*: GM VI, 235). He agreed that God is present in the world, but operationally rather than substantially, and metaphysically rather than physically: God is an *intelligentia supramundana* who has no business in pulling and pushing bodies like a stevedore. Rather, as for many Scholastics, God keeps an active nature in existence by continually conserving it (Lz II, 5–12). He agreed that nature and its laws are contingent, but denied to God a libertarian contra-causal will, and claimed that the laws of nature are not prescriptive to the divine will, but descriptive of the operations of the active natures God placed in things (*De Ipsa Natura*: GP IV, 504–16). He agreed that the soul is immaterial, but strongly denied that it is extended and that it interacts with the body (*Monadology*: GP VI, 607–23). The first three points guaranteed that nature is not a self-sufficient system (indeed, strictly speaking, matter is not even a substance); the fourth guaranteed that the soul is not a part of nature.

Clarke and Leibniz viewed their respective antinaturalist theories with deep suspicion. For Clarke, Leibniz had separated God from nature both too much and too little. Too much in making God an *intelligentia supramundana* and nature a mechanism that never needs rewinding, thus starting down the slippery slope leading to the independence of nature from God (Cl I, 3–4). Too little in denying a contra-causal libertarian will to God, thus making nature the inevitable outcome of the divine essence (Cl IV, 1–2). The result, then, was a view that failed to provide a solid ground for the radical contingency of nature. Clarke's suspicions were confirmed by Leibniz's attribution of activity to matter, his claims that matter is infinite in extension and that motive force is conserved, and the identification of motive force with *vis viva*, which Clarke traced to Leibniz's alleged belief that every part of matter is ensouled and can be considered a corporeal substance and, hence, potentially endowed with consciousness (Cl IV, 21–23; WB 546, 562; W IV, 738).

Leibniz thought that Clarke had tied God and nature too closely, thus debasing the divinity. God's constant physical intervention showed him a bad engineer, unable to produce a self-moving nature; God's spatio-temporal presence and literal dimensionality destroyed divine simplicity; God's placement of nature in necessarily arbitrary spatio-temporal coordinates by mere fiat was an unwarranted fiction which, if true, would turn the divinity into an irrational being. Leibniz's suspicions were confirmed by Clarke's insistence that divine thoughts, like ours, are successive and that God cognizes what is in space (the world) in a way analogous to that in which the soul cognizes what is in the *sensorium*, the space that the soul occupies or, worse, the organ of perception.

The Leibniz-Clarke correspondence has been translated in all major European languages and in some non-European as well, including Chinese and Japanese. I have primarily used four editions: Clarke's own edition in W IV, 575–710; *The Leibniz-Clarke Correspondence: With Extracts from Newton's "Principia" and "Opticks,"* edited by H. G. Alexander (Manchester: Manchester University Press, 1956); *Correspondance Leibniz-Clarke présentée d'apres les manuscripts originaux des bibliothéques de Hanovre et de Londres*, edited by A. Robinet (Paris: Presses Universitaires de France, 1957); *Der Leibniz-Clarke Briefwechsel*, edited and translated by V. Schüller (Berlin: Akademie Verlag, 1991). Each edition has advantages and drawbacks, which can be noted by considering the following components that an ideal edition should, in my opinion, have: the text of the letters, Clarke's appendix containing excerpts from Leibniz's works, Leibniz's drafts of the letters (Clarke's do not survive), Clarke's marginal references to the appendix and direct references to the letters in later editions of other works, and finally, related material, such as, letters to Caroline, passages from Newton's and Lebiniz's works, and contemporary reviews. Of course, all four editions have the text of the letters and some related material (Schüller's edition has a great wealth of related material), but Robinet's misses Clarke's appendix. It has, however, Leibniz's drafts, which the other three lack. Of course, Clarke's edition has his marginal notes, which the other three lack. No edition has Clarke's direct references to the letters in other works. In general, the best course of action is to use all four editions, complementing their strengths and obviating their weaknesses.

Before launching into an examination of the correspondence it may be helpful to give its outline. Leibniz wanted to write an account of the correspondence for *Acta Eruditorum*, but he never did (To Erskine, 22 June 1716: NC VI, 358). However, a contemporary summary was provided by the anonymous reviewer (probably Wolff) of Clarke's edition in the October 1717 issue of the same journal.[16] The review is clearly partisan, but since it highlights many of the points of contention, I provide a rather free translation of the relevant parts.

> At the beginning of this collection is an excerpt from a letter . . . to Her Highness the Princess of Wales. Leibniz laments the worsening of the state of natural religion in England, since many imagine the soul corporeal and others claim that even God is corporeal. He thinks that Locke and his followers at least doubt the soul's immateriality, and that Newton in the appendix to *Optice* claims that space is the divine *sensorium*, which entails that the world is neither dependent on, nor is the production of, God. Leibniz also reproaches Newton for claiming that things need correction by extraordinary divine concourse in the world's machine (a view of those who do not discern the human from the divine).
>
> Defending Newton's views, Clarke states that for Newton God does not use space as an organ of perception but perceives everything because of his presence everywhere. Newton, he continues, considers the brain and the sensory organs the mediums through which the images present to the mind are formed, not the mediums through which the mind perceives them. Attacking Leibniz's view, he objects that if the world is taken to be a machine and motion to continue without divine intervention, then one introduces fatality, and that if Leibniz declares God an *intelligentia supramundana*, he eliminates divine providence and makes the world eternal.

In his second letter ... Leibniz replies that mere presence is not sufficient for perception, that God perceives things in the world not through mere presence but through operation, and that *"sensorium"* has always meant 'the organ of sensation.' He claims that divine providence is not eliminated but confirmed by the fact that in the world's machine everything occurs by preestablished design without the need of any correction, since it entails that God has foreseen and predetermined everything. For if there is a need for correction, then either God must be the soul of the world, or the correction must occur supernaturally, and therefore miraculously. Moreover, at the beginning of his letter, Leibniz notes that the foundation of Mathematics from which the whole of Arithmetic and Geometry can be demonstrated is the Principle of Contradiction or Identity, namely that the same statement cannot be true and false at the same time. However, he continues, in Physics and Metaphysics one must add the Principle of Sufficient Reason, which allows to demonstrate almost the whole of Metaphysics and even the principles of Dynamics.

In his second reply, Clarke ... acknowledges that nothing happens without a sufficient reason why it happens rather than not. But this reason can be the mere will of God, for example as when one asks why this body has been placed by God in this location rather than another. He adds that if the divine will could not act but by being predetermined by another cause, it would not be free, and therefore fatality would be introduced. He denies supposing that mere substantial presence is sufficient for perception; he rather holds that in addition the substance must be alive. Hence, God perceives things neither by mere presence nor by operation, but by being present to them, and in addition alive and intelligent. He adds that the word "correction" must be understood not with respect to God but with respect to us, and claims that the word *"sensorium"* denotes not the organ but the place of sensation. Finally, he attacks Leibniz's characterization of what is done by God as miraculous because it eliminates divine rule from the universe.

There follows Leibniz's third letter, which from the beginning shows that Clarke has not understood the Principle of Sufficient Reason. In fact, a decision without an inclining reason is incompatible with this Principle. Leibniz points out that the example given by Clarke is based on a chimerical notion of space, which some contemporary English, and most people, consider an absolute entity, while in reality it is but a mere relative entity, namely, the order of coexistences, as time is that of successions. Without doubt the Principle of Sufficient Reason abundantly shows that space and time cannot be absolute entities. In fact, since they are uniform, no reason can be given why bodies are placed in this rather than that location, or why the positions are not reversed, or why things have not been created by God a year earlier or later. But according to Leibniz's view of space and time, no reason is needed why things are not placed in inverted positions because the two states are indiscernible, and consequently no reason can be given why one should be preferred to the other.

Leibniz claims that the fatality Clarke fears is the best order of providence, for brute necessity is avoided when a wise choice occurs. As for the meaning of the word "*sensorium*" he refers to Rudolf Glocenius, who in his philosophical dictionary defines "*sensorium*" as the organ of sensation. He also denies that the simple presence of an intelligent substance is sufficient for perception, giving the counterexample of a blind or distracted man who does not see. God is present to things not by situation but by essence, and his presence is shown by immediate operation; by contrast, the presence of the soul is altogether different. That the natural and the supernatural do not differ with respect to God, a view Clarke takes from Locke and Locke from Spinoza, will not be approved by theologians, continues Leibniz, agreeing with them in considering miraculous what exceeds the natural power of bodies.

In his third letter, Clarke replies that even if space were but the order of coexisting things, there would be no reason but the divine will for a body's placement in this rather than that space, and therefore no argument is here given against the absolute reality of space. Clarke seems to have convinced himself of the falsity of Leibniz's view when he says that it entails that the Sun and the Moon would be in the same place they are now even if they were recreated where now the fixed stars are, and that the world moved from its place would still be in it. He believes to have shown the same about the Leibnizian notion of time when he claims that it entails that God could not have created the world earlier even if one supposes him to have created it some millennia before he actually did.

Clarke adds that if there should always be an external reason for the divine will's determination to action, then God would be determined like a machine. After close consideration, he admits that God could be called an *intelligentia supramundana* in the Leibnizian sense. However, he himself a theologian, does not accept the notion of miracle generally used by theologians (a fact which would be amazing if it did not stem from his prejudice in favor of Locke's authority), which he deems false because it would seem to entail that animal motions are miraculous.

In his fourth letter, Leibniz claims that a mere will without a motive is fictitious and contradictory, as he has amply shown in the *Theodicy*: choice does not take place among indifferent things because there is no reason why one should be preferred to the other. Moreover, he claims that indiscernibles are not given, and that the Principle of the Identity of Indiscernibles, which destroys atoms, should be added to that of Sufficient Reason if one wants real notions and demonstrations in metaphysics. The same principle is used to show that the notion of this universe in another place or time is an impossible fiction. In addition, he shows that God is not determined by an external cause because he was determined by his understanding before things existed. He also points out the difference between the cognitions of God and soul, since the former knows things because he produces them, while the latter knows them because God has placed in it a representative principle of what is external to it.

Leibniz argues that the notion of miracle as anomalous occurrence is wrong because otherwise strange events would be considered miracles, and he does not see why animal motions should be inexplicable in terms of natural forces. He adds a *postscriptum* showing the absurdity of atoms and the void from the notion of divine perfection and the Principle of Sufficient Reason. Assuming God has given things every perfection which could be given without prejudice to others, Leibniz infers both the plenum and the infinite division of every corpuscle, so that each contains an entire universe of new creatures. Secondly, he assumes that there is no principle determining a ratio between the plenum and the vacuum. In fact, as matter is more perfect than the vacuum, there should be a geometrical proportion so that the quantity of matter exceeds that of vacuum as the perfection of the former exceeds that of the latter. But matter is to the vacuum as something is to nothing. Hence, there is no vacuum. Similarly, he argues that there is no reason why the force of nature could be terminated in the progression of subdivision.

As Clarke's fourth answer adds little to the issues and shows he does not understand the force of the Leibnizian principles, intending to see whether his opponent is moved by the love of truth or the desire to contradict, Leibniz explains everything more distinctly and at greater length. Hence, he shows the difference between physical and moral necessity already clearly explained in the famous *Theodicy*. He elegantly demonstrates how neither divine foreknowledge and providence nor moral necessity destroy liberty, and why the motive does not necessitate since the opposite is possible as well. Leibniz obtains moral necessity from the Principle of Sufficient Reason, but metaphysical necessity from the Principle of Identity or Contradiction, and declares Christian Fate the decree of divine providence, distinguishing it from Mohammedan and Stoic fate. By "motive" he understands all the dispositions a spirit can have by which it can act freely, namely not only reasons, but also inclinations arising from passions or previous impressions.

Leibniz does not admit simple or indiscernible bodies, which he claims result from the wrong positing of atoms and the void, or the *lazy philosophy* which, not proceeding sufficiently deeply into analysis, believes to have arrived at the first elements. He claims that indiscernible bodies are not absolutely impossible; however, by the Principle of Sufficient Reason he shows they cannot exist because of the power of the divine wisdom, while mere mathematicians, dealing only with figments of the imagination, can admit a real space beyond the material world. He locates the cause of resistance not in the quantity of matter, but in the difficulty with which it gives way: for example, floating timber contains less matter than an equal volume of water, and yet it offers more resistance to a ship.

Leibniz also shows that the consideration of the situation (and its changes) among things is sufficient to form the notion of space, and that there is no need to assume the reality of anything beyond the things the situation among which is considered. He then obtains the nominal definition of both place and space, and since Clarke could not understand how space could be a quantity if it is nothing but an order of coexistences, he shows how relations can have quantity.

We have already indicated how the soul and God perceive things differently; here Leibniz, that very perspicacious man, explains it more clearly, and takes this occasion to show both that preestablished harmony is possible and that it does not impinge on liberty. He opposes the attractions of Newton and his followers with good arguments and correctly notes that the natural forces of bodies are subject to natural laws, the forces of spirits to moral laws; the former follow the order of efficient, the latter that of final, causation. Since Clarke claimed that the Principle of Sufficient Reason had been merely assumed and not proved, although he himself (as was above noted) had appeared to admit it before he had understood its force against Newtonian and common views, Leibniz notes that its truth can be seen *a posteriori*, since one can adduce innumerable examples in its favor and none against it. It is in the fecundity of truths which are advanced in this letter by Leibniz that we believe the value of the work is found. Clarke answers Leibniz's last letter with no less prolixity . . . but since he persists in defending common hypothesis by now sufficiently known, it is not necessary that we repeat them here.

1

GOD

Even a cursory reader of the correspondence between Clarke and Leibniz cannot fail to notice that theology was one of the areas in which the exchange was most lively and, at times, pointed. Prima facie, the eagerness that both correspondents displayed may appear rather surprising. Both were theists who believed in the integration of natural and revealed religion; both believed in a free, simple, omnipotent, omniscient, omnibenevolent, omnipresent deity who created the world; both were convinced that they could prove its existence.[1] To be sure, Clarke was sceptical of one of Leibniz's preferred arguments for the existence of God, the ontological argument, and certainly Leibniz did not approve of Clarke's argument from the nature of absolute space and time to divine existence. Even so, both employed the cosmological argument, and both believed, although Clarke more tentatively than Leibniz, that most of the arguments proposed for the existence of God could be made sound.[2]

Clarke and Leibniz were sharply divided, however, on both the nature and the metaphysical prerequisites of many of the divine attributes, in particular eternity, omnipresence, and omniscience. Their deep disagreement on these issues manifested itself in the less than urbane exchange on the relation God has with space, time, and the world. Undoubtedly some of the animosity displayed was grounded in the contentious climate in which the exchange developed, but, as we shall see, the philosophical disagreement was substantial. This chapter is divided into two parts: the first deals with divine immensity and eternity and their relation to space and time; the second deals with the relation between God and the world.

1. God's Immensity and Eternity

It is part of traditional Christian theology that God is eternal and immense (omnipresent). Theologians have been usually quick to point out that divine eternity and immensity arc shrouded in mystery and cannot be adequately comprehended by us; in spite of this, or perhaps because of it, the notions of eternity and immensity can be, and have been, understood very differently. The claim that God is eternal can be taken to mean two very different things. In one sense it means that God is a timeless being whose duration is not successive, with no before or after: past, present, and future are all timelessly present to God in ways to be specified. In another sense, it means that God is sempiternal, that is, a being existing throughout time but whose duration is successive and for whom there is a before and an after.[3]

Similarly, divine immensity or omnipresence can be understood in different ways. One might say that God is present everywhere by operation but not by situation. In this sense, God is present in a place not by being there like a human would be, but by acting there. God fills this room by causing the room and its contents in a way remotely analogous to that in which I can fill a glass by pouring water in it.[4] By contrast, one could claim that divine operational presence requires situational presence and hold that the divine substance is, in some sense to be specified, coextended with what it fills. However, divine extension can itself be taken in two ways. It can be understood in terms of local extension; God, then, would be extended like, say, a stone or perhaps space are, with the proviso that God, unlike a stone, could penetrate all other extended things. Or, it can be understood in nonlocal terms, in accordance with what More dubbed "holenmerism"; the divine substance, then, would be whole in the whole of space and whole in each and every place.[5]

1.1 Leibniz

The main features of Leibniz's theology are relatively well known, and therefore we can be brief. According to Leibniz, divine independence manifests itself in the unique features of divine existence. Divine existence is eternal, that is, metaphysically necessary (*Causa*

Dei § 5: GP VI, 439). Leibniz, like Spinoza before him, took eternity to consist in necessary existence and not in continued temporal existence.[6] God is a timeless being in the radical sense that it is not one of the substances out of whose properties time is ultimately constructed. Therefore, there is no succession in God, no before or after. A second consequence of divine independence is immensity (*Causa Dei* § 5: GP VI, 439). Contra Spinoza, Leibniz held that God's immensity does not consist in infinite extension because the perfect being is immaterial and without parts (NE II,15). Rather, divine immensity consists in the fact that God can, and does, act everywhere: God's presence is by operation and not by situation (NE II, 15, 2).[7]

One might question Leibniz's commitment to this view in light of his remark against Malebranche that if God's general volition does not exist at present in the things themselves as their natures, then

> it can accomplish nothing . . . and whoever thinks otherwise renounces any distinct explanation of things, if I am any judge, for if that which is remote in time and space can operate here and now without any intermediary, anything can be said to follow from anything else with equal right. . . . Some connection, either immediate or mediated by something, is necessary between cause and effect. (*De Ipsa Natura* § 6: GP IV, 507 500)

However, Leibniz's point against Malebranche revolves completely around the spatio-temporal requirements that need to be satisfied for the divine will to be efficacious (it has to be here and now), not around what Clarke took to be the spatio-temporal requirements that the divine substance needs to satisfy for its operation to occur spatio-temporally. In other words, Leibniz's point is that the divine will can operate only where and when it is, not that it can operate where it is only if the divine substance is there by situation.[8]

So, no temporal or spatial features apply to God; holding the contrary amounts to diminishing divine greatness by denying divine omnipotence, as the Socinians do (*Causa Dei* § 2–3: GP VI, 439).[9] Moreover, space and time are also world-dependent, and consequently the attempt to associate them with divine existence could only lead to the conclusion that God is part of the world, perhaps as the *anima mundi*.

1.2 Clarke

While Leibniz felt comfortable with the traditional view of God as substantially removed from space and time, Clarke found it unintelligible at best and contradictory at worst. To be sure, he argued that the manner of divine existence "infinitely transcends" that of creatures, even sempiternal ones, and that we cannot have an adequate notion of the divine being and attributes because they involve the infinite (WB 539, 525). Nevertheless, he maintained that divine eternity involves both necessary existence and a "Duration of inexhaustible and never failing permanency," which, however, could not be identified with the traditional notion of the *nunc stans* according to which God exists in an unchanging permanent present without any "Succession of Duration" (WB 539). Clarke considered such a view unintelligible, as he clearly intimated in *A Demonstration* by approvingly providing quotations from Gassendi and Tillotson that charged it with unintelligibility if not outright inconsistency (WB 539–40, n. n).[10] And while there his criticism was restrained, in his sermon on the eternity of God it was considerably more forceful:

> 'Tis worthy of observation, as to the *Manner* of our conceiving the Eternity of God; that the Scholastick Writers have generally described it to be, not a *Real* Perpetual *Duration*, but *One Point* or *Instant* comprehending Eternity, and wherein all things are really co-existent at once. But unintelligible Ways of Speaking have (I think) never done any Service to Religion. The true Notion of the Divine Eternity, does not consist in making past things still present, and all things future to be already come; [which is an express contradiction]. (W I, 22)

Clarke did not explain why he thought it contradictory to think of all events as co-present to the divine eternity, but perhaps he had in mind the following. If two events occurring at different times are simultaneous with the whole of eternity, then they ought to be simultaneous with each other because the relation of simultaneity is transitive, and this contradicts the assumption that they occur at different times.[11]

The attribution of successive duration to God might suggest that for Clarke, God, like us, is in time but unlike us does not change. However, this was not Clarke's view. For one thing, as we shall see, Clarke made clear in his exchange with Butler that God is not in space and time. Moreover, Clarke was ready to attribute successive thoughts to God. To be sure, he held that divine knowledge is unchanging because "all things past, present and to come" are known and represented to God "in one single Thought or View . . . as if all things *had been* (not that they really *are*) actually present at once" (W I, 22).[12] However, he also chided Collins for holding that "Thinking in God cannot be successive, nor have any Modes or distinct Acts of Thinking." If it were so, he continued, then "God cannot vary his Will, nor diversify his Works, nor act successively, nor govern the World, nor indeed have any Power to will or do anything at all" (W III, 896). Clarke did not develop his argument, but the claim that the will of an eternal being could have no variety or produce any change seems based on a confusion between a change of will and a will to change: an eternal God could will (eternally) that up to a certain date a land be a desert and after it be a meadow.

God, then, has successive thoughts; his psychological life, one might say, is successive like ours. Some thoughts, namely his volitions, have even different intentional contents; others, namely his thoughts encompassing all knowledge, presumably have the same intentional content. Of course, if God has successive thoughts, one might wonder about divine immutability, especially with respect to the divine will. But Clarke was ready to weaken its requirements dramatically: God is immutable with respect to his will and his general and particular decrees in the sense that he does not change his mind (W I, 40–41). The divine will inerrantly follows the good.

Clarke's treatment of divine immensity or omnipresence was similar to his treatment of eternity. He criticized the view that "the immensity of God is a *Point*, as his Eternity (they think) is an *Instant*" as unintelligible. All we can say, he continued, is that whereas creatures can be present only in one definite place at a time,

> The Supreme Cause on the contrary, being an Infinite and most simple Essence, and comprehending all things perfectly in himself, is *at all times equally* present, both in his Simple Essence, and by the Immediate and Perfect Exercise of all his Attributes, to *every Point* of the Boundless Immensity, *as if* it were really but one single Point. (WB 541)

While for Clarke, God's temporal presence is analogous to ours by involving temporal succession, his views about God's spatial presence are somewhat less clear. McGuire and Grant, analyzing the same issue with respect to Newton, have reached different conclusions. According to McGuire, Newton rejected More's suggestion that God is locally extended and adopted holenmerism, the view that God is whole in each place. Grant, by contrast, claims that Newton did accept More's point that God is locally extended and dimensional. In addition, he correctly points out that McGuire does not provide any substantial textual evidence for his conclusion, and argues that holenmerism is unintelligible or, worse, contradictory. But one could reply that for Clarke and Newton, God is wholly in each place in a way analogous to that in which for them each instant of time is wholly in each place, and consequently they could well accept holenmerism.[13] However, the fact that Clarke so vigorously denied Leibniz's charge that extension is incompatible with divine simplicity because it introduces parts in God without making any reference to holenmerism intimates that he was ready to think of divine omnipresence in terms of local extension and dimensionality. In fact, there is some evidence that Newton took God to be literally dimensional.[14]

Clarke's reaction to the Scholastic notions of eternity and immensity was based on more than their alleged unintelligibility or inconsistency. There were four further main reasons behind Clarke's position. The first was broadly systematic. He criticized the view that God is an *intelligentia supramundana* as ultimately leading to materialism and libertinism (WN 600). One way to block such a view is to tie God's existence with space and time by equating them with divine immensity and eternity. Then, given divine infinity, God could be thought of as substantially present, although in ways to be specified, to the spatio-temporal world.[15] Second, Clarke thought of time and space as necessarily existing entities (WB 527; W II, 745). As such, they could not be creatures, since no created being can exist necessarily, otherwise God's will would not be free to destroy them. In order to avoid a contraposition between them and God, Clarke had to claim that they somehow depend on the divine substance, and he did so by equating them with divine immensity and eternity.

Third, Clarke held that "no Being can act *Where* it is not, any more than *When* it is not." Hence, he concluded, "the scholastick Fiction of a Being *acting* in all Places, without being *present* in all places, is either making the notion of God an express contradiction, or else supposing him *so* to act by the ministry of Others, as not to be Himself present to understand and know what they Do" (W I, 46).[16] Clarke did not explain why no being can act where it is not, but a strong argument was readily available from More's critique of Descartes: since the operations of a substance are but its modifications, a substance must be where it operates.[17]

The same argument can be repeated concerning divine duration: in order to produce anything in time, divine operations must occur in time, and therefore a timeless being cannot act.[18] But given Clarke's views on space and time, being unable to act in space or in time entails being unable to act at all. And of course a God unable to act would be a God in name only; in fact, it would not even be a spirit. One could maintain, as Collins seemed ready to do, that infinite perfection excludes "Successive Thoughts in God: And that the Essence of God is one perfect Thought: And that though his Transient Acts are done in a Succession of Time, yet his Immanent Acts, his Knowledge and his Decrees, are one with his Essence."[19] But this, Clarke held, shows the "pernicious Effects of Scholastick Jargon" that uses "Words which have no Signification" (W IV, 731). A supporter of a timeless God could object that God is present when his actions take place in the world because all moments of time are present to eternity. But as we saw, Clarke rejected the view of co-presence of past and future in the eternal now as contradictory. In sum, the possibility of divine activity, a precondition for divine spirituality, requires the rejection of the traditional Scholastic view of eternity and immensity.

Fourth, Clarke held that God exists by absolute necessity, and consequently must be *"everywhere* as well as *always,* unalterably the same."* If he did not, he would exist merely by consequential necessity, that is, a necessity depending on some external cause, since "a Necessity absolutely such in itself, has no relation to Time or Place, or any thing else" (WB 540). Clarke sought to reinforce his conclusion by providing another argument for its contrapositive equivalent, namely, that a finite being, that is, one that is not ubiquitous or eternal, is not a self-existent being. For, he argued, if a being "can without a Contradiction be absent from one Place, it may without a Contradiction be absent likewise from another Place, and from all Places: And whatever Necessity it may have of Existing, must arise from some External Cause, and not absolutely from itself; and consequently, the Being cannot be Self-Existent" (WB 540). So, assuming the equivalence of self-existence with absolutely necessary existence, Clarke's argument moves from finitude, to possible lack of existence in one place, to possible lack of existence in all places, to contingent existence, to lack of self-existence.

Butler did not find the argument convincing, and in 1713 wrote to Clarke that, from the fact that something can be absent from one place at one time, it does not follow that it can be absent from all places at the same time, that is, go out of existence. Suppose one were to demonstrate that a certain man will live 1,000 years. Then such man could be absent from all places at different times, but he could not be absent from all places at the same time, that is, go out of existence, since by hypothesis he will live 1,000 years. It would be the same, Butler concluded, "if instead of a Thousand Years, I should say, for ever; And the proof seems the same, whether it be applied to a Self-Existent or a Dependent Being" (W II, 738).

Butler's objection was well taken and demolished Clarke's argument, such as it was. In his answer, Clarke repeated that what is absolutely necessary is so

> in every Part of Space, and in every Point of Duration. Whatever can at any time be conceived *possible to be absent* from *any One part of Space,* may for the same Reason, [*viz.* the implying no Contradiction in the Nature of Things,] be conceived *possible to be absent* from *every Other part of Space* at the *same time;* either by *ceasing to be,* or by supposing it *never to have begun to be.* (W II, 739)

In sum, what can be absent from one place is a contingent being, and consequently can be absent from all places at one time just by not existing. In effect, then, Clarke, without saying it, reformulated the argument Butler had criticized: while originally he had gone from possible lack of existence from one place at one time to possible lack of existence from all places at one time, to contingent existence, he now switched the third with the second, in effect inferring contingent existence directly from lack of ubiquity. The man of Butler's example, Clarke argued, cannot go out of existence but on the supposition that he will live 1,000 years. But such a supposition is not a necessary truth, and therefore absolutely speaking Butler's man could vanish (W II, 739).

Butler doubted the soundness of Clarke's retort because it rested on a questionable premise, namely that "the idea of *Ubiquity* is *contained in* the idea of Self-Existence . . . any otherwise than as, whatever exists, must exist *somewhere*" (W II, 741). This objection went to the heart of the matter, and in response Clarke merely repeated that since necessary existence is not limited by any external cause, it must come about "*everywhere* for the same reason it is *anywhere*" (W II, 743). The reason is that

> Necessity *absolute,* and *antecedent* (in order of Nature) to the Existence of any Subject, has nothing to *limit* it; but if it operates at all, (as it must needs do,) it must operate (if I may so speak,) *everywhere and at all times alike. Determination* of a *particular Quantity,* or *particular Time* or *Place* of Existence of any thing, cannot arise but from somewhat *external* to the thing itself. (W II, 745)[20]

Clarke in effect kept repeating to Butler that ubiquity and eternity pertain to a necessary being because its existence cannot be subject to any external condition or limitation. As we saw, at one time he expressed this thought with the claim that "Necessity absolutely such in itself, has no relation to Time or Place, or anything else" (WB 540). But from such premise philosophers like Leibniz or Aquinas concluded that God is beyond space and time, not that he is everywhere and always in Clarke's sense.

Not only is Clarke's move from necessary existence to spatiotemporal presence questionable, but holding that divine duration is successive and God extended throughout space calls for clarification. It also invites immediate charges of having done away with divine simplicity and moreover opens the problem of explaining the ontological relation between God and space-time. These issues played an important role in the debate with Leibniz.

1.3 God, Space, and Time in the Correspondence

In the early stages of the exchange with Clarke, Leibniz toyed with the idea that for Clarke space might be God, and he told Conti that if God were space, then the divine being would have parts (6 December, 1715: NC VI, 252=R 42). However, by the time he wrote the third letter, Leibniz had become aware that this was not Clarke's position, probably by reading *A Demonstration*. Nevertheless, he found that Clarke's view could be subjected to the same critique simply by broadening the basis of his attack. Those who believe in the existence of absolute space, he pointed out, also believe that space "must be eternal and infinite. Hence some have believed it to be God himself or, one of his attributes, his immensity. But since space has parts, it is not something which can properly pertain [convenir] to God" (Lz III, 3).[21]

Clarke replied by rejecting Leibniz's first alternative. He had already argued that space is not the essence of God:

> Infinite space, is nothing else but abstract Immensity or Infinity; even as infinite Duration is abstract Eternity. And it would be just as proper, to say, that Eternity is the Essence of the Supreme Cause; as to say that Immensity is so. Indeed, they both seem to be but Modes of an Essence or Substance Incomprehensible to Us. (WB 538)[22]

But while in *A Demonstration* Clarke seemed somewhat tentative in claiming that space is a mode of the divine substance, he did not show any hesitation in telling Leibniz that space is a property of God.

Moreover, he claimed, since space is essentially indivisible, it does not introduce any parts in the divine being (Cl III, 3).[23]

In the fourth letter, Leibniz produced a new criticism: if absolute space existed, he said, not even God could change it because it would be immutable and eternal in every part (Lz IV, 10). Consequently, he concluded, space and all its infinitely many parts would be eternal things besides God. Clarke's reply was that although space, like time, is immense, immutable, and eternal, nevertheless "it does not at all from hence follow that anything is eternal *hors de Dieu*. For space and duration are not *hors de Dieu*, but are caused by, and are immediate and necessary consequences of his existence. And with them, his eternity and ubiquity (or omnipresence) would be taken away" (Cl IV,10). In effect, then, Clarke provided Leibniz with two accounts of the relation between space, time, and God. On the one hand, they are divine properties; on the other, they are both necessary effects of God's existence, and necessary requirements for divine eternity and ubiquity.

Clarke supplied no argument to show that these two accounts are equivalent, although if they are, they are not obviously so. Indeed one may reasonably wonder whether they are even compatible. Since eternity and ubiquity are metaphysically necessary attributes of the necessary being, their preconditions must be part of the divine essence. But one can hardly see how God can cause its own essence, given that effects must be distinguished from their causes, as Clarke acknowledged (WB 527).[24] However, Leibniz chose not to ask Clarke for clarification, and preferred to keep on the offensive by deepening his criticism that space and time would be eternal things besides God. He told Clarke that "If the reality of space and time is necessary for the immensity and eternity of God . . . God will in some measure depend on space and time, and stand in need of them. For I have already prevented that subterfuge, that space and time are (in God like) properties of God" (Lz V,50). As Leibniz himself noted, his critique could get off the ground only if he could show that space cannot possibly be a property of God.

Leibniz was not the first to attack Clarke's view that space and time are divine properties. In 1713, answering a query from Butler, Clarke had argued, as he had done in *A Demonstration*, that God must exist because although space and time exist necessarily, they are clearly not substances but properties or modes, and therefore the substance "without which these Modes could not subsist, is itself *much more* (if that were possible) *Necessary*" (W II, 745; WB 527). Butler took Clarke to be claiming that space and time inhere in God, and protested that it is unintelligible, or at least not evident that God is the "*Substratum* of Space, in the *common sense* of the Word" (W II, 746). Butler did not elaborate, although the sequel of the exchange suggests that he took space to be a substantial or quasi-substantial entity, which therefore could not inhere in anything.

Clarke replied by admitting that the claim that God is the *substratum* of space or that space is a property of God "are *not* perhaps very *proper Expressions;* nor is it easy to find such" (W II, 748). He then attempted to clarify his position: "The idea of *Space,* (as also of *Time* or *Duration,*) is an *Abstract* or *Partial Idea;* an Idea of a certain *Quality* or *Relation,* which we evidently see to be *necessarily-existing;* and yet which (not being itself a *Substance,*) at the same time necessarily *presupposes* a *Substance,* without which it could not exist" (W II, 748).[25] Not surprisingly, Butler was not convinced and replied that he could not see why space is a property or something dependent on God, since even upon the supposition that God did not exist, space and time would exist. Nevertheless he humbly, or ironically, pointed out that he did not understand the nature of space and time and could not say that he did not believe Clarke's argument conclusive (W II, 748–49). Clearly, Clarke was intent on impressing upon Butler that space and time are not self-subsisting entities, but he also seemed dissatisfied with the idea that space and time are properties of God in the proper sense of the term, although unable to formulate a clear alternative. This lack of clarity cost him dearly in the controversy with Leibniz.

Leibniz addressed several objections against the view that space and time are divine properties. They can be broadly divided into three groups. The first set of objections attacked the very presupposition of Clarke's view, namely, that immensity and eternity, which, Leibniz agreed, certainly are divine attributes, can be equated with space and time. On the contrary, he claimed, immensity and eternity are logically prior to space and time, as most divines hold (Lz V, 36,106). Moreover, as we shall see in the chapter on space and time, for Leibniz space and time are not only *entia rationis* but even world dependent because they are constructed out of the relations among creatures, and consequently their association with divine existence leads to the conclusion that God is part of the world. Leibniz's alternative, as we saw, is that eternity is necessary existence and divine immensity the full presence of the divine power everywhere. Clarke's reply was direct and scornful: denying that immensity is boundless space and eternity time without beginning or end is literally talking nonsense (Cl V, 106). Moreover, for Clarke the view that space and time are world dependent is as "senseless" as saying that time depends "on the turning or not turning of an hourglass" (W II, 752).

Leibniz's second set of objections was based on an analogy between the triplets God, immensity, and space on one hand, and creatures, extension, and space on the other. If infinite space as a whole is a property of God by being God's immensity, then some finite part of space will be a property of some finite creature by being its extension (Lz V, 37,46). But the space a thing occupies cannot be its extension, since something can leave its space but not its extension (Lz V, 37). Nor can the space a thing occupies be one of its properties, since the same space can be occupied by different things. But a property can belong only to one subject; to maintain the contrary is to give up the distinction between substance and property (Lz V, 39). Finally, since space is made up of its parts (presumably because a real existent that has parts must be composed of them), a property of God would be constituted by the properties of things, which is unacceptable (Lz V, 40–41). In sum, Leibniz diagnosed, Clarke is guilty of a confusion: he takes the space things occupy for their extension (Lz V, 46).

Clarke's reply was that the space a thing occupies is not its property. Indeed, even if the whole of space were to be filled by infinite matter, it still would not be a property of that matter (Cl V, 36–41). His point can be clarified by considering his reply to the following criticisms advanced by Butler and Leibniz. Since for Clarke divine immensity makes God actually present everywhere, God must be in space. Hence, Butler claimed, as space and each of its parts exist necessarily, Clarke's view ultimately entails that every substance exists necessarily, since every substance is in space and the subject of a necessarily existing property must exist necessarily as well (W II, 744). Leibniz, playing on the ambiguity of the word "in," was more sarcastic: "we have often heard that a property is in its subject; but we have never heard that a subject is in its property" (Lz V, 45).

Clarke answered Leibniz as he had done Butler: God

> does not exist in space, and in time; but his existence causes space and time. And when, according to the analogy of vulgar speech, we say that he exists in all space and in all time; the words mean only that he is omnipresent and eternal, that is, that boundless space and time are necessary consequences of his existence; and not, that space and time are beings distinct from him, and IN which he exists. (Cl V, 45)[26]

So, neither the whole of space, nor any section of it is a property of what is in it, nor is that of which space is a property in space at all. Ultimately, Leibniz's and Butler's parallels fail because while things are in space, God is not.[27] Clarke did not clarify his position further, but perhaps he had in mind the following. Space is extended, otherwise extended objects could not be in it. But space is not, properly speaking, in space. Hence, one can think of God as extended but not in space. Presumably an analogous point could be made with respect to divine succession and time. As Newton had claimed in the scholium on space and time, time flows uniformly, each instant regularly succeeding another. But time is not in time. So one can think of divine thoughts uniformly succeeding each other without having to assume that God is in time.

Alternatively, with respect to time, one might be tempted to gloss Clarke's position as follows. Creatures enjoy a tensed existence because they live in time, which flows equitably from the past to the future. By contrast, God's existence is successive, ordered on the basis of the asymmetrical relations "before" and "after", but tenseless, and consequently outside time. However, although tempting, this interpretative line is difficult to evaluate. There is no evidence that Clarke had in mind anything similar to McTaggart's distinction between A-series and B-series. Morover, while an appeal to the distinction between tense and date might work with respect to divine eternity, it would not with respect to divine immensity.

Leibniz's third set of objections against space being a property of God tries to link Clarke's position to an unacceptable view of the divine nature. Denying that infinite space has parts leads to the absurd conclusion that infinite space would exist even if all finite spaces were destroyed (Lz IV, 11). But since space has parts, God would have parts as well (Lz III, 3; V 42–43).[28] Moreover, since the parts of space are at times full and at times empty, God would change. In sum, God would look very much like the Stoic God, "which was the whole universe considered as a divine animal" (Lz V, 42–43). In addition, since things are in space and move in it, one could say that literally they are in God's essence and move about it (Lz V, 44, 50, 79). Finally, any oddly shaped part of empty space would be a property of God, which is just preposterous (Lz V, 38).

Clarke rejected all of Leibniz's criticisms. Since space has no parts, he reiterated, there are no parts in God (Cl V, 42). Nor does motion in space, with the effect that some spaces are now empty now full, engender any change in God (Cl V, 43). Clarke did not provide any argument, but perhaps what he had in mind is that space is impenetrable: objects in space do not penetrate it; rather, it penetrates them.[29] As for the objection that on his view any oddly shaped part of empty space would be a property of God, Clarke replied that "there is no such thing in reality as bounded space; but only we in our imagination fix our attention upon what part or quantity we please, of that which itself is always and necessarily unbounded" (Cl V, 38). In sum, Clarke's reply implied, Leibniz was confusing imagination and understanding. Absolute space has no partitions or boundaries and it is changeless and homogeneous, although in our imagination we can distort its nature by picturing space partitioned and bounded by objects. But of course it is absolute space, not the space of our imagination, which is a property of God. Finally, there is nothing strange in saying that things move in God, since St. Paul himself said that in God "we live and move and have our being" (Cl V, 44).[30]

Clearly Clarke did not think much, or so he feigned, of Leibniz's objections, and in his last letter he noted that they "do not seem to contain any serious arguments, but only represent in an ill light the notion of the immensity or omnipresence of God" (Cl V, 36–48). However, it is hard to share such a dismissive judgment because Leibniz had put his finger on a sore spot in Clarke's own theory by insisting that if space were a property of God, then God would have parts.[31] Leibniz's objection was formidable although not new. Bayle had chided the Newtonians for identifying space with divine immensity in order to solve the ontological problem created by the positing of an infinite space and had compared this solution to Malebranche's placement of "intelligible extension" in God. Such a view, he had claimed, is patently absurd, as Arnauld had shown. In effect, Arnauld had held that Malebranche's view leads to the destruction of divine simplicity. Malebranche had replied that extension is in God not formally but ideally or intelligibly, and had distinguished intelligible extension from divine immensity, and yet at the end he had taken refuge in divine mystery.[32] Even Spinoza, who had made extension one of the infinite attributes of God, had worried about the possibility that an extended substance would be divisible and had expressly argued against it by appealing to the necessary existence of substance and the inconceivability of two substances with the same attribute.[33]

For obvious strategic reasons, in his replies Clarke, like Spinoza, chose to focus on divine indivisibility rather than divine simplicity, and tried to answer Leibniz's charge by making a point he had al-

ready made against Collins's accusation that if the soul were extended, it could not be one. The parts of space, he said, are called
"parts" only improperly because they cannot be separated even in
thought from each other (Cl III, 3; IV, 11–12).[34] Hence he concluded,
as he had in *A Demonstration*, that "there is no difficulty here, but
what arises from the figurative abuse of the word *parts*" (Cl III, 3; W
II, 753–54). Leibniz was not convinced. In some comments written
to his own fourth letter, Leibniz pointed out that it is certainly true
that the parts of space are indivisible, but the reason is that space is
an *ens rationis*, not an actually existing thing. For if space and time
were actually existing things,

> God could produce changes in them. Time and space, like numbers
> and other ideal things, belong to the essences and not to the exis-
> tents. And as God cannot bring about that the ternary number not
> be between the binary and the quaternary because that would be
> absurd, similarly God cannot bring about that an hour like that in
> which we are be taken out from in-between the previous and the
> following hours and reduced to nothing or placed elsewhere. It is
> the same with place or space. (R 101)

So, if space and time were actual existents, it would be logically
possible for their structure to be altered, and consequently they cannot be in God. Just how far Leibniz was ready to go in this direction
is evidenced by his comments to his copy of Clarke's letters to Collins, where he asked whether God could not destroy a part of space.[35]

However, instead of sending Clarke these objections, Leibniz
tried to show that his opponent's view was problematic on its own
terms. Clarke had explained in *A Demonstration* that God's infinity
and necessity entail that he is "a most Simple, Unchangeable, In-
corruptible Being; without Parts, Figure, Motion, Divisibility, or any
other such Properties we find in Matter" (WB 540). As a result, God
does not have parts in two related senses. First, he is not divisible
either in fact or in thought because, Clarke claimed, that would be
equivalent to setting bounds within the divine nature, which is incompatible with divine infinity. Second, he is not the result of composition, otherwise he would not be necessary (WB 540–41). But even
granting Clarke's point that space is indivisible because its parts cannot be separated from each other, all he could argue for is that space
has no separable parts, not that it has no parts. And indeed, parts it
must have, since a line or a surface divide it into distinct regions (Lz
V, 51). Leibniz's point was both powerful and strategically well
taken. For Clarke himself had told Leibniz that "different spaces are

really different or distinct from one another, though they be perfectly alike" (Cl III, 3; IV, 11–12).

Clarke dismissed Leibniz's point as a "quibbling upon words" and referred his opponent back to his previous remarks on the topic (Cl V, 49–51). However, Clarke was well aware that his position was not in tone with some of the traditional views of divine simplicity. To be sure, he was ready to tamper with those views, but attributing extension to God does seem to destroy divine simplicity altogether. He answered an anonymous critic of *A Demonstration* who had argued that God's immensity à la Clarke is incompatible with divine simplicity by claiming that the objection

> arises merely from the *Jargon* of the Schoolmen: Who (in order to help out *Transubstantiation*) have used themselves to speak of This and of many other things, in *Phrases* which had no *Meaning* or *Ideas* belonging to them. By denying the *real Immensity* and the *real Eternal Duration* of God, they in true *Consequence* . . . denied his Being. The *Immensity* of Space, (it being throughout *absolutely uniform* and *essentially indivisible,*) is no more inconsistent with *Simplicity*, than the *uniform successive flowing of the Parts of Duration*, (as you rightly observe,) are inconsistent with *Simplicity*. There is no Difficulty at all in this Point, but a mere *Prejudice*, and *False Notion* of *Simplicity*. (W II, 753)

Here Clarke employed a double strategy. On the one hand, he dismissed the view of divine simplicity incompatible with his own ideas about the relation between space, time, and God as a piece of popish philosophy. But, on the other hand, in effect he argued that those who are ready to maintain that time pertains to God should not have any problem in believing that God is extended because both space and time are indivisible and absolutely uniform, the same point he had intimated to Leibniz (Cl III, 3).

The seam of Clarke's argument consists in claiming parity between spatial and temporal extendedness: since the former is not a problem for the simplicity of what "stretches" temporally, so the latter is not a problem for what stretches spatially. One might object that at each moment of time the whole thing is given, but at each point of space only a part of the thing is, and therefore a simple thing can be temporal but not spatial: a temporal "stretch" is a stretch only metaphorically. For example, consider an object A stretching from one side of the room to the other; then, the middle of the room is occupied by a part of A. By contrast, consider A "stretching" from noon till midnight; then, barring an appeal to temporal stages, which would be incompatible with Clarke's substance metaphysics, what is found at four o'clock is not part of A, but the whole of A.

Clarke, I think, could attempt the following reply. As at each moment of time the whole thing is given spatially, so at each point in space the whole thing is given temporally: if we are allowed to consider the thing's spatial extendedness at any moment of time, then we should be allowed to consider the thing's temporal extendedness at any point in space. There is, then, parity after all. The problem with this reply is that rather than showing that spatial extendedness is not detrimental to a thing's simplicity because temporal extendedness is not, it seems to show that the latter is detrimental to a thing's simplicity because the former is. Someone of Leibniz's opinion could use the point to argue for the notion of an atemporal God. In Clarke's defense, it might be pointed out that he was not arguing under the assumption that the subject whose simplicity is at issue is in space and time, since he explicitly denied that God is in space and time. But then, either Clarke's point is unintelligible, or it must be interpreted as referring to what is in space after all, in spite of his denial that God is in space, or at least extended although not strictly in space, like space itself. But in this case the objection stands because space does have parts, albeit inseparable.

However, perhaps Clarke could have found a way of partially accommodating Leibniz's objections without giving up any of his own views. Paraphrasing Newton's point in the General Scholium, Clarke told Leibniz that space is "absolutely indivisible, even so much in thought; (to imagine its parts moved from each other, is to imagine them moved out of themselves)" (Cl II, 4). From the indivisibility of space, he inferred that the parts of space are interdependent. So, he told Collins that space is "an extension whose parts (improperly so called) depend on each other for their existence . . . because of the contradiction which a separation of them manifestly would imply" (W III, 794). Then, one can say that Clarke was close to the Leibnizian view that space is not a *totum syntheticum*, that is, a totality that is logically dependent on its parts, but a *totum analyticum*, namely, a totality whose parts presuppose it.[36] If this is correct, then Clarke could have gone at least some way toward solving the problem of divine unity, although Leibniz would not have accepted such a move because he denied that anything existent is a *totum analyticum*; that space is such a totality was for him evidence that it is an *ens rationis* (GP VIII, 467; NE II, 17, 3). Moreover, even a *totum analyticum* can be taken to have parts, albeit potentially, and it may be argued that even potential parts would destroy divine simplicity.

The same anonymous reader who had argued that divine immensity à la Clarke is incompatible with divine simplicity, also argued that it is incompatible with divine "spirituality," as Clarke put it, namely with the claim that God thinks. This too was an attack aimed at showing that Clarke's God is not a unity. For, according to Clarke, only an essentially simple substance can think, and consequently matter, being a compound, cannot possibly be the subject of consciousness (W III, 730). Clarke replied that "the individual Consciousness of One Immense Being, is as truly *One*; as the present Moment of Time is *Individually ONE* in all Places at once. And the One can no more properly said to be an *Ell* or a *Mile* of *Consciousness*, . . . that the other can be said to be an *Ell* or a *Mile* of *Time*" (W II, 753).

While unfortunately we do not have the letter of Clarke's critic, presumably the objection was that if the divine consciousness were extended, then it would be possible to consider a spatial part of it as being itself conscious. But this possibility shows that an extended consciousness is not a unity because if a spatial part of consciousness were a consciousness, then the whole consciousness would be a multitude of consciousnesses. And this would not only be incompatible with divine simplicity, but with Clarke's point that consciousness is a unity in the sense of not being composed by several consciousnesses (W III, 784). As before, Clarke's reply invoked the symmetry between space and time. He started by pointing out, with Newton, that an instant of time is the same everywhere.[37] But, Clarke thought, the spatial extension of one instant of time does not affect its unity and does not justify the claim that it stretches for, say, 1 mile. The evidence for this conclusion, Clarke seemed to hold, is given by the fact that one does not think, or talk, about time in terms of, say, miles. Similarly, he concluded, from the fact that the divine consciousness is extended, one should not infer that it is proper to talk about it in terms of its spatial parts. This argument especially satisfied Clarke, who told his interlocutor to give it particular thought; however, it has problems of its own. For if one assumes that an instant of time is infinitely extended, one is implicitly assuming that it is extended for at least 1 mile. That is, if time is spatially extended, then it is a four-dimensional entity, embodying a temporal coordinate and three spatial coordinates. But then it is far from clear why one should be allowed to apply metric considerations along one coordinate but not along the other three.

In spite of all these difficulties, Clarke's commitment to the idea that space and time are properties of God was evident not only in his defense of the view from Leibniz's criticisms, but also in his attempt to prove it. In his fifth reply, Clarke appended a note with an argument by cases concluding that space, like time, is a divine property (Cl V, 36–48, footnote). There are only six possible views of space, Clarke claimed, namely, first, that space is absolutely nothing; second, that it is a mere idea; third, that it is a relation of one thing to another; fourth, that it is a body; fifth, that it is some substance other than a body; sixth, that it is a property of a substance. Clarke did not associate these views with any philosopher; however, it is possible to surmise what Clarke's immediate targets were. The first view was held by Toland, whose belief that motion is essential to matter had been the subject of criticism in *A Demonstration*. The second view had been held by Hobbes, a primary target with Spinoza of the *A Demonstration*. Leibniz was clearly the author of the third view and Descartes of the fourth. The fifth view had been advocated by More and those who identified space with God; of course, the sixth was Clarke's own.[38] Now the first alternative is unacceptable because space has properties, for example, quantity and dimensions, while nothing has no properties. The second alternative cannot be accepted because while space is actually infinite, "no idea of space can possibly be framed larger than finite." Nor can space be a relation, as Leibniz claimed, since a relation cannot be a quantity. Moreover, space cannot be a body, as the Cartesians thought, because otherwise body would be infinite, which is incompatible with the fact that there is space that does not offer any resistance to motion. Last, space is not any kind of substance, since it is immensity and not the immense; denying this amounts to confusing the abstract with the concrete. Consequently, it must be a property, and the same holds for time.

Clarke's argument was criticized on several counts. Leibniz himself, as we shall see in the chapter on space and time, had attempted to show that relations can be quantities. Others found problems with Clarke's dismissal of the view that space might be an idea or a substance. Moreover, a case can be made for the claim that the six views of space Clarke used in his main premise are not exhaustive. For example, Clarke failed to include Gassendi's influential position that space is neither a substance nor a property, a position Newton himself had apparently accepted in "De gravitatione."[39]

Even aside from the argument allegedly establishing that space is a property of God, Clarke and Newton must have felt somewhat

unhappy with the way in which the issue of the relation between
God and space and time had been handled in the exchange with
Leibniz. For one thing, since Clarke insisted that space and time are
quantities, making them divine attributes leads to the subsumption
of God under the category of quantity, a view Newton opposed.[40] So,
Clarke asked Des Maizeaux to append an *Avertissement au Lecteur*,
in which Newton had more than a hand, and which allegedly clarified the relation between space and time and God. Des Maizeaux did
as asked by inserting it verbatim in the preface of his edition of the
correspondence, which appeared in 1720. When Clarke speaks of immensity and eternity as properties or qualities of God, the *Avertissement* stated,

> he does not take the terms "quality" or "property" in the same
> sense in which those who treat of Logic or Metaphysics take these
> terms when they use them in relation to matter. But, he merely
> wants to say that space and duration are modes of existence in all
> beings, and infinite modes and consequences of the existence of the
> substance which is really, necessarily and substantially omnipres-
> ent and eternal. This existence is not a substance and could not be
> reduced [*raportée*] to any type of quality or property; but it is the
> substance itself together with all its attributes and qualities. Place
> and duration are the modes of this existence in such a way that one
> could not reject them without rejecting this existence itself. It is
> difficult to speak of things which do not fall under our senses with-
> out using figurative expressions.[41]

While it can hardly be said that the *Avertissement* is clear, its main
point seems to be the following: space and time, that is, immensity
and eternity, are not qualities inhering in their subject as a substratum (the matter of logicians and metaphysicians), but rather express
how God and the divine qualities exist, namely, immensely and eternally.

The point is somewhat clarified by Clarke's statement to Wa-
terland that

> Immensity is not an *Attribute*, in *the Sense* that Wisdom, Power,
> and the like are strictly so called; but 'tis [*Sui generis,*] a *Mode of
> Existence*, both *of the Substance*, and *of All the Attributes*. In like
> manner; *Eternity*, is not an *Attribute* or *Property*, in *the sense* that
> other Attributes, inhering in the Substance, and supported by it, are
> properly so called; but 'tis [*Sui generis*] the *Duration of Existence*,
> both *of the Substance*, and of *All the Attributes*. Attributes or *Prop-
> erties* strictly so called, cannot be *predicated* one of another. *Wis-
> dom* cannot properly be said to be *Powerful*; or *Power* to be *Wise*.

But *Immensity*, is a *MODE of existence*, both *of the Divine Substance*, and *of all the Attributes. Eternity*, is the *DURATION of existence*, both *of the Divine Substance*, and *of all the Attributes*. (W II, 758)[42]

The proper grammatical expressions of space and time, one might say, are neither proper names, as for Kant, nor adjectives, as for Clarke in his exchange with Butler and Leibniz, but adverbs, so that while divine attributes properly apply to the divine substance and not to each other, immensity and eternity apply not only to the existence of the divine substance, but to that of the divine attributes as well. However, such a move hardly helps: if space and time are quantities and they characterize the way in which God exists, then God is again subsumable under the category of quantity.

2. God and the World

Leibniz was dissatisfied not only with the Newtonian view of the relation between God and space and time, but also with that of the relation between the divinity and the world. On this issue the confrontation between Leibniz and Clarke revolved around three connected topics: the divine role in the maintenance of the world, whether God is an *intelligentia supramundana* or the soul of the world (or neither), and how God cognizes the world. These are the topics we consider now.

2.1 God and the Maintenance of the World

The issue of the divine maintenance of the world was a point of contention since Leibniz's first letter. According to the Newtonians, he said, from time to time God must rewind, clean, and even mend the clockwork of the world by extraordinary intervention. Such a view, he continued, diminishes God by resembling him to a worker whose lack of skill is measured by how frequently he must intervene to repair and reset his machine. The proper position, Leibniz concluded, is that the same "force and vigor" are always present in the world, and consequently God need not intervene extraordinarily and miraculously to regulate the world's machinery (Lz I, 4).[43]

Clarke's reply did not address the physical underpinnings of Leibniz's claim that the the same amount of force is conserved in the world. Nor did it mention the links between Newton's millenarism, which Clarke shared at least in part, and his views on the progressive disorder of the solar system.[44] Rather, it focused on theological issues in a twofold way. On the one hand, Clarke denied the adequacy of Leibniz's analogy. A human artisan does not create the forces that are involved in his machine; that is, the forces of springs and weights driving the machine are merely adjusted by him to that end and consequently continue to operate without his direct and constant intervention. God, by contrast, is the creator of these forces, which could not continue to operate without constant divine support. Consequently, Clarke concluded, the fact that the running of the world requires continuous divine "government and inspection," far from diminishing God, is the sign of his true greatness.

On the other hand, Clarke used Leibniz's clockwork analogy to unload against his interlocutor the accusation of crypto-materialism. The idea of a clockwork world regularly ticking without the need of continuous divine intervention

> is the notion of materialism and fate, and tends, (under pretence of making God a *supra-mundane intelligence*), to exclude providence and God's government in reality out of the world. And by the same reason that a philosopher can represent all things going on from the beginning of the creation, without any government or interposition of providence; a sceptic will easily argue still farther backward, and suppose that things have from eternity gone on (as they do now) without any true creation or original author at all, but only what such arguers call all-wise and eternal nature. (Cl I, 4)

Clarke rounded up his point by providing an analogy of his own. A king who does not actively intervene in the affairs of his kingdom is a king in name only, and those who depict him so can be justly suspected of desiring to set him aside. The same is true in relation to divine government; the doctrine that denies God's continuous direct intervention in nature "does IN EFFECT tend to exclude God out of the world" (Cl I, 4).

Leibniz replied by retorting the charge against his interlocutor. True divine providence, he claimed, requires both perfect foreknowledge and perfect provision; denying the latter, as Clarke does, amounts to holding a view of God that borders on Socinianism, according to which God neither foresees nor foreordains and consequently, as it were, "lives from day to day" (Lz II, 8–9). Nor could Clarke's emphasis on God's creative power help him to avoid dangerous theological consequences, since a God characterized merely by power and not by wisdom is nothing but the God of the materialists and of Spinoza (Lz II, 6–7).[45] As far as his own views were concerned, Leibniz continued, he most certainly did not hold that the machine of the world can go on turning without constant divine intervention; on the contrary, his view was that God conserves everything (Lz II, 6,8,11). What he emphatically denied is that the clockwork of the world needs correction.[46] Taking up Clarke's own analogy, Leibniz explained that far from being a king in name only, God is like a king who has so well inculcated his good wishes in his subjects that he does not need to intervene to mend their ways, a figurative expression of the point made in *De Ipsa Natura* that the natures of things are the result of the divine will (Lz II, 11; *De Ipsa Natura* § 5–10: GP IV, 506–10=L 500–503).

Leibniz's association of Clarke's and Newton's positions with those of Socinianism must have been particularly galling to them, since both did lean toward Arianism.[47] To be sure, while Arianism rejected the deity of Christ but not his divinity (Christ is divine but created), Socinianism rejected both, but historically the charge of Socinianism against Latitudinarians was rather common.[48] Worse, although Newton avoided a public stance on trinitarian issues, some members of his circle did not share his prudence in the least. For example, in 1707 Whiston, who four years earlier had been designated by Newton himself as his successor to the Lucasian Chair, delivered the Boyle Lectures launching an explicit attack against the Nicene Creed. Refusing to retract his views, he was admonished and finally expelled from the university in 1710. The seriousness with which Newton looked upon the incident can be gauged by the fact that around the same time he not only withdrew his support for Whiston, but in 1713 even effectively opposed his admission to the Royal Society.[49] However, these attempts on Newton's part to distance himself from Whiston did not prevent his name from being publicly associated with that of the Arian heretic.[50] As for Clarke, in 1712, he wrote *The Scripture-Doctrine of the Trinity*, in which, although he denied that the Son was a creature made out of nothing, in effect he also denied that he was the self-existing substance.[51] The publication of the book generated such a controversy that the Church of England, by threatening official censure, made him promise he would not preach and write on the issue any longer.[52]

No surprise, then, that in his reply to Leibniz Clarke emphasized that far from living from day to day, God has a detailed plan for the maintenance and possible renovation of the world (Cl II, 6–8). From this Clarke inferred that, properly speaking, divine interventions in the maintenance of the world can be viewed as repairs only in relation to us (Cl II, 8). But with regard to God, "there are no disorders, and consequently no remedies, and indeed no powers of nature at all, that can do any thing of themselves, (as weights and springs work of themselves with regard to men); but the wisdom and foresight of God, consist . . . in contriving at once, what his power and government is continually putting in actual execution" (Cl II, 9). In sum, God follows his own plan providing the power in nature according to his own free decrees; God's wisdom does not consist in making a world that never needs mending, but in making one that lasts as long as he thinks fit (Cl II, 8). Finally, Clarke indicated his readiness to allow Leibniz's account of divine conservation of nature; he told his interlocutor that "if God's conserving all things, means his actual operation and government, in preserving and continuing the beings, powers, orders, dispositions and motions of all things; this is all that is contended for" (Cl II, 11).

From the third letter on, the issue of divine maintenance of the world became less central, being overshadowed by the burgeoning topic of the nature of space and time. Leibniz argued that if the active forces in nature diminished, since God could avoid it, his workmanship would be de facto, and not only apparently, deficient (Lz III, 13). In his reply, Clarke attempted to move the discussion to the metaphysical level by insisting that the diminution of force, by which he understood motive power, namely, mv, stems from the very nature of dependent beings (Cl III, 13–14; IV, 40). His point brought under scrutiny the contrasting physical theories about the nature and conservation of forces that underpinned Leibniz's and Clarke's views and which we shall study in the last chapter.

However, the theological dimension of the issue under discussion did not disappear. The radical dependence of the world on God, Leibniz argued, far from explaining why the clockwork of the world needs mending or recharging, is the reason why such imperfection cannot be present, for it would badly reflect on divine craftsmanship (Lz IV, 40). Clarke replied by resurrecting the spectre of Spinozism; if Leibniz's argument were any good, he said, it would prove "that the material world must be infinite, and that it must have been from eternity, and must continue to eternity: and that God must always have created as many men, and as many of all other things, as 'twas possible for him to create; and for as long a time also, as 'twas possible for him to do it" (Cl IV, 40). When Leibniz asked Clarke how on earth he could draw such an inference, Clarke repeated a point he had already made: for Leibniz the universe cannot diminish in perfection, and no possible reason can be given to limit the quantity of matter because divine perfection compels God to produce as much matter as he can (Cl IV, 21–23; V, 103; Lz V, 103). He then concluded with a rhetorical point: "whether . . . my inferring, that (according to these notions) the world must needs have been both infinite and eternal, be a just inference or no, I am willing to leave to the learned, who shall compare the papers, to judge" (Cl V, 103; IV 21–23).

Clarke's objection was rather weak. Certainly, Leibniz did hold that "no possible reason . . . can limit the quantity of matter," and that "the whole universe . . . cannot diminish in perfection" (Lz IV 20,40).[53] But Leibniz's point was not that it is metaphysically necessary that the quantity of matter be infinite and the world not diminish in perfection, as Clarke implied, but merely that the Principle of the Best requires it. Here was the true point of disagreement; as we shall see in the chapter on free will, Clarke believed that Leibniz's stern application of the Principle of Sufficient Reason to divine choice itself amounted to a destruction of divine freedom, which, in effect, turned God into a necessary agent bound to produce the world as it is.

The nature of the exchange on the divine role in the maintenance and regulation of the world clearly indicated Clarke's fear that Leibniz had made the world independent of God. However, Clarke's understanding of the nature of this alleged independence underwent a change during the correspondence. At first, he believed it consisted in divine absence from the world either in the sense that God had not created the world, or in the sense that he did not care about it at all. Clarke abandoned this view once faced with Leibniz's mounting insistence that divine conservation was required for the very continuation of the world. Although, as we shall see, Clarke and Leibniz did not agree on the nature of divine conservation, Clarke was in effect compelled to drop his accusation. However, later in the exchange, Clarke found new ground for his distrust of Leibniz's position. He became convinced that the way in which Leibniz applied the Principle of Sufficient Reason to the divine will turned God into a necessary agent. But since for Clarke, who was a libertarian, a necessary agent is really no agent at all, the world would be independent of God in the sense that it would follow inexorably from the divine nature without being subject to any divine choice.[54]

According to Leibniz, Clarke had a mean view of God because he had a mean view of God's creation. In effect, Leibniz resurrected the traditional argument that if the imperfection of the world goes beyond what is required by the necessary dependence of creatures on God, then God is not omniscient, omnipotent, and omnibenevolent. Clarke resisted the argument on philosophical and theological grounds. At the philosophical level, he ultimately adopted the position that the world's winding down depends on the very nature of a created material entity. When challenged to support this point, he appealed to the inertness of matter: as we shall see in the last chapter, inertia and the lack of elasticity of atoms guarantee that motion is constantly lost (Cl IV, 39).

However, such a reply can work on its own only if the loss of motion is metaphysically necessary, something which Clarke did not accept. For, as we shall see in the chapter on miracles and nature, even if inertia belongs to the essence of matter, the world's active principles, such as gravitation, are the result of constant and direct divine intervention fully determined by God's mere will, and consequently God could have arranged them so as to make up for the loss of motion, without any need for special intervention.[55] Of course Clarke could reply that such an arrangement would create a more imperfect world than the actual one, and this leads to Clarke's theological reply. Clarke held that God made the world as he thought "fit." The nature of God guarantees that the world is just what it should be.[56] However, such a reply is hardly satisfying, especially coming from a philosopher ready to argue from the "Exquisite Perfection and Consummate Excellency of his Works" to the infinite wisdom of God (WB 569–70). For if the excellency of Clarke's world proves divine greatness, so its deficiencies show divine imperfection, unless, of course, they are illusory or unavoidable, and Leibniz pointed out that there are good reasons for saying that they are neither.

2.2 *God as a Supramundane Intelligence and as the Soul of the World*

In his first reply, as we have seen, Clarke insinuated that Leibniz wanted to make the world independent of God under the pretense of making God an *intelligentia supramundana* (Cl I, 4). No doubt, part of the reason behind Clarke's accusation was to put Leibniz on the defensive. But it would be a mistake to let it go at that. Clarke was convinced that Newtonianism could be used for apologetic purposes by showing that the world is not a vast mechanical system of bodies moved merely by other bodies because attractive forces cannot be explained mechanically and require constant divine (or angelic) intervention. It is, then, not surprising that in *A Discourse*, Clarke inveighed against those deists who admit the existence of a

God who created the world but, like the Epicureans, deny that he concerns himself with its government (WN 600). In a note appended later, Clarke widened his attack: "nor is the doctrine of *Modern* Philosophers, much different; who ascribe every thing to Matter and Motion, excluding Final Causes; and speak of God as an *Intelligentia Supramundana*: which is the very Cant of Epicurus and Lucretius" (WN 600 n. a). Of course Leibniz did not fit the bill, but Clarke was merely expanding on the Newtonian party line, which had surfaced in Cotes's preface to the second edition of the *Principia*. There, without being mentioned by name, Leibniz had been implicitly charged, with all plenists, with getting rid of divine providence and holding that matter is eternal and infinite.[57]

Leibniz's response to Clarke's charge was twofold. On the one hand, he denied that the world is independent of God (Lz II, 6, 8, 11). On the other, he went on the attack by rhetorically asking Clarke whether by denying that God is a supramundane intelligence he intended to say that God is a mundane intelligence, "that is, the soul of the world" (Lz II, 10). Clarke replied that God is "neither a *mundane intelligence* nor a *supra-mundane intelligence*, but an omnipresent intelligence both in and without the world. He is in all, and through all, as well as above all" (Cl II, 10). Prima facie, Clarke's point was certainly not perspicuous, because one would think that since God is an intelligence, he must be either a mundane or a supramundane intelligence. However, Clarke's position becomes somewhat clearer if one understands that it was grounded in his views concerning the relation between God and space. Space is a divine attribute or a way in which God exists. But space is in all and through all, since it penetrates all things; it is also above all in the sense that the finite world is surrounded by the infinite space. Since divine substantial presence is through all of space, God can be said to be neither a supramundane intelligence, since he pervades the world, nor a mundane intelligence, since his presence extends beyond it.

Leibniz chose not to ask Clarke for an explanation of his point, presumably because he was already engaged in a discussion on the relation between God and space. Instead, he reiterated that holding that God is an *intelligentia supramundana* does not involve denying that he is in the world (Lz III, 15). At last, in his reply, Clarke acknowledged the appropriateness of Leibniz's conception of *intelligentia supramundana* "as it is here explicated," although he insisted that the term was not appropriate (Cl III, 15). This concession effectively brought the issue to an end. In effect, then, the outcome of the exchange on the characterization of God as an *intelligentia supramundana* was similar to that of the exchange on divine conservation. In both cases, Clarke grudgingly conceded that his opponent's position was in fact acceptable (Cl II,11; III,15). However, these concessions must not be overemphasized, since Clarke and Leibniz disagreed both on the nature of the divine conservation of the world (as we shall see) and on the nature of the divine presence in the world (as we have seen).

While Clarke's opposition to Leibniz's characterization of God as a supramundane intelligence subsided rather rapidly, Leibniz's accusation that Clarke's views at worst entailed, and at best led to, the idea that God is the soul of the world was repeated to the very end of the correspondence. Leibniz seemed quite ready to saddle other philosophers with this charge. In his opinion, Aristotle, Averroes, Spinoza, and Malebranche, just to name a few, were either fully or partially guilty of believing in a divine world soul, or at least of holding views that lead to it.[58] Whatever the historical accuracy of Leibniz's judgement, clearly the view that God is the soul of the world is incompatible with one of Leibniz's deepest theological commitments, namely, that God is the creator of the world, since he held that the cause of the world must be extramundane (*De Rerum Originatione Radicali*: GP VII, 303=L 487). It also runs against another deep Leibnizian commitment, namely, the individual immortality of souls. For, although the doctrine of a divine world-soul is compatible with the view that individual souls are immortal, Leibniz believed that many of its supporters held that it is the only soul (*Considerations sur le doctrine d'un Esprit Universel Unique*: GP VI, 530=L 555). On this view the world-soul

> animates the whole universe and all its parts, each according to its structure and the organs which it finds there, just as the same wind current causes different organ pipes to give off different sounds. Thus . . . when an animal has sound organs, this spirit produces the effect of a particular soul in it but . . . when the organs are corrupted, this particular soul reduces to nothing or returns, so to speak, to the ocean of the universal spirit. (GP VI, 529=L 554)

But such a position, Leibniz claimed, "destroys the immortality of souls and degrades the human race" (GP VI, 530=L 555).

Leibniz's suspicions were aroused by Clarke's original critique of the characterization of God as *intelligentia supramundana*. Those who advance this criticism, he claimed, must be careful not to fall into the view that God is the soul of the world (Lz II, 10). His misgivings were reinforced by the belief that Clarke and Newton held that space is the *sensorium* of God, and that they conceived divine action on the world on the model of the vulgarly understood action of the soul on the body. We shall look at Leibniz's first belief in the section devoted to God's knowledge of the world. Here we shall consider the second belief. It was clearly connected with the issue of the divine maintenance and regulation of the world. At the end of the second letter, Leibniz presented Clarke with a dilemma. If God intervenes to mend the clockwork of the world, such intervention is either supernatural or natural. If the former, miracles are invoked to explain natural phenomena, which is unacceptable; if the latter, God is not an *intelligentia supramundana*, but part of the "nature of things, that is . . . the soul of the world" (Lz II, 12). Leibniz believed that Clarke's position was the latter, as he indicated in his last letter (Lz V, 111). Indeed, in the early stages of the correspondence, he seriously entertained the thought that Newton was ready to go well beyond the mere idea that God is the soul of the world. In December 1715, he told Bernoulli that Newton had strange views about the divinity, namely, that God "is extended and has a *sensorium*. I fear that he inclines towards the view of Averroes and some others, and also attributed to Aristotle, about a Soul or general agent Intellect operating in whatever body on account of the organs of that body" (GM III, 952=R 45). Here Leibniz was ready to attribute to Newton the full implications of the theory of a single universal spirit.

Clarke's reaction to Leibniz's charges was twofold. On the one hand, he pointed out that in the General Scholium Newton had explicitly denied that God is the soul of the world (Cl II, 12). On the other, he kept repeating that while the soul and the body constitute a compound, a unity, because they interact on each other, God and the world form no such thing, since the former acts on the latter but not vice versa (Cl II, 12; IV, 29, 32; V, 79–82). However, Clarke's points failed to satisfy Leibniz, who, at the very least, kept believing that his opponent's position was dangerously linked to the view that God is the soul of the world. In June 1716, he told Arnold that

> according to these gentlemen [Clarke and Newton] God becomes imperfect, and resembles too much the soul of the world of the ancient philosophers because he needs a *sensorium*, lives in a machine as imperfect as our bodies, and keeps up his machine through the force he impresses on it from time to time in the same way in which the vulgar imagines the soul does with the body. (R 103)[59]

Here Leibniz seemed to overplay his hand. For although Clarke's constant denial that space is the *sensorium* of God was perhaps disingenuous, both the characterization of the divine recharging of the clockwork of the world as analogous to the vulgarly conceived transmission of force from the soul to the body, and the depiction of God's presence in the world in terms of his "living" in it, were clearly prejudging the issue.

However, Leibniz did not claim that he could prove that Clarke's position entailed that God is the soul of the world. Rather, what he had in mind is indicated by another view of Clarke's, which he adduced as evidence for his suspicions, namely, the denial that the divine conservation of things is really their continuous production (Lz V, 88). For Leibniz believed that if God is the soul of the world, then his preservation of things cannot be a continuous production of them.[60] That is, Clarke's position on the conservation of things is not only compatible with the view of the world-soul, but it follows from it. In effect, then, Leibniz found himself facing a set of views, such as God's alleged need of a *sensorium*, the denial of divine continual production of creatures, God's substantial presence in the world, the attribution of successive thoughts to God, and the claim that the universe as a whole is not a perfect machine, which he reasonably thought to be entailed by the view that God is the soul of the world. From this, Leibniz concluded that at some level or other, Clarke had either actually inferred these views from the idea that God is the world-soul, or at least had not sufficiently understood the link between them and the view of the world-soul. This conclusion was probably further supported by Leibniz's belief that it is natural for man to think that God acts in the world like an artisan in his shop (GP VII, 134).

2.3 *Divine Cognition of the World*

Both Leibniz and Clarke held that omniscience is one of the metaphysical attributes of God. What we consider here is the topic of God's knowledge of the world. The discussion about it revolved around the metaphysical presuppositions that have to be satisfied for it to occur. Leibniz took the view that any cognition, divine or otherwise, requires a causal link between the cognized and the cognizer. The link need not be a direct relation of cause and effect (Lz II, 4; III,11). For example, the soul perceives the body even if there is no causal interaction because the link is provided by the fact that both have been harmoniously arranged by a common cause, namely, God. However, the causal link that makes God's knowledge of the world possible is direct and given by his continual causal activity on it. By contrast, in spite of some ambiguities, Clarke's position was that cognition requires the simple presence of a living substance to the object cognized (Cl II, 4). Therefore, since God is omnipresent and infinitely intelligent, he must "necessarily have a thorough prospect of the inmost nature and essence of everything" (*On the Omniscience of God*: W I, 67).

No surprise, then, that Leibniz asked Clarke for an explanation of how a substance can perceive what is not in itself (Lz III, 11). Clarke replied that how this happens is a mystery (Cl III, 11). However, he also drew analogies between the soul's awareness of material images in its *sensorium* and the divine awareness of the world:

> God perceives things, not indeed by his simple presence to them, nor yet by his operation upon them, but by his being a living and intelligent, as well as omnipresent substance. The soul likewise, (within its narrow sphere,) not by its simple presence, but by its being a living substance, perceives the images to which it is present; and which, without being present to them, it could not perceive. (Cl II,5)

The result, of course, far from convincing Leibniz, was to confirm his suspicion that for Clarke, God is the soul of the world.

According to Leibniz, God knows the world because he continuously produces it (Lz II,5; IV, 30). That is, God's knowledge of creation is in fact a form of self-knowledge; it is by being aware of his will that God knows the world. As Leibniz told Clarke, "God perceives things in himself" (Lz II, 29). For Leibniz, since there must be a causal link between the knower and the known, Clarke's denial that God knows creation by continual production entails that God is to some extent passive by being acted upon by creatures. As such, of course, it resembles the soul of the world (Lz V, 82). Clarke was little moved by this sort of objection. After denying that the world acts on God, he told Leibniz that "God discerns things, by being present to and in the substances of the things themselves. Not by producing them continually; (for he rests now from his work of creation:) but by being continually omnipresent to every thing which he created at the beginning" (Cl IV, 30).

Leibniz's indignant reply to Clarke's not too veiled reference to Genesis was that his interlocutor was abusing the Scriptures (Lz V, 88). However, Leibniz must also have understood that his attempts at showing Clarke that cognition requires a causal link were to no avail. Consequently, he changed strategy by trying to force his interlocutor to accept continual preservation as the only way to maintain the radical dependency of creatures on God: "It is true that there is no production of new substances. But one would be wrong to infer that God is now in the world but as the soul is conceived to be in the body, governing it merely by his presence, without any concourse being necessary to continue its existence" (Lz V, 88). If one of Clarke's main worries was to deny that the world continues without divine intervention, certainly he could accept continual production. Indeed, in Leibniz's eyes, he had already implicitly done so in his second reply, when he had not objected to Leibniz's claim that God conserves all things (Cl II, 11). However, Clarke did not accept Leibniz's shift of focus. In his reply, he claimed that the view that God knows things by continually producing them is a "mere fiction of the schoolmen, without any proof" (Cl V, 83–91).[61] In effect, the confrontation between Clarke and Leibniz on this issue hinged upon which divine attribute to emphasize in relation to the divine knowledge of the world. For Leibniz, it was omnipotence; for Clarke it was omnipresence. The former insisted on nonlocal causation, the latter on substantial presence. This difference was based not only on a disagreement of the preconditions for cognition, but also on a disagreement on the preconditions of causation, which for Clarke, but not for Leibniz, required spatio-temporal substantial presence.

One important aspect of the controversy over the requirements for the divine knowledge of the world centered around the attribution of a *sensorium* to God. Already in March 1715, Leibniz had told Johann Bernoulli that upon examining the 1706 *Optice* he had "laughed at the idea that space is the *sensorium* of God, as if God, from whom everything comes, should have need of a *sensorium*" (GM III, 939). Not surprisingly, then, at the outset of the correspondence, Leibniz complained that for Newton "space is an organ, which God makes use of to perceive things by. But if God stands in need of any organ to perceive things by, it will follow that they do not depend altogether upon him, nor were they produced by him" (Lz I,3). One can see the reason for Leibniz's inference: if God is the creator, he must continuously produce creatures because they, as it were, have no ontological inertia. Hence, he knows them by producing them, by inspection of his own will, not through an organ. Consequently, since for Newton God needs an organ, he is not the creator. Worse, if God needs a *sensorium*, then divine cognition of the world is sensuous and essentially passive, that is, caused by creatures. This, Leibniz claimed, makes God the soul of the world (Lz V, 82).[62]

Throughout the correspondence, Clarke insisted that Newton

did not say that space is an organ God uses to perceive the world, for God, being omnipresent,

> perceives all things by his immediate presence to them . . . In order to make this more intelligible, he [Newton] illustrates it by a similitude: that as the mind of man, by its immediate presence to the pictures or images of things, form'd in the brain by the means of the organs of sensation, sees those pictures as if they were the things themselves; so God sees all things, by his immediate presence to them; he being actually present to the things themselves . . . as the mind of man is present to all the pictures of things formed in his brain . . . And this similitude is all that he [Newton] means, when he supposes infinite space to be (as it were) the *sensorium* of the Omnipresent Being. (Cl I, 3)

To show the truth of his view, in his edition of the correspondence, Clarke hastened to append a note in which he provided a quotation from query 20 of the 1706 *Optice*, which indeed confirmed his point. However, Leibniz had claimed that he found "in express words, in the Appendix to Mr. Newton's *Opticks*, that space is the *sensorium* of God" (Lz II, 3). There is no question that Leibniz was right that for Newton space is the divine *sensorium*. In the 1706 *Optice*, Newton described God as "more able by his Will to move all Bodies within his boundless uniform *Sensorium*, and thereby to form and reform all the Parts of the Universe, than our soul, which is in us the image of God, is able by its will to move the Parts of our own Bodies"(NO *quaestio* 23, 346).

Furthermore, there is no question that at one time Newton did attribute a *sensorium* to God also in the very same passage Clarke used to show he did not. Koyré and Cohen have discovered a few copies of the 1706 *Optice* in which infinite space is described as "the *Sensorium* of the Incorporeal, Living and Intelligent Being," instead of as that in which God, "as it were in his *Sensorium*, [tanquam Sensorio suo] sees the things themselves intimately," as the standard version says. Koyré and Cohen have surmised that the change occurred after printing but before the binding of the volume, and that some unrevised copies somehow made it to the market, concluding that possibly Leibniz owned an unrevised copy.[63]

Be that as it may, obviously Clarke knew that even in the amended version of *Optice*, God had been given a *sensorium*. This explains his certainly less than candid double strategy: on the one hand he denied that Newton attributed a *sensorium* to God in the passage he had chosen to do battle about by constantly referring to the famous *tanquam*; on the other, he tried to read away the other attribution, without ever mentioning it. He attempted this second task in two ways. At first he claimed that "the word *sensory* does not properly signify the organ, but the place of sensation" (Cl II, 3). When a clearly irritated Leibniz quoted Goclenius's *Dictionarium Philosophicum*, which unequivocally defined *sensorium* as the "organ of sensation," Clarke quoted Scapula's *Lexicon Graeco-Latinum*, which said that at times it means the "place where the sense resides" (Lz III, 10; Cl III, 10). However, in a part of the definition of "sensorium" that Clarke failed to mention, Scapula gave "instrument of sensation" as the principal meaning of the word.[64] Perhaps feeling that the battle of the dictionaries might end ignominiously, finally Clarke resorted to the claim that the issue was not what Goclenius meant, but what Newton meant (Cl III,10). It was a rather hurried retreat, as Leibniz did not fail to remark by pointing out that Newton should have been more careful in his terminology, since "the design of dictionaries is to show the use of words" (Lz IV,28).[65]

In his reply, Clarke clearly indicated he did not want to discuss the issue any further. Nevertheless, he took the time to repeat that Newton merely talked of space being, "as it were," the sensory of God (Cl IV, 24–28). At last, probably out of exasperation, Leibniz decided to take the bull by the horns: "The author alleges, it was not affirmed that space is God's *sensorium*, but only *as it were his sensorium.* The latter seems to be as improper, and as little intelligible as the former" (Lz V, 78). The point, as Leibniz had explained in the previous letter, is that no comparison can be made between "God's knowledge and operations, [and] the knowledge and operations of souls" (Lz IV, 30). Not only does God not have a *sensorium*, and consequently any comparison involving the *sensoria* of animals or man cannot stand, but he does not have anything even remotely analogous to one. In other words, divine cognition is radically different from that of creatures. As we saw, in Leibniz's eyes even the institution of an analogy between the relation the soul has with the images in the brain and the relation God has with the world presupposes a fundamentally mistaken and mean view of God. Clarke's reply merely reasserted the aptness and intelligibility of Newton's analogy and referred the reader to previous letters (Cl V, 78).

Ultimately, Clarke's attempt to explain the relation between God and the world in terms of that between the soul and the body, not surprisingly, backfired. At the beginning of the eighteenth cen-

tury there was, to put it mildly, no settled view of the relation between the mind and the body. Hence, appealing to that relation as
the analogical counterpart of that between God and the world did
little to clarify the issue. The problem was compounded by Clarke's
inability to present a clear picture of his own of how the soul acts
on the body or how the mind knows what is in its *sensorium* because
both activities, he claimed, are mysterious. What was left, then, was
the "vulgar" account of the mind-body relation, and this could not
but confirm Leibniz's worst suspicions about the degradation of
Newton's God into the world-soul.

For both Clarke and Leibniz, as for Locke, reason is the arbiter of
faith because we are not to accept irrational religious claims, like
those often advanced by religious enthusiasts.[66] However, Leibniz
and Clarke disagreed on what reason teaches us, and therefore their
theologies were at odds. While Leibniz, especially in relation to divine immensity and eternity, accepted much of the view put forth
by Scholastics like Aquinas and Suarez, Clarke rejected it. In its
place, he put a picture of God modeled in large part on that of finite
spirits like us. To a large extent then, their theological confrontation
de facto revolved around the interpretation of the biblical claim that
we are made in God's image.[67]

Leibniz and Clarke rejected Spinoza's view that a word can refer
both to human and divine properties only equivocally, and were even
prepared go beyond the Thomistic position that it can do so only
analogically, for in spite of some ambiguity, both held that human
and divine attributes have the same nature, although God's are infinite.[68] However, Clarke was ready to push the similitude between
God and us considerably farther than Leibniz. Certainly he did claim
that being self-subsistent, the divine spirit is different in nature from
created ones and denied that God is in space and time like us (*On
the Spirituality of God*: W I, 28–29; Cl V, 45). But he also attributed
successive thoughts to God and made him extended, just as he
thought we are. Nor was he bothered by the fear of destroying divine
simplicity and immutability because he was ready to reinterpret
them as mere indivisibility and psychological steadfastness. Finally,
he was also prepared to explain the relation between God and the
world through analogies to that between the soul and the body.

By contrast, Leibniz's approach to theology was much more traditional. To be sure, he was ready to admit a multiplicity of ideas in
God, although he confessed that no system could explain how this
is compatible with divine simplicity (GP VI, 576). But he certainly

denied any succession of thoughts in God: while our thoughts are ordered both logically and temporally, divine ideas are ordered only with respect to logical priority (*Theodicy* §192, 390: GP VI, 230; 346–47). Moreover, not only he denied that God is extended, but he also opposed the use of the relation between the mind and the body to illustrate the relation between God and the world. Newton's reference to space as the divine *sensorium* incensed Leibniz because divine cognition of the world is not even remotely analogous to ours: God knows creatures by creating and conserving, not mirroring, them.

2

THE SOUL

On the topic of the soul, Clarke and Leibniz shared several important views. Both firmly held that the belief in an immaterial and hence naturally immortal substance is necessary to religion and morality. Both thought that this belief was under a concerted attack and attempted to defend it against Hobbes, Spinoza, Locke, and their followers. However, they also disagreed on two important issues. Clarke believed that the soul is extended while Leibniz denied it. Leibniz put forth preestablished harmony to explain the relation between the soul and the body, while Clarke was an interactionist, although at times a somewhat reluctant one. These two areas of disagreement ran very deep, involving broad metaphysical concerns. For Leibniz, extension entails divisibility, which precludes any hope of showing that the soul is naturally immortal. Moreover, he saw with deep suspicion his opponent's analogy between God and the world on one side, and the soul and the body on the other, because he felt that it could lead to a mortalist view of the soul. Clarke saw preestablished harmony as a fairy tale, which not only did not do justice to the data of introspection, but also engendered a determinist view of the soul that would deprive us of liberty and even ultimately lead to materialism. In this chapter, we shall first consider Clarke's and Leibniz's views and then their exchange.

1. *Clarke*

In 1706, Henry Dodwell published a book in which he defended conditional immortality: our souls are naturally mortal and upon the death of the body can be kept in existence only by divine supernatural intervention.[1] Since Dodwell was one of the most respected scholars of his time, the reactions to his book were considerable, not only in England, but on the Continent as well.[2] Clarke's reaction was not late in coming. He wrote an open letter to Dodwell complaining that he had let wide the floodgates to Libertinism by providing an excuse for the wicked not to fear eternal punishment (W III, 721). He then argued that the soul, being immaterial, is naturally immortal by giving his own version of the traditional argument for the immateriality of the soul from the alleged unity of consciousness:

> That the Soul cannot possibly be *Material* . . . is demonstrable from the single consideration, even of bare Sense or Consciousness it self. For *Matter* being a divisible Substance, consisting always of separable, nay actually separate and distinct parts, 'tis plain, that unless it were essentially Conscious, in which case every particle of Matter must consist of innumerable separate and distinct Consciousnesses, no System of it in any possible Composition or Division, can be any individual Conscious Being: For, suppose three or three hundred Particles of Matter, at a Mile or any given distance one from another; is it possible that all those separate parts should in that State be one individual Conscious Being? Suppose then all these particles brought together into one System, so as to touch one another; will they thereby, or by any Motion or Composition whatsoever, become any whit less truly distinct Beings, than they were when at the greatest distance? How can their being disposed in any possible System, make them one individual conscious Being? If you will suppose God by his infinite Power superadding Consciousness to the united Particles, yet still those Particles being really and necessarily as distinct Beings as ever, cannot be themselves the Subject in which that individual Consciousness inheres, but the Consciousness can only be superadded by the addition of Something, which in all the Particles must still it self be but one individual Being. The Soul therefore, whose Power of thinking is undeniably one Individual Consciousness, cannot possibly be a *Material* Substance. (W III,730)[3]

This was a very ambitious argument, as one can see by comparison with Locke's argument from consciousness to immateriality. Locke agreed that matter on its own cannot possibly produce thought either in itself or in anything else. Therefore, from the fact that we think he concluded that God, our maker, must be immaterial.[4] However, Locke was ready to admit that God could superadd thought to matter, and consequently that we could not exclude with metaphysical certainty that our minds are material.[5] By contrast, Clarke's argument attempted to prove not merely that matter cannot possibly produce thought, but also that it would be metaphysically impossible for matter to be the subject of inherence of thought. Not only matter could not possibly think on its own, but not even God could make it think, since God is bound by the laws of logic and metaphysics (W III, 841).

Clarke's argument failed to convince Anthony Collins, whose intervention in defense of Dodwell started a protracted controversy. While Dodwell had been content with upholding conditional immortality mostly on the basis of scriptural exegesis, to Clarke's displeasure Collins made no bones about his materialist view of the soul. Clarke told Collins that if thinking in humans were a mode of matter, then "it [would] be but too natural a Consequence, to conceive that it may be only the same thing in all Other Rational Beings likewise; and even in God himself. And what a Notion of God This would give us, is not difficult to imagine" (W III, 851). For then, Clarke continued, every thinking being, including God, would be governed by "absolute necessity, such as the motion of a clock or a watch is determined by." The result would be the destruction of every possibility of self-determination and the undermining of the very foundations of religion.

In the course of the exchange with Collins, it became clear that Clarke's argument for the immateriality of the soul revolved around three premises. First, necessarily consciousness is an individual power (W III, 784). Second, an individual power cannot result from, or inhere in, a divisible substance (W III, 784); or, alternatively, an individual power can only be produced by, or inhere in, an individual being (W III, 760).[6] Third, matter is not, and cannot possibly be, an individual being (W III, 791). The conclusion is that consciousness cannot possibly be the product of, or inhere in, matter.

The first premise, Clarke explained, must be understood as expressing the obvious truth that consciousness is "truly one undivided Consciousness, and not a Multitude of distinct Consciousnesses added together" (W III, 784, 790). Collins was ready to accept Clarke's claim that consciousness is an individual power, namely, that it is not an aggregate of consciousnesses (W III, 800). He was also ready to accept the third premise not with respect to matter per se, but with respect to systems of matter such as the brain. However, he disagreed with Clarke's claim that an individual power such as consciousness cannot but inhere in an individual subject, namely a being which, as Clarke put it, is "essentially one, i.e., such that any division in it destroys its essence" (W III, 795). Consequently, he disagreed with Clarke's contention that only an individual substance like an immaterial soul can be the subject of consciousness.

Certainly Collins's reservations were justified. Clarke tried to transfer a feature of a property (being individual) to the subject of that property. Such a transfer seems quite plausible in some cases. For example, duration seems to be a transferable feature: while a property lasts, so must its subject. But counterexamples are easily found. Inherence is not a transferable feature because a property inheres in something, but its subject need not, and an apple is not composed of blue and yellow, although its green color is. However, Clarke thought he had a powerful argument for the permissibility of the transference at issue. Against Collins's accusation that he had simply assumed that an individual power like consciousness could not inhere in a nonindividual subject like matter, he replied:

> I think it is *proved* strongly, that Consciousness cannot reside in a Being that consists of a Multitude of separate and distinct Parts: Because if it could, it must necessarily follow, either that it would become a Multitude of distinct Consciousness, contrary to the Supposition which you yourself allow; or else that an Individual Quality of each single Particle, would become the Individual Quality of every one of the rest likewise, which is a Contradiction in Terms; or else, that Consciousness would be one Power resulting from the contributing Powers of all the several separate and distinct Particles; in which case, it would be, as I have before proved in enumerating the several kinds of Powers, a mere *abstract Name* or *complex Notion* and not a real Quality residing in any Subject at all. (W III, 791)

While not clear, presumably Clarke's argument can be rendered as follows. If consciousness resided in a composite being C, then either it would be constituted by a multitude of consciousnesses or not. If the former, then the unitary nature of consciousness would be lost. If the latter, then two cases would be possible. In the first case, the consciousness of C would be the consciousness of one of its parts P. But this is impossible because then C, P, and, Clarke seemed to hold, all the parts of C would have the same numerical consciousness, which contravenes the principle that the properties or powers of different subjects are numerically different. In the second case, the consciousness of C would be a supervenient feature. But then that consciousness would not be a power in the true sense of the term, that is, a quality inhering in the composite C.[7] The reason is to be found in a principle of "homogeneity": a power can really inhere in a composite only if it is of the same kind as the powers of the parts (W III, 759). For example, a composite has weight only insofar as its parts do; it can have shape only insofar as its parts do, and so on. But certainly "Intelligence is *not* Figure, and Consciousness is *not* Motion," by which one was presumably to understand that mental and material attributes are of different natures (WB 544, 545).

Clarke had a causal argument for the principle of homogeneity in the case in which the power of the whole is caused by the powers of the parts. If supervenient or nonhomogeneous powers could arise, then "the Effect would contain more than it was in the *Cause*; that is, something would without any Efficient [cause], be produced out of nothing" (W III, 786).[8] However, the principle of homogeneity held in the case of superaddition as well. If a power were superadded to a composite, then it would have to inhere proportionally in its parts because a composite is merely the sum of its parts, and consequently its powers can only be the sum of the powers of the parts (W III, 759, 827). In sum, the principle of homogeneity guarantees not only that matter cannot produce consciousness on its own, but that it cannot even be the type of subject to which consciousness can be superadded.

Although prima facie Clarke's causal principle seems to intimate that the soul cannot act on the body, he always maintained that the soul does causally affect the body. One can appreciate the theological, moral, and broadly philosophical motivations for such a position. He clearly wanted to leave the door open for arguing that God, the maker of matter, is immaterial, and the claim that a thinking immaterial substance can produce material modifications is an essential component of his argument. Moreover, for Clarke, the capacity of the soul to affect the body causally is a consequence of our being endowed with liberty. He chastised Leibniz for denying that we can generate new force, for example, move our bodies. If we could not move our bodies, then we would not be agents but, barring the view that our actions are supernatural, we would be machines like clocks and our actions, if one could call them so, would be ruled by determinism (Cl IV, 32, 33; V, 92, 93–95). But for Clarke, who was a strict libertarian, determinism is incompatible with freedom (W III,

905). Hence, the consequence of denying that our souls move our bodies would be disastrous, since Clarke was convinced that freedom is a necessary condition for morality and religion (W III, 905; IV, 735). In addition, as we shall see, Clarke thought that we experience the causal power by which we move our body (WB 558).

Being convinced that the soul acts on the body, Clarke tried to explain the possibility of this action by resorting to the traditional metaphysical view of the levels of perfection of qualities. In contrast to qualities such as consciousness and intelligence, the qualities of matter such as figure, divisibility, mobility "are not real, proper, distinct Positive Powers, but only *Negative* Qualities, Deficiencies or Imperfections" (WB 545). As imperfections, they can be in the effect without being in the cause if higher qualities are in the cause. Therefore, intelligent beings, and more generally conscious beings, can produce modifications in matter.

While Clarke unequivocally held that the soul acts on the body, the same cannot be said of the converse. When Collins pointed out that since Clarke allowed that matter acts on the soul without contact, matter must have powers of which we are not aware, and consequently we cannot rule out that it has the power of thinking, Clarke replied that "the Power by which Matter acts upon the Soul is not a *real Quality* inhering in Matter, as *Motion* inheres in it . . . but it is only a Power or Occasion of exciting certain *Modes* or *Sensations* in another Substance" (W III, 897; WB 545). Such statement might lead to the conclusion that Clarke was ready to adopt, or at least toy with, Occasionalism.[9] But such a conclusion would be hasty. Clarke continued by claiming that in the same way in which we don't know how matter acts on the soul, so we don't know how matter acts on matter. Given the pressure Collins put on him to limit the powers of matter, not surprisingly Clarke trotted out some Occasionalist jargon in order to deemphasize the activity of matter on the soul, much in the same way in which Descartes had used the term "occasion" in his tirade for innate ideas against Regius.[10]

However, at other times, Clarke was ready to do exactly the contrary. To an anonymous opponent who, as Leibniz was to do, charged him with turning God into the soul of the world, Clarke replied: "This is a great Mistake. For the Word, *Soul*, signifies a *Part* of a *Whole*, whereof *Body* is the *Other* Part; And they, being united, *mutually affect* each other, as *Parts* of the same *Whole*" (W II, 753). By contrast, he continued, nothing acts on God. Here, certainly, Clarke meant to emphasize the activity of the body on the soul by stressing their interaction and their union.

The reason for this ambivalence probably can be found in the different contexts in which Clarke adopted these two positions. He held both that matter cannot possibly produce thought and, as we shall see, that the soul, like God, is extended. He employed the first claim to argue for the immateriality of God and the soul, and in this context he tended to emphasize the utter inability of matter to cause perception even in a conscious substance. It is, therefore, not surprising that Clarke's account of the activity of the body on the soul as merely an "occasion" for perceptions occurs primarily in the *Demonstration* and in his answers to Collins. But as the second claim earned him the charge of upholding the view that God is the soul of the world, Clarke reacted by emphasizing the close relation between the soul and the body in order to distance it from that between God and the world. In particular, he tended to contrast the absolute inability of the world to act on God with the capacity of the body to affect the soul.

Collins not only rejected Clarke's argument from the unitary nature of consciousness to the immateriality of its subject, but also wondered how an immaterial substance like the soul can be indivisible if one assumes, as Clarke had obliquely intimated, that it is extended (W III, 758). To Collins's apparent surprise, instead of rejecting the view that the soul is extended, Clarke replied that,

> How far such *Indiscerpibility* can be reconciled and be consistent with some kind of *Expansion*; that is, what *unknown Properties* are joined together with these *known ones* of Consciousness and Indiscerpibility; is another Question of considerable Difficulty, but of no Necessity to be resolved in the Present Argument. Only This: As the Parts of *Space* or *Expansion* itself, can demonstrably be proved to be *absolutely Indiscerpible*; so it ought not to be reckoned an insuperable Difficulty, to imagine that all *Immaterial Thinking Substances* (upon Supposition that *Expansion* is not excluded out of their Idea,) may be so likewise. (W III, 763)

One can sympathize with Clarke's guarded reply. On the one hand, he understood the problems involved in the claim that the soul is extended and is also an individual, essentially indivisible, immaterial being, and consequently tried to separate the issue of immateriality from that of extension. More's difficulties were indicative of the problem. He had vigorously attacked Descartes's claim that the soul could be considered extended only in the sense that its operations can affect the body, by arguing that since the operations of a substance are nothing but its modifications, spirits must be substantially present where they operate, and consequently must be extended.[11] However, when faced with the problem of reconciling the extension and the indivisibility of the soul, traditionally taken to be the direct consequence of its immateriality, at times he seemed satisfied with merely claiming that there is no contradiction in the notion of a soul which is both extended and indivisible, that is, such that its parts are so tied together as to be inseparable.[12] At other times, he tried to prove that the soul is indivisible by dubious arguments revolving around the notion of necessary emanation from the "*Center of the Spirit*, which is not a Mathematical point, but Substance, so little in magnitude, that it is *indivisible*."[13] However, in spite of More's protestations to the contrary, it seemed clear that the infinite littleness of the centers of spirits could at most guarantee de facto indivisibility and would fall short of the essential indivisibility which was traditionally attributed to the soul.[14]

On the other hand, Clarke did indeed maintain that the soul is extended. He held that while God is not in space, everything else , including souls and thoughts, is (Cl V, 79–82). As he eventually told Leibniz, not only is the soul in space, but it is in a particular place, the *sensorium*, which a part of the brain occupies (Cl IV, 37). Clarke inferred the presence of the soul in the *sensorium* through an argument that employed two independent premises: first, that something can act only where it is substantially, and second, that the soul interacts with the body. The conclusion is that the soul is substantially present where (at least) a part of the body is (Cl III, 11–12).

Saying that the soul must be substantially present where a part of the brain is does not fully determine how the soul is present. It certainly rules out mere Cartesian operational presence, but it fails to determine whether the soul's presence is to be understood in terms of holenmerism or in terms of mere extension. However, there is cumulative evidence that for Clarke the soul is merely coextended with a part of the brain. As we shall see, Clarke used an analogy with space, which he took to be both extended and indivisible, to explain how the soul could be extended and indivisible; but certainly holenmerism does not apply to space. He did not address More's critique of holenmerism, as one would expect him to do had he adopted it. He did not address Leibniz's accusation that the extension of the soul destroys its unity by appealing to holenmerism; rather, he defended the claim that, as he put it, the soul "fills the sensorium" (Cl V, 98). Finally, as we shall see, Leibniz clearly attributed to Clarke the view that the soul is extended. In sum, Clarke's views on freedom, with their ties to morality and religion, conjoined with his views on causality, pushed him toward the thesis that the soul is extended. No surprise, then, that he did not tell Collins that the soul is unextended and preferred the diplomatic answer that the issues of extension and immateriality were separate and that at any rate, the soul could be both extended and indivisible just like space is.

Clarke's reference to space did not impress Collins. He still could not see how an extended substance could be essentially indivisible. All finite extended things, he claimed, must

> so far consist of Parts, that the part of one side is not the part of the other side. . . . Suppose the substance of the soul to be four inches square . . . it does not appear to me, that an inch on one side . . . is more dependent on an inch on the other side, as to each other's existence, than two sides of a perfectly solid Particle of matter are. (W III, 775)

In Collins's eyes, Clarke's attribution of extension to the soul undermined the argument for its immateriality and consequently rendered his own materialist position more attractive. True, space has parts and yet it is indivisible, but this, Collins claimed without explaining, is due to its infinity and to the fact that space is "mere Absence or Place of Bodies" (W III, 775).

In his reply, Clarke reasserted that the issue of the extension of the soul is logically independent of the argument for the immateriality of the soul (W III, 794). Furthermore, he claimed, even if the supposition that immateriality (and consequent indivisibility) and extension are compatible entails difficulties that one could not clearly solve, the proof for the immateriality of the soul would not be weakened unless one could show that the proof itself is defective. The reason is that "there are many Demonstrations even in abstract Mathematicks themselves, which no Man who understands them can in the least doubt of the Certainty of, which yet are attended with difficult Consequences that cannot perfectly be cleared. The infinite Divisibility of Quantity, is an instance of this kind" (W III, 794). As further examples, Clarke gave divine eternity and immensity, which, although self-evident, involve considerable difficulty.

One can hardly see the strength of Clarke's point, since there is no parity between the cases he discussed. For him, it is demonstrable that a geometrical line is infinitely divisible, and if we are sure of the proof, the difficulties surrounding the composition of the continuum can be set aside. This position is completely correct. Suppose, however, that the infinite divisibility of a geometrical line were a mere hypothesis, as the extension of the soul is allegedly taken to be by Clarke; then, the difficulties surrounding it would be a good reason for rejecting it outright. Therefore, if the supposition of the extension of the soul involves one in difficulties, for example, with respect to the soul's indivisibility, then one should give it up, unless, of course, the claim that the soul is extended, far from being a mere supposition, is taken to be demonstrated. Clarke showed no sign of being ready to jettison the view that the soul is extended, although for strategic reasons he emphasized its independence of the proof for the soul's immateriality. The reason, I believe, was that he felt as certain of the soul's extension as of its immateriality. The analogy with the infinite divisibility of quantity worked not with respect to the position Clarke prudently put forth against Collins, but with respect to his true one. In this sense, his analogy betrayed his true views.

Clarke continued by plausibly remarking that, at any rate, the difficulties surrounding the ascription of extension to the soul are not so grave as those surrounding the attribution of infinite divisibility to quantity or eternity and immensity to God. Space, Clarke claimed, is not mere absence of bodies and it is extended and yet indivisible because it is "an extension whose parts (improperly so called) depend on each other for their existence, not only because of its infinity, but because of the contradiction which a separation of them manifestly would imply" (W III, 794). All one has to do, Clarke continued, is to think of the soul as a substance whose parts depend on each other, like those of space (W III, 795). This answer left Collins dissatisfied, and Clarke, who perhaps had grown impatient, cut short this part of the debate by refusing to discuss the issue further (W III, 821, 851).

2. *Leibniz*

Since Leibniz's views on the soul are well known and relatively clear, a brief overview of the relevant issues will suffice. Leibniz believed that a soul is an individual immaterial substance. From this he inferred that a soul is naturally immortal, and consequently, barring divine miraculous annihilation, immune from destruction. Like Clarke, he thought that the natural immortality of the soul plays a very important role in natural religion and ethics.[15] Like Clarke, he also believed that it had come under attack. Leibniz identified two types of threats: the attack on the immateriality of the soul, and the attack on its substantiality.

Among those who attacked the immateriality of the soul, not surprisingly Leibniz mentioned Epicurus and Hobbes (GP VII, 333–34). However, he saw the germs of materialism in less suspicious quarters as well for he was quite prepared to read Locke's sceptical remarks about the nature of the mind and his views on thinking matter as a sign of carelessness at best and incipient materialism at worst. Moreover, Leibniz saw a sinister connection between what he took to be Locke's uncritical acceptance of Newtonian gravitation and the undermining of the immateriality of the soul:

> After that [admitting attraction] it will be permissible to feign everything which one wishes: one will be able to give to matter the power of thinking, and undermine the soul's immateriality which is one of the principal foundations of natural theology. Thus one saw that Mr Locke who was not too convinced of this immateriality seized eagerly on the opinion of Mr Newton as soon as it appeared, and whereas he had formerly believed with reason that a body cannot move another immediately except by touching and pushing it, he retracted his opinion on the subject in one of the subsequent editions of his book on the understanding as if Mr Newton showed that matter is capable of higher faculties than one believes.[16]

If Epicurus and his overt or covert followers threatened the immateriality of the soul, others threatened its substantiality by absorbing it into a single universal spirit,

> which . . . animates the whole universe and all its parts, each according to its structure and the organs which it finds there, just as the same wind current causes different organ pipes to give off different sounds. Thus they also hold that when an animal has sound organs, this spirit produces the effect of a particular soul in it but that when the organs are corrupted, this particular soul reduces to nothing or returns, so to speak, to the ocean of the universal spirit. (*Considerations sur le doctrine d'un Esprit Universel Unique*: GP VI, 529=L 554)

Such a view, Leibniz thought, "destroys the immortality of the soul and degrades the human race" (GP VI, 531=L 555). Leibniz's list of offenders was quite long, ranging from Aristotle to Spinoza and the Occasionalists, the last two being guilty of holding that only one substance exists, the former explicitly, the latter ones unawares insofar as they maintained that only God acts (GP VI, 531=L 555).

Not only did Leibniz find fault with his contemporaries' views on the nature of the soul, but he also disapproved of the way in which the issue of the relationship between the mind and the body had been handled. To be sure, at times he presented himself as a developer of principles present in Occasionalism. However, his considered and often repeated view was that Occasionalism, aside from endangering the substantiality of the soul, required the intervention of the first cause when that of second causes was all that was needed, and consequently confused the miraculous with the natural (GP IV, 483=L 457).[17]

While at times Leibniz seemed ready to look upon Occasionalism with some favor, the same cannot be said for interactionism. Whether Descartes' causal views entitled him to adopt interactionism is an open question.[18] However, there is little doubt that Leibniz found Cartesian interactionism both unintelligible and at odds with the laws of physics. He could not see how created substances could interact (*Systeme Nouveau*: GP IV, 483=L 457). Hence, even assuming matter were a substance, it could not interact with the soul. Nor could he see how body and soul, "which differ *toto genere*," could have any sort of "physical communication" between them (*Theodicy* § 59: GP VI, 135). Moreover, such interaction ran afoul of the principle of conservation of force, which precludes the introduction of new force in the universe (*Considerations sur les Principes de Vie . . . par l'Auteur du Systeme de l'Harmonie preétablie*: GP VI, 540–41=L 587).[19]

3. The Correspondence

In spite of the facts that the exchange between Clarke and Collins on whether matter can think had been well known in England, and Clarke's side of the controversy, which Le Clerc had approvingly summarized in his *Bibliotheque Choisie* in 1713, had gone through several editions, Leibniz seems to have paid little if any attention to it.[20] However, this state of affairs was to change quite dramatically. In October 1715, he received from Rémond some letters by Conti, a Leibnizian then visiting England, which briefly explained the positions of Newton and Clarke on the soul. Newton, Conti said,

> talks of the soul and the body only in relation to experience [*aux les phenomenes*]. He claims to ignore completely the nature of these two things. By body, he understands merely what is extended, impenetrable, heavy, etc. By soul, what thinks, what feels in us, etc. He claims to know nothing more about it. Dr. Clarke goes further and says that one could not prove that the soul is something which belongs to the body. Here is his argument: one can show that

every body is divisible; but one knows from experience [*par les phenomenes*] that the thinking substance is something indivisible. Since these two properties are contradictory, they cannot be found in the same subject. Consequently, one cannot prove that the soul and the body are the same thing. (18 October 1715: GP III, 653 19)

Clarke and Newton had, then, two different, albeit compatible, positions, and it is reasonable to assume that Leibniz was much more interested in the latter than in the former. Newton's position sounded very much like Locke's, who, in Leibniz's eyes, had professed ignorance of the nature of the soul only to prepare the way for his crypto-materialist views. This explains the letter Leibniz sent to Caroline, which became the first letter of his exchange with Clarke: "Natural religion itself seems to decay very much. Many will have human souls to be material; others make God himself a corporeal being. Mr. Locke and his followers are uncertain, at least, whether the soul be not material, and naturally perishable" (Lz I, 1–2). The letter continued with the explicit charge that for Newton, God needs a *sensorium* and the implicit one that the Newtonian God is the soul of the world. Because of Leibniz's innuendos, at the end of the letter, Newton looked a bit like Locke and Spinoza rolled into one.

In the meantime, Princess Caroline had sent Leibniz two works by Clarke who, she thought, might translate the *Theodicy* into English (3 November 1715: KLC 50= R 21). Among them were Clarke's letters to Dodwell and Collins. Presumably, while he was reading them, came Clarke's first reply, in which he and Newton distanced themselves from Locke (Cl I, 1–2). By the end of November 1715, Leibniz was ready to give a preliminary judgment of Clarke's letters to Collins:

[Clarke] often says very good things, but he falls short of following or envisaging my principles. He is right in holding against Mr. Dodwell and against an anonymous opponent that the soul is immaterial because of its indivisibility, and that all that is composed of parts cannot have anything in it which is not in its parts. Given this, I cannot see how he can maintain that the soul is extended, since everywhere there is extension there are parts, unless one takes that word in an unusual sense. (R 32)

Leibniz continued by obliquely criticizing the Newtonian position on the soul. Caroline had told him that according to Newton and Clarke, God can annihilate the soul. She disagreed: God can no more annihilate the soul than he can bring it about that what I hold in my fist is bigger than my fist (25 November 1715: R 27). Leibniz replied that Caroline had done well in holding that the soul is naturally immortal and therefore God could annihilate it only by miracle, thereby tactfully correcting the princess and de facto agreeing with Clarke. However, he continued by claiming that those who lower the idea of God by resembling him to the soul of the world, also lower that of the soul to the extent that they seem to hold that it could perish by natural divine operation. Worse, some of their followers could be easily convinced to adopt a full-blown theory of a single universal spirit. Leibniz's implication was clear: Newton's position either amounted to a form of crypto-averroism, or could insensibly lead to it.

Leibniz's letter to Caroline offered hints to two of the lines of criticism he pursued immediately and vigorously in the correspondence, namely, the issue of the relation between Clarke's views of the soul and of God and that of the extension of the soul. The third main issue, that of the interaction between soul and body, became prominent later. Since we dealt with the first issue in the chapter on God, here we shall look at the remaining two.

3.1 *The Extension of the Soul*

Leibniz's opposition to the view that the soul is extended was both general and specific. For one thing, he could not agree with the motivation behind Clarke's acceptance of it. For Clarke's principal reason for making the soul extended was to guarantee the possibility of its interaction with the body, which both experience and piety demanded. But for Leibniz this was a wrong-headed attempt, since he denied that any such interaction takes place. However, aside from this general metaphysical criticism, Leibniz had more specific ones. In his second letter, he presented Clarke with a puzzle: since the soul is indivisible, as Clarke himself showed, it must be present to the body at most at one point. Then, how can it perceive what goes on outside that point (Lz II, 4)? It is not easy to understand Leibniz's reasoning. Since for him anything extended is divisible, one can reasonably assume that he was not claiming that the soul can be both indivisible and extended. Perhaps he was looking at Clarke's position in light of More's views, such as they were, that the center of a spirit is infinitesimally small and consequently, indivisible. But clearly, the heart of Leibniz's objection consisted in the inference from indivisibility to lack of extension. Clarke's answer was to the point:

indivisibility does not exclude extension; for example, space is indivisible and yet extended (Cl II, 4–5).

Leibniz was not satisfied. He replied by focusing more sharply on the spatial relation between the soul and the body. Saying that the soul "is diffused through the body is to make it extended and divisible; saying that the whole of it is in each part of the body is to make it divisible from itself. Attaching it to a point, spreading it out through several points, all these are nothing but abusive expressions, *idola tribus*" (Lz III, 12). Leibniz's strategy was, then, to foreclose any possible interpretation of the claim that the soul is extended by showing that all the traditional readings led to the divisibility of the soul. In addition, the reference to the Baconian *idola tribus* was probably not too subtle a comment on what Leibniz took to be the deplorable English tendency, from More on, to think of the soul as extended. Moreover, Leibniz had correctly taken Clarke to hold the principle of homogeneity (To Caroline, November 1715: KLC 60= R 32). Consequently, since the soul has parts, its consciousness, according to Clarke himself, must be the aggregation of the consciousnesses of its parts, which is inconsistent with Clarke's principle of the unity of consciousness. In sum, giving extension to the soul or, worse, to God, amounts to destroying their unity.

Clarke followed a two-pronged strategy in his replies. One showed some embarrassment at Leibniz's criticism. For, he began restricting the extension of the soul, first by claiming that it is present not in the whole body but in the brain, and finally by saying that it is not present in the whole brain, but merely in a place where part of the brain is, the *sensorium* (Cl III,12; IV, 37). His defense looked very much like a retreat, and Leibniz was quick to indicate that the problems surrounding Clarke's position did not depend on the amount of the soul's extension, but on its extension *simpliciter* (Lz V, 98).

Clarke's second strategy was more promising. He repeated that Leibniz's criticisms were based on a misconception of the nature of the soul, which, he claimed, is like space in being both extended and indivisible. In addition, Clarke made a point he had already hinted at in his replies to Collins: the parts of space, unlike corporeal parts, are called "parts" improperly because they cannot be separated from each other (Cl III, 3; IV, 11–12; W III, 794). Again, Leibniz was not convinced. He had already mentioned to Caroline his dissatisfaction with Clarke's use of the term "part," and he had also noticed that Clarke had told Collins on the one hand that space has parts, and on the other that these parts are so called only improperly (Lz IV, 12; W III, 763, 794). At the end, Clarke made a concession of sorts:

> If the soul be a substance which fills the sensorium, or place wherein it perceives the images of things conveyed to it; yet it does not thence follow, that it must consist of corporeal parts, (for the parts of the body are distinct substances independent on each other;) but the whole soul sees, and the whole soul hears, and the whole soul thinks, as being essentially one individual. (Cl V, 98)

However, Clarke's reply is hardly satisfactory, since Leibniz's criticism does not revolve around the assumption that for Clarke the soul or its parts are material or, for what matters, separable.[21] And the admission of parts in the soul, combined with the principle of homogeneity, does seem to entail the conclusion that each part of the soul has consciousness, thus leading to the destruction of the unity of consciousness on which Clarke had built his argument for the immateriality of the soul.

We shall never know what Clarke would have replied, had Leibniz pressed the point. However, we can guess. As we noted in the discussion of God, Clarke held that space is indivisible and therefore that the parts of space are interdependent, so that the positing of one entails the positing of all the others, and ultimately the positing of space as a whole (W III, 794, 795). Against Leibniz, who was ready to admit that the parts of space presuppose the whole of space because space is merely an *ens rationis*, Clarke consistently maintained both the priority of space over its parts and its real existence. Therefore, pursuing the analogy between the soul and space, he could maintain that the soul is not merely indivisible, but that it is a totality in which the whole logically antecedes the parts. Hence, at least some of its powers as a whole could not depend on those of its parts. Clarke could then claim that consciousness is one of these powers, and consequently that the extension of the soul is compatible with his argument for the soul's immortality. For the objection against their compatibility was based on the alleged dependence of the composite subject's consciousness on the consciousnesses or powers of the parts.

3.2 *The Relation Between the Soul and the Body*

Leibniz did not content himself with attacking the view that the soul is extended; he also challenged Clarke on the issue of how the soul senses. In his first reply, Clarke had claimed that God by his presence sees all things in a way analogous to how the soul, "by its immediate presence to the pictures or images of things, form'd in the brain by means of the organs of sensation, sees those pictures as if they were the things themselves" (Cl I, 3). Given the theological setting of the analogy, not surprisingly Clarke avoided any causal reference in his account of sensation. Leibniz found the lack of reference to causality unsatisfactory, and told Clarke that mere presence is not sufficient for sensation, as "Father Malebranche and all the Cartesians," he hastened to say, would hold as well (Lz II, 4). For Leibniz, as for Malebranche, there is a causal story to be told about how the mind perceives what goes on in the body. Of course, Leibniz's own story was to say that God is the artificer of preestablished harmony. Indeed, for Leibniz, not even God could be aware of the states of the world merely by being there, diffused through the world, as it were. On the contrary, God knows the world because he made it and continually preserves it (Lz II, 4). Leibniz's motives for pressing the issue seem reasonably clear. If Clarke denied any sort of causal link between soul and body in sensation, he could be charged with hopeless obscurity. If he admitted a casual influence, then he could be charged either with de facto admitting a causal influence of the world on God, which of course would sit very well with the charge that he had turned God into the soul of the world, or with using a bad analogy.

Clarke replied that the soul perceives not only because it is present to the brain, but because it is a living substance (Cl II, 4). Presumably, then, a living substance perceives what goes on where it is, although Clarke did not explain how that could happen. When Leibniz objected that the mere presence of a living substance is not sufficient for sensation, since neither a blind nor a distracted man see, Clarke replied that a blind man does not see merely because the organs of sight do not convey the images to the brain (Cl III, 11). He continued by claiming that we do not know how the soul "sees the images to which it is present." When he repeated that the soul senses because the images of things are conveyed to it, Leibniz charged him with revamping the obscurantist Scholastic doctrine of intentional species "passing from the organs to the soul" (Cl IV, 30; Lz V, 84). In his last letter, Clarke rejected the accusation, claiming that Leibniz had failed to show that the conveyance of images to the *sensorium* where the soul perceives them is unintelligible (Cl V, 84). Clarke's answer, however, failed to address Leibniz's charge, since the issue was not the transmission of images from objects to the *sensorium*, but that of images from the sensorium to the soul, or better, how the soul becomes aware of the images in the *sensorium,* and of this Clarke provided no explanation.

Leibniz's mention of intentional species might sound out of place, but it was not unjustified. He thought that, lacking any understanding of the union between mind and body, we are prone to imagine that our souls receive species as messengers as if they had "doors and windows" (GP IV, 451=L 320). His analysis was not without foundation.[22] Moreover, he had some textual evidence for his charge against Clarke. In his letters to Collins, Clarke held that the soul, being indivisible, is also not alterable by any natural power. When Collins objected that then the soul could not sense, Clarke replied that his view does not entail that the soul cannot be "acted upon at all" by any power of nature (W III, 793). He endeavored to clarify his position by way of an analogy. Imagine some atoms whose intrinsic qualities such as hardness, shape, size, could not be altered by any natural means. But, Clarke continued,

> these Particles might be *acted upon,* might be *struck* by each other, might be moved this way, upwards or downwards; all which makes no Alteration in them: So, an indiscerpible immaterial thinking Substance, though it may be transferred from one point of the Universe to another, though it may be *acted upon* by a Multitude of things, though it may have different Ideas represented to it, though the Organs of the Senses may at times transmit different Species, or hinder them from being transmitted to it; yet all this makes no real Alteration either in the Substance or its inherent Powers. (W III, 793)

In his copy of Clarke's letters to Collins, Leibniz underlined the word "Species," which found its way into his fifth letter.

While Clarke's analogy between souls and atoms was not transparent, presumably the gist of it lay in the claim that the only powers and qualities any natural power can change in a soul are extrinsic. More generally, Clarke may be understood as trying to individuate two different types of qualities in the soul: intrinsic, mental or intentional modifications (e.g., sensations) and extrinsic modifications (e.g., spatial positions). This might open the possibility of reconciling his claim that the body acts on the soul with the view that matter cannot produce thought either in itself or in another substance. For, although Clarke's hierarchical view of the ontology of qualities entails that matter cannot directly produce sensation, it is compatible with the claim that matter could induce sensation in a sentient substance. Matter could cause a modification of the same sort it has itself in a sentient substance that is capable of such modification, and this modification, in turn, could be a concause (not the full cause) of sensation.

However, what modification could do the trick is far from clear. Certainly, the body could not cause changes in the shape of the soul, since he held that the parts of the soul, like those of space, cannot be moved with respect to each other (W III, 794–95). Force would seem a more likely candidate. To be sure, Clarke seemed to restrict force to the activity of souls (Cl IV, 33; V, 93–95). But what he had in mind was not the transmission of force, but the production of new force, since for him, like for Locke, a body can only transmit as much force as it loses (Cl V, 93–95).[23] So, nothing in his system prevents him from holding that a body can transmit force it has itself received.

If an appeal to force is what Clarke had in mind, unfortunately he did not explain, preferring to point out that since it is a mystery to us how bodies act on each other, we should not deny that matter acts on the soul simply because we do not understand how that comes about (W III, 897). Perhaps he was trying to argue in a way analogous to Newton, who in the general scholium to book 3 defended universal gravitation by separating the issue of its existence and its mode of operation from that of the "mechanism" underlying it. However, whereas in the *Principia* Newton had mounted a powerful case for the existence of universal gravitation, the same cannot be said for Clarke's action of the body on the soul, since both Leibniz's preestablished harmony and Malebranche's Occasionalism could give a reasonable account of appearances. The action of the body on the soul was not one of the strong points of Clarke's system.

Whereas on the topic of sensation Clarke remained on the defensive, on that of the activity of the soul on the body he was much more outspoken. He repeatedly told Leibniz, as he had Collins, that denying that the soul imparts new force on the body amounts to saying that the soul does not act, which leads to fatalism and moreover conflicts with our everyday experience (Cl IV, 32; V, 92).[24] Clarke's appeal to experience might seem strange, since Malebranche had already pointed out that at most, all we experience is our volition and the effort to move our body usually followed by the appropriate bodily motion.[25] However, Clarke seemed to think he had an answer to Malebranche's point, since he claimed that "there is no one thing that . . . a Man can imagine *ought* to follow from the Supposition of Self-Motion, which every Man does not now as much feel and *actually* experience in Himself, as it can possibly be imagined any Man *would* do, supposing the thing were true" (WB 558).

The only reason for doubting we originate motion in matter, Clarke continued, would be either if the notion of such a power were shown to be per se inconsistent, which it is not, since God did originate motion in matter; or if the notion of such a power in creatures were inconsistent, which it is not, since, Clarke claimed, this power is not essentially associated with "self-existence and absolute independency" (WN 588).[26]

Indeed, so wedded was Clarke to the idea that we experience the power whereby we move the body that he ventured to claim that even if we had an apparently strong argument against the existence of originative causal powers in us, it would not be inappropriate to doubt our reasoning rather than the obvious evidence from experience (WN 588). After Hume, we might find it hard to share Clarke's confidence that we actually experience the force whereby we move the body. However, it would be unfair to criticize Clarke too harshly on this point. That we have a direct experience of the causal power of the mind does have an intuitive appeal. Locke had found in the experience of moving our limbs at will one of the sources of the idea of active power. Indeed, Leibniz himself was ready to attack Occasionalism with the claim that the denial that we cause our own thoughts is inconsistent with the data of experience.[27]

To Clarke's claims on the causal activity of the mind on the body, Leibniz objected that the production of new force is incompatible with the laws of physics, and that action does not require transmission of force, as when two equal bodies upon meeting rebound with the same speed each had before but with opposite direction (Lz V, 93–94). Clarke briefly dismissed Leibniz's point about impacting bodies by claiming that each body rebounds not with its own force, but with that received through the elasticity of the other (Cl V, 93–95). He was right to dismiss Leibniz's example since the issue at hand was not what impels what in impact, but what the soul's action on the body consists in. Clarke followed Locke and common sense by claiming that true action requires the production of new motion: "Action is the beginning of a motion where there was none before from a principle of life or activity" (Cl V, 93–95). Of course such a view requires the denial of the conservation of motive force, and on this Clarke and Leibniz disagreed, as we shall see in the chapter on matter and force.

Clarke was not impressed by Leibniz's metaphysical objections to interactionism. In the appendix to the correspondence, he quoted a passage from the *Theodicy* § 59 in which Leibniz argued that there could not be any causal link between the soul and the body because such action could not "be deduced from the Notion of anything we can conceive in the Body and Soul; though nothing be better known to us than the Soul, because it is intimate to us, that is, to itself" (W IV, 706, appendix 5). In sum, interactionism is unintelligible at best and impossible at worst, and consequently must be rejected. Clarke disagreed. He attached a note to Leibniz's passage in which he distanced himself from Leibniz's rather ebullient Cartesian statements about our knowledge of the soul: "As the Eye sees not itself; and if a Man had never seen Another's Eye, nor the Image of his own in a Glass, he could never have had any Notion what an Eye is; So the Soul discerns not its own Substance" (W IV, 706). One might object that if Clarke denied that the introspective powers of the soul could reach its substance, then he effectively undercut his appeals to introspection in the defense of interactionism. But such an objection would be misplaced. Clarke, like Malebranche, could consistently hold that introspection is reliable, even infallible, without holding that it provides any direct access to the nature of the soul. Certainly one could know, by argument, that the soul must be immaterial and extended, but even argumentation cannot disclose the substance of the soul to us. As we shall see in the chapter on miracles, for Clarke, as for Locke and Newton, we just do not know the substance of things.[28]

Moreover, our inability to explain how the soul acts on matter is not peculiar. We cannot explain how an immaterial God acts on matter and yet we do not deny that he does. In addition, Clarke rhetorically asked in his last letter,

> Is it not as easy to conceive how certain parts of matter may be obliged to follow the motions and affections of the soul, without corporeal contact; as that certain portions of matter should be obliged to follow each other's motions by the adhesion of parts, which no mechanism can account for; or that rays of light should reflect regularly from a surface which they never touch? Of which Sir Isaac Newton in his *Opticks* has given several evident and ocular experiments. (Cl V, 110–16)

So, the fact that we cannot understand how the soul acts on matter is not sufficient reason for rejecting it, since the world is full of things we do not understand. To be sure, Leibniz's claim was that interactionism is not merely not understood, but that it is outright unintelligible. However, as we saw, Clarke denied that Leibniz had in any way proved his point (Cl V, 83–88).

To Clarke's interactionism, Leibniz opposed preestablished harmony. In December 1715, apparently still stung by Conti's report that the *Commercium Epistolicum*, published anonymously but written by Newton, held that Leibniz's philosophy was conjectural while Newton's was experimental, Leibniz told Bernoulli that preestablished harmony, far from being a conjecture, was demonstrated (December 1715: NC VI, 260–61 = R 44). No surprise, then, that when he read Newton's letter to Conti stating that preestablished harmony is contrary to our experience of seeing with our own eyes and moving our bodies with our will, Leibniz told Conti that Newton had misinterpreted his view (Newton to Conti, 26 February 1716: NC VI, 285=R 63; Leibniz to Conti, 9 April 1716: NC VI, 307= R 65). Perhaps chagrined at what he took to be Newton's superficial criticisms, Leibniz introduced the issue of preestablished harmony in his fourth letter (Lz IV, 30–31, 35). The context was essentially theological, and Leibniz's efforts were directed at showing how his opponent's analogy between divine and human cognitions of the world was completely ill taken. Leibniz's move provided Clarke with the opportunity to shift the discussion from the shortcomings of interactionism to those of preestablished harmony.

Following Newton, Clarke accused Leibniz's theory of involving a perpetual miracle and of failing to explain the cause of the correspondence between soul and body (Cl IV, 31). Clarke's first point was ill taken. Leibniz effectively replied that in pressing his charge, Clarke was contradicting his own account of miracles as unusual phenomena, since the correspondence between the soul and the body could by no means be considered unusual (Lz IV, 42). To be sure, preestablished harmony was due to an original miracle (Lz V, 89). However, one must distinguish the institution of preestablished harmony from specific occurrences of it. That the body and the soul at time t_1 are so disposed that at time t_2 their states will match can be fully explained on the basis of secondary causes. By contrast, the planning and production of substances that by purely natural means would effect preestablished harmony are of course supernatural; indeed, Leibniz was ready to infer the existence of God from that of preestablished harmony (*Considerations sur les Principes de Vie . . . par l'Auteur du Systeme de l'Harmonie preétablie*, GP VI, 541=L 584). Clarke, probably realizing his mistake, did not react.

Clarke's charge of failing to explain the cause of the correspondence between soul and body prompted Leibniz to accuse Clarke of pretending not to know what preestablished harmony is; he gave Clarke a brief lecture on the theory in his last letter (Lz V, 83, 87, 90, 124). Leibniz's account did not satisfy Clarke, who saw in it further confirmation that his interlocutor's philosophy, in contrast with Newton's and his own, was conjectural. For not only did he find central notions such as mirroring and representing according to a point of view hopelessly obscure, but also thought it amazing that someone could reject gravitation, which is an "actual phenomenon," and accept "so strange an Hypothesis, as *Harmonia Praestabilita*" (Cl V, 110–16).

In fact, Clarke found Leibniz's theory more than strange. At times he even seemed to doubt its possibility, rhetorically asking whether it would be possible for a mere machine to produce all the movements a human body performs (Cl V, 110–16). Clarke's objection was quite natural and not new. It had been advanced by Bayle, who had claimed that not even the divine power could organize a material system capable of playing its role in preestablished harmony.[29] Leibniz had disagreed, asking Bayle for a proof of such impossibility, and claiming that "a man could make a machine capable of walking about for some time through a city and of turning exactly at the corners of certain streets," and consequently God could construct the harmonic material counterpart of the soul (*Reponse aux Reflexions . . . de M. Bayle*, GP IV, 555–56=L 575). Of course, Leibniz could not prove that there exists a set of initial conditions, which joined to the actual laws of motion yields the appropriate movements of all the ensouled bodies in the universe, but his reply was certainly convincing.

In addition to rejecting preestablished harmony as impossible, Clarke also claimed that it ran counter to our experience of moving the body and being causally affected by the senses. If Leibniz were right, he claimed, "a Man does not indeed *see*, nor *hear*, nor *feel* anything, nor *moves his Body*; but only *dreams* that he sees, and hears, and feels, and moves his Body" (Cl V, 110–16). He did not develop the point, but presumably part of what he had in mind was the sort of arguments from introspection for the causal activity of the mind that we considered above. Moreover, there are signs that Clarke viewed Leibniz's dismissal of the alleged intimations of introspection as being part of a wider position that involved a determinist theory of the soul. In his edition of the correspondence, he attached a marginal note to the passage just cited, asking the reader to look at the appendix, number 12, where he provided a quotation from the *Theodicy* § 50 in which Leibniz dismissed Descartes's appeal to inner sense as a way to establish contra-causal freedom and compared our decisions to the motions of a compass (W IV, 697, 710).

In fact, the charge that preestablished harmony would lead to fatalism had already surfaced (Cl IV, 32, 92; V, 92). In a sense, Clarke was right because for him the paradigmatic case of fate and necessity (these, for him, being interchangeable notions) was the deterministic behavior of a machine like a clock, and a Leibnizian body is no doubt like a clock in this respect. However, it is certainly possible that two sequences A and B, such that A is constituted by Clarkeian free, that is, contra-causal, indeterministic, volitions regarding bodily motions and B is constituted by mechanically determined bodily motions, match up in the appropriate way, for example, the volition at time t_1 to move my arm with the appropriate motion of my arm at time t_2. In other words, the performance of contra-causal free actions need not involve the breach of the laws of mechanism. So, the harmony between soul and body need not lead to any form of determinism, or, to use Clarke's word, fatalism.

Of course, Clarke could object that in Leibniz's theory A and B do not just happen to match up; rather, they have been planned to match up, and the planning destroys freedom. Again, in a sense Clarke would be right. For Leibniz held that the divine plan for our world involves that minds are immaterial automata ruled by deterministic laws, and this is incompatible with Clarke's views of freedom. However, that the soul is a deterministic system is independent of preestablished harmony. Indeed, the institution of preestablished harmony is even compatible with Clarke's own views on freedom. For he never denied divine foreknowledge of our future free actions (W IV, 732–33). Consequently, God could match up my volitions, which he foresaw, to the movements of a machine, assuming such a machine could be built. But of course, my actions would not cease for all that to be contra-causally free.

Clarke denied that such a machine could be built, and this explains why he saw a link between his qualms about the possibility of preestablished harmony and fatalism. If mechanism is not adequate to produce all the bodily movements needed to match the appropriate volitions, then preestablished harmony, which Leibniz wanted on the basis of wrong physical views and misguided criteria of intelligibility, could be obtained only by adjusting the latter to the former. In other words, since deterministic mechanism cannot mimic the freedom of the soul, the soul must be turned into a deterministic automaton in order to obtain preestablished harmony.

Clarke was even ready to go beyond the charge of fatalism and link preestablished harmony with a materialist view of the soul. To be sure, he did not explicitly say that Leibniz was dangerously close to a materialist view of man. Rather, he phrased his charge in a historical context:

> If the world can once be persuaded . . . that [a man's] seemingly voluntary motions are performed by the mere necessary laws of corporeal mechanism, without any influence, or operation, or action at all of the soul upon the body; they will soon conclude, that this machine is the whole man; and that the harmonical soul, in the hypothesis of an *harmonia praestabilita,* is a mere fiction and a dream. (Cl V, 110–16)

Clarke had some justification for his worries. In the fourth letter, while charging Leibniz's theory with fatalism, he compared a Leibnizian body to a Cartesian animal. But the Cartesian *bete machine,* certainly against the intentions of its creator, did open the way for *l'homme machine.*[30] Leibniz's theory, then, could provide more ammunition for the materialists. Indeed, when coupled with Clarke's suspicion, which we shall consider in the chapter on miracles, that Leibniz either approved of the view that bodies are substances because they are active and consequently perceive, or did not take sufficient care to reject it, Clarke's worries seem quite reasonable (WB 546, 562). In fact, Newton was prepared to go even further than Clarke and explicitly link Leibniz's mechanism to materialism. In a draft published by Koyré and Cohen, he called the idea that phenomena in nature are "caused by mere matter and motion and man himself is a mere machine [and] his body is not actuated by any mind " the "hypothesis of the materialists." And he concluded that "[Leibniz's] zeale for this precarious hypothesis makes him rail at Mr Newton's universal gravity."[31] Ironically, Newton saw Leibniz's denial of universal gravitation as a consequence of incipient materialist leanings much in the same way in which Leibniz had viewed Locke's acceptance of universal gravitation as a prelude for materialism.

3

FREE WILL

Both Leibniz and Clarke attached great importance to the issue of free will, and like many philosophers agreed that the highest form of freedom involves willing as one should, namely, having one's will in step with one's right values. Unlike Spinoza, they also agreed that freedom of the will is a necessary condition for that higher form of freedom, and that Hobbes's and Spinoza's official necessitarian view that everything happens by metaphysical necessity destroys it (NE II, 21, 8; *On the Liberty of Moral Agents*: W I, 218–20). Both held that God, like us, is endowed with free will and follows his judgment of what is good, as we do when acting wisely (*Theodicy* § 234: GP VI, 256–57; W I, 218–20). In spite of these points of agreement, the controversy on free will was sufficiently heated to lead Leibniz in his last letter to accuse his opponent of being disingenuous. Certainly, the intensity of the exchange was partially due to the fact that Clarke was a libertarian who believed in agent causation and contra-causal freedom, while Leibniz was a compatibilist. It was around this difference that the dispute revolved. However, as we shall see, behind the issue of free will were others that involved different but equally substantial philosophical and theological questions. We shall first look at Clarke's and Leibniz's views and then at their exchange.

1. Clarke

That the issue of freedom was dear to Clarke can be easily discovered by considering that he dealt with it at some length in his
Boyle Lectures. Moreover, in the dedicatory letter to his edition of
the correspondence, Clarke explicitly identified "questions concerning liberty and fate" as one of the most important points discussed in it (W IV, 582). The topic attracted him not merely
because of its philosophical importance, but also because of its
many ramifications. In 1717, just months after the exchange with
Leibniz came to an end, Clarke published his edition of the correspondence and appended to it two works on free will, namely, his
brief epistolary exchange with Bulkeley and his remarks on Collins's book against liberty.[1] He closed his remarks on Collins with
an impassioned appeal:

> I cannot make an End, without earnestly desiring this Author se-
> riously to consider with himself, *what* it is he has all this Time
> been pleading for . . . *Superstition and Bigottry* . . . can never be
> rooted, but by persuading Men to look upon themselves as *rational*
> Creatures, and to implant in their Minds *rational Notions of Reli-*
> *gion: Religion* there can be none, without a *moral Difference of*
> *Things*: a *moral Difference of Things there cannot be*, where there
> is no Place for *Action*: And *Action* there can be none, without *Lib-*
> *erty.* (W IV, 735)[2]

According to Clarke, the principal enemies of freedom were Spinoza,
Hobbes, and their followers, all of whom denied the libertarian views
he espoused (WB 559).[3] At the end of proposition IX of *A Demon-*
stration, after a protracted attempt to show that God is a free agent,
Clarke felt ready to deliver the coup de grâce against his opponents:

> The Principal Argument used by the Maintainers of Fate against
> the possibility of Liberty, is this: That, since every thing must have
> a Cause, every Volition or Determination of the Will of an Intelli-
> gent Being, must, as all other things, arise from some Cause, and
> That Cause from some other Cause, and so on infinitely. But now
> (besides that in This sort of Reasoning, these Men always ignorantly
> confound *Moral Motives* with *Physical Efficients*, between which
> Two things there is no manner of relation: Besides This, I say,) this
> very Argument really proves the direct contrary to what they in-
> tend. For since every thing must indeed have a Cause of its Being,
> either from without, or in the Necessity of its own Nature; and 'tis
> a plain Contradiction (as has already been demonstrated) to suppose

an infinite Series of dependent Effects none of which are Necessary in Themselves or Self-Existent; therefore 'tis impossible but there must be in the Universe some Being, whose Existence is founded in the Necessity of its Own Nature; and which, being acted upon by Nothing beyond itself, must of Necessity have in itself a Principle of Acting, or Power of beginning Motion, which is the Idea of Liberty. (WB 552–53)[4]

In sum, the causal version of the Principle of Sufficient Reason entails that God is free in Clarke's sense of the term. Clarke's argument is not only bold, but disconcerting. If the Cosmological Argument shows anything, it shows that the first cause cannot be acted upon by any other cause and consequently must be an original causal principle. Spinoza knew this and pointed out that God is self-existent and self-determined, that is, a free cause in his sense, and that its essence is power.[5] But whether the divine power operates in accordance with metaphysically necessary laws themselves arising from the divine nature or not, is left open by the causal version of the Principle of Sufficient Reason. Moreover, to the extent that the Principle of Sufficient Reason is viewed as requiring a reason for everything and engendering explanatory rationalism, it seems to entail that divine actions must be ultimately determined by self-explanatory, and consequently necessary, laws.[6]

Clarke thought he had an answer to this sort of objection based on what presumably is a conceptual analysis of the notion of being an agent. He claimed that "to Act necessarily is really and properly not to Act at all, but only to be Acted upon" (WB 548). The very notion of a necessary agent, he stated, is contradictory (WB 566; Cl IV, 22–23). Therefore, since God must be an agent, he cannot operate necessarily. Clarke did not produce any explicit argument in favor of his view and contented himself with claiming that an agent acting necessarily would be like a stone falling to the ground by the necessity of its own nature, that is, Clarke concluded, no "Agent or Cause at all" (WB 548). It is hard to escape Leibniz's conclusion that he simply had no argument to offer for the claim that the very notion of a necessary agent is inconsistent and consequently resorted merely to brandishing his own intuition of what an agent is (Lz V, 77).

Not only was Clarke ready to say that an agent cannot act necessarily, but he also claimed outright that being an agent and being free are the same thing. A person's liberty "consists in his *being an Agent*, that is, in his having continual Power of *choosing*, whether he shall *Act* or whether he shall *forbear Acting"* (WB 565–66). Of course, the identification of agency with the capacity to choose provided further ammunition against the view that Spinoza's god is an agent, as Clarke did not fail to point out (WB 586). But even granting his views on agency, Clarke could not explain why the first cause ought to be an agent in his sense rather than just a Spinozistic cause that produces all that can be produced without choosing. Ultimately, the causal version of the Principle of Sufficient Reason cannot yield the conclusion Clarke wanted.

However, Clarke had other arguments against the view that the ways of divine operation are necessary. He held that since necessity must be everywhere and always the same, it cannot produce any variety, and consequently that if the divine operation were necessary it could not produce a diverse world (WB 540, 549). This argument, however, is not convincing since metaphysical pronouncements about necessity are hard to defend, and a mathematical function, such as an ellipse, can have variations—for example, different degrees of curvature—in spite of presumably embodying a type of necessity akin to the metaphysical one. A further argument was that if God operated necessarily, things could not be different from how they are. But the number of planets, their orbits, indeed, the law of gravitation itself could have been different, as any reasonable person (but not Spinoza) could plainly see. Further, the obvious fact that final causes are at play in the world indicates that divine activity follows not necessary but architectonic patterns. True, Spinoza denied final causes, and ridiculed those who claimed that eyes were designed to see with, teeth to chew with, and the sun to give light. However, Clarke concluded,

> I suppose it will not be thought, that, when once a Man comes to this, he is to be disputed with any longer. Whoever pleases, may for Satisfaction on this Head, consult *Galen De Usu Partium, Tully de natura Deorum, Mr Boyle of Final Causes,* and *Mr Ray of the Wisdom of God in the Creation.* I shall only observe this one thing; that the larger the Improvements and Discoveries are, which are daily made in Astronomy and Natural Philosophy; the more clearly is this Question continually determined, to the Shame and Confusion of Atheists. (WB 551)

Spinoza and the opponents of the Newtonian project to support religion with the help of the new science were not merely bad philosophers but also scientific *ignoremus.*

Clarke did not content himself with attacking necessitarianism with arguments drawn from general metaphysical considerations, but he also criticized the specific theories of volition that leading necessitarians had put forth, in particular the view that volition is caused by, or even identical with, the last evaluative judgment. He did not identify whom he had in mind, but probably the targets were Spinoza and Hobbes. Spinoza had argued that "will and intellect are one and the same thing," by which he meant that every act of volition is an act of affirmation and vice versa. Presumably, what he had in mind is that every volition is identical with a value judgment: to will to do X is to judge that X is the best thing to do.[7] Hobbes had not identified the volition with the evaluative judgment, but had told Bramhall that the latter was the final and decisive cause of the former, since the last judgment of the understanding "may be said to produce the effect *necessarily*, in such manner as the last feather may be said to break a horse's back, when there were so many laid on before as there wanted but that one to do it."[8]

Clarke was ready to grant that the understanding is fully determined to assent to a proposition that is perceived to be true, in the same way in which an open eye is fully determined to see objects. In this sense, the assent is necessary (W IV, 714). However, the necessity of the last evaluative judgment is totally immaterial to the issue of freedom. His opponents, Clarke thought, were guilty of basic philosophical errors. If they maintained that the content of the evaluation, the evaluative proposition, is identical with the volition or causes it, then they were confusing reasons with causes or, as he put it, "Moral Motives with Physical Efficients" (WB 553). Properly understood "the *last Judgment of the Understanding* is not itself a *physical Efficient*, but merely a *Moral Motive*, upon which the *physical Efficient* or *Motive Power* begins to Act" (WB 565).[9] The understanding presents the agent with a value judgment, for example, "doing X is better than doing Y," which the agent has the actual power to follow or not. The reason, Clarke explained to Collins in 1717, is that the motive, for example, the proposition "doing X is better than doing Y," cannot cause anything because it is an abstract entity. Holding the contrary is taking an abstract entity for a substance (W IV, 723, 725).

On the other hand, if Clarke's opponents maintained that not the evaluative proposition, but one's perceiving, judging or otherwise believing it, is identical with, or a concause of, volition, then they were falling foul of a basic causal principle. Against Descartes, Clarke insisted that judging, that is, assenting to what appears true and dissenting from what appears false, is not an action but a passion (W IV, 727). However,

> Nothing can possibly be the *Cause* of an *Effect* more *considerable*
> than *itself*. Nothing that is *passive*, can possibly be the *Cause* of
> anything that is *Active*. An *Occasion* indeed it *may* be; and an
> *Action* may be *consequent* . . . upon *Perception* or *Judgment* . . .
> and yet at the same time there be no manner of *Physical* or *Nec-
> essary Connection* between them. (W IV, 723)

Presumably, the same argument could be used to show that strictly
speaking the passions cannot cause our volitions. So, there is no
causal link between evaluation and volition, or as Clarke put it "ap-
probation and action" (W IV, 714). Nor is there any causal link between previous nonvolitional mental states and any volition.
Clarke's view was not that all the evaluations, passions, and char-
acter traits merely causally underdetermine the volition, but that
they do not have any causal role at all. For Clarke, denying this
conclusion entails being guilty of an egregious category mistake, or
of ill-conceived views about causality. What causes the volition is
the principle of action itself, which Clarke identified with the agent,
that is, the spiritual substance. In sum, he believed in a strong version of agent causation in which the agent is the sole cause of volition.[10]

If in Clarke's eyes piety and philosophy alike required lack of
causal influx between evaluation and volition, they also required
that God be supremely benevolent, so that we may rest assured that
God always does what is best and that, therefore, the great ends of
morality are safeguarded. Consequently, Clarke hastened to try to
provide some unbreakable link between divine evaluation and volition. Since it is metaphysically necessary that God is omniscient
and omnipotent, it is similarly necessary that his evaluation be correct and "He must of necessity, (meaning, not a *Necessity of Fate*,
but such a *Moral Necessity* . . . consistent with the most perfect
Liberty,) *Do* always what he *Knows* to be *Fittest to be done*" (WB
572). The reason is that since God lacks nothing and understands
everything, he has no passions leading him to act contrary to his
(necessarily) best judgment (WB 565, 572). So, although the moral
attributes of God do not belong to him with metaphysical necessity,
we know that "*Free Choice*, in such a Being, may be as *Certain and
Steddy* a Principle of Action, as the Necessity of Fate" (WB 573).[11]

Although for Clarke the causal version of the Principle of Sufficient Reason entails that God is necessarily endowed with liberty,
it does not entail that humans are endowed with it as well. Hence,
he tried to give evidence that we, like God, are free. His argument

was based both on metaphysics and experience. It is clear that liberty is a communicable power because it does not entail such incommunicable qualities as total causal independence and self-existence (WB 559). We do not know how the power of action can be transmitted, but, as Clarke told Collins in 1717, considerations drawn from experience assure us that is has been, since "all our Actions do now in Experience *seem* to us to be *free*, exactly in the *same manner*, as they *would* do upon the *Supposition* of our being really *Free Agents*" (W IV, 726).[12] Of course, Clarke continued, this does not amount to a strict demonstration; it is possible that we are not free agents much in the same way in which it is possible that our perceptions are illusory because the external world does not exist. But such eventuality is only a "bare Possibility," and just as nobody in his senses would deny that experience provides evidence for the existence of the external world, so no reasonable person would deny that experience provides evidence for our liberty. In sum, the burden of proof is not on the supporter of liberty, but on its denier.

Clarke's argument was both attractive and in line with his desire to make experience the basis of his considerations about the mind. That we have a prima facie feeling of being free in Clarke's sense can hardly be denied, and other philosophers before him had appealed to it.[13] However, by 1717, Clarke's knowledge of the literature against agent causation included not only Occasionalist tracts but also the *Theodicy*, and it is unfortunate he did not think he had to confront Leibniz's arguments based on the alleged existence of minute perceptions.

In addition to providing evidence for the libertarian position, Clarke also endeavored to answer arguments against it. He addressed the Hobbesian argument that, since thought is a mode of matter and "'tis manifest that Matter has not in itself the Power of Beginning Motion, or giving it self any manner of Determination whatsoever; therefore 'tis evident likewise, that 'tis impossible there should be any such thing as Freedom of Will," by advancing two objections (WB 559). One consists in a complex argument, which we discussed in the chapter on the soul, for the claim that thought cannot possibly inhere either naturally or supernaturally in matter. The other consists in the claim that Hobbes and his followers were "guilty of a most shameful fallacy," which Clarke endeavored to expose with a dilemma. If by "matter" Hobbists meant a

Solid Substance endued only with Figure and Motion, and all the possible Effects of the Variations and Compositions of these Qual-

> ities; then the Soul cannot be mere Matter; because (as Mr *Hobbes* himself confesses) Figure and Motion can never produce anything but Figure and Motion. . . . But *if*, on the other Hand, they will by *Matter* mean *Substance in general*, capable of unknown Properties totally different from Figure and Motion; then they must no longer argue against the Possibility of *Liberty*, from the Effects of Figure and Motion being all unavoidably necessary. (WB 564–65)

Clarke's argument cannot be easily evaluated. No doubt, if his dilemma was historically accurate, he had a powerful dialectical point. But certainly he was forcing the issue in the first horn of the dilemma, since a materialist merely had to hold that thought is ultimately matter in motion in order to resist the argument. Of course, Clarke believed he had shown that the notion of conscious matter is incoherent, but, as we saw, his argument was hardly watertight.[14]

Another objection Clarke considered is that a free agent cannot choose whether to have a will or not; "but (the two Contradictories of *Acting* or *not Acting*, being always *necessarily* before him,) he must of *Necessity*, and *essentially to his being a Free Agent*, perpetually *Will* one of these two things, either to *Act* or to *Forbear Acting*" (WB 565). This fact, Clarke continued, induced even "some considerate Persons" to entertain "great *Doubts* concerning the *Possibility* of *Liberty*." Clarke did not identify the philosophers he had in mind, but probably one of his targets was Locke, who in the chapter on power in the *Essay* seemed to move from the claim that an action can take place or not only if the agent wills it or not, and the claim that necessarily an action must take place or not, to the conclusion that the will of the agent is determined.[15] Clarke's reply was that the

> Essence of *Liberty* consists, not in the Agents choosing whether he shall have *a Will* or *No Will*. . . . But . . . in his *being an Agent*, that is, in his having a continual Power of *choosing*, whether he shall *Act*, or whether he shall *forbear Acting*. . . . Nor is this *Free Agency* at all diminished, by the *impossibility* of his choosing two *Contradictories* at once; or by the *Necessity*, that *one* of *Two Contradictories* must always be done. . . . For a Free Agent *may* be, and indeed essentially every Free Agent *must* be, *necessarily* Free. (WB 565–66)

In criticizing Locke's argument, for once Clarke sided with Leibniz, who in the *New Essays* had reasonably noticed that the nonoccurrence of an action does not require a volition to that effect, but merely the absence of one (NE II, 21, 23). However, Clarke's objection was both different from Leibniz's and more general. For it pointed out that Locke's argument was guilty of confusing *de dicto* and *de re* necessity. It might be true that if I think about doing A, then it is necessary that either I will to do A or will not to do A. However, from this it does not follow that if I think about doing A, then necessarily I will to do A. Nor does it follow that if I think about doing A, then necessarily I will not to do A.

2. *Leibniz*

As Grua's considerable collection of Leibnizian papers on liberty indicates, Leibniz's interest in the topic of freedom spanned most of his life, and a substantial part of his other major philosophical correspondence, that with Arnauld, was devoted to the issue of the compatibility of liberty with the existence of complete concepts.[16] At the end of the preface to the *New Essays*, Leibniz pointed out that the issue of freedom was among the most important in Locke's work, and entitled his discussion of Locke's chapter on power, "On Power and Freedom." In that chapter, after providing a systematic but brief overview of his position on freedom, he concentrated on freedom of the will, of which he individuated two components, namely, the mastery over the passions, which allows us to will as we should, and the lack of necessity in volition. The first component, Leibniz continued, "is a kind of freedom which pertains strictly to our understanding," presumably because passions are inversely proportional to the amount of clear and distinct ideas in one's mind. The second component,

> the freedom of the mind which is contrasted with necessity pertains to the bare will . . . [and] is what is known as 'free will': it consists in the view that the strongest reasons or impressions which the understanding presents to the will do not prevent the act of the will from being contingent, and do not confer upon it an absolute or (so to speak) metaphysical necessity. It is in this way that I always say that the understanding can determine the will, in accordance with which perceptions and reasons prevail, in a manner which, although it is certain and infallible, inclines without necessitating. (NE II, 21,8)

What Leibniz meant by "inclines" is not clear. In particular, it is not obvious whether the antecedent conditions merely "incline" the will because they are themselves not absolutely necessary, or whether they "incline" it because the causal link between them and the will is not metaphysically necessary. However, the passage makes it abundantly clear that Leibniz rejected necessitarianism, the view that events, including volitions, are metaphysically necessary.

Leibniz's explicit rejection of the thesis that volitions are necessitated set him in conflict with the declared views of both Hobbes and Spinoza. However, while Clarke's opposition to Spinoza and Hobbes was public, vocal, and without nuances, Leibniz's stance was more complex, since at times he was ready to entertain the idea that Hobbes's, and perhaps even Spinoza's, principles did not entail necessitarianism. According to Leibniz, Hobbes was certainly right in holding that every event has a cause and that when the cause is given the effect will follow. However, he was wrong in inferring from the causal principle that everything happens by absolute necessity. On this issue Leibniz was ready to defend Bramhall's thesis that the causal principle entails at most a form of hypothetical necessity (*Reflexions sur l'ouvrage que M. Hobbes a publié en Anglois de la Liberté, de la Necessité e du Hazard*: GP VI, 389–90; *Theodicy* § 172: GP VI, 216–17). Indeed, there are indications that according to Leibniz not even Spinoza could derive necessitarian conclusions from his own principles, since finite modes, being finite, cannot follow from the divine nature, and consequently cannot partake of its necessity.[17]

In spite of his belief that the necessity of the causal link does not lead to necessitarianism, when the *New Essays* were composed, Leibniz was quite ready to hold that the the causal link involved in the transition from antecedent conditions to volition is not metaphysically necessary. In the chapter on power and freedom, barely three pages after the passage just quoted, he claimed that

> we must distinguish what is necessary from what is contingent though determined. Not only are contingent truths not necessary, but the links between them are not always absolutely necessary either; for it must be admitted that when one thing follows from another in the contingent realm, the kind of determining that is involved is not the same as when one thing follows from another in the realm of the necessary. Geometrical and metaphysical followings necessitate, but physical and moral ones incline without necessitating. (NE II, 21,13)

By the end of 1707, Leibniz gave a fuller account of the view that the transition from cause to effect is not metaphysically necessary.

To Coste, who wanted his opinion on free will with respect to the exchange between Locke and Limborch on liberty of indifference, he expained that

> When we present a choice to ourselves, for example, whether to leave or not to leave, given all the internal or external circumstances, motives, perceptions, dispositions, impressions, passions, inclinations taken together, there is a question as to whether I am still in a state of contingency, or whether I make the choice to leave, for example, by necessity—that is, whether in fact this true and determined proposition, that *in all these circumstances taken together, I will choose to leave*, is contingent or necessary. I reply that it is contingent, because neither I nor any other more enlightened mind could demonstrate that the opposite of this truth implies a contradiction. (GP III, 401)

If we denote the proposition "I will choose to leave" with L and the conjunction of the propositions expressing all the antecedent circumstances with C, Leibniz seemed to deny both (1) "Necessarily, L" (necessitarianism) and (2) "Necessarily, if C then L" (hypothetical necessitarianism) and assert (3) "If C, then L." Presumably, the acceptance of (1) amounts to what Leibniz called *fatum mahometanum*, namely, the view that something would happen "even though its cause should be avoided; as if there was an absolute necessity" (Lz V, 13; *Theodicy* § 55: GP VI, 132–33). By contrast, (2) amounts to what, according to Leibniz, Spinoza and Hobbes were entitled to, namely, the claim that since the transition from cause to effect is metaphysically necessary the volition follows necessarily from its causes. Presumably, the acceptance of (2), if coupled with Spinoza's brand of ethical theory, corresponds to what Leibniz called *fatum stoicum*, namely the view that one should "have patience perforce, since it is impossible to resist the course of things" (Lz V, 13; *Theodicy* Preface: GP VI, 30). The identification is reinforced by noticing that Leibniz, not unreasonably, did tend to view Spinoza as a reviver of the ancient Stoic doctrines about the world-soul and the frank recognition of the necessity of all events as a prerequisite for the achievement of happiness (GP VII, 333–34). Finally, (3) is the view according to which the transition between cause and effect is certain and law-like but contingent because it ultimately depends on God's will.[18] It corresponds to what Leibniz called *fatum christianum*, the position that every event is certain and part of a providential plan (Lz V, 13).

If Spinoza and Hobbes were wrong in overemphasizing the link between antecedent conditions and volition, others had committed the opposite mistake of detaching them, as if the will could be causally undetermined even with all the antecedent conditions in place. This was the error of allowing freedom of indifference, the view of Molina which Leibniz associated with thinkers as different as Descartes, King, and, at times, Locke (*Theodicy* § 365: GP VI,331–32; *On King* 1: GP VI, 440–41; NE II, 21, 40). As we shall see later, for Leibniz, freedom of indifference is incompatible with the Principle of Sufficient Reason, and consequently cannot exist; worse, were it to exist, far from guaranteeing freedom, it would destroy it.

Whether for Leibniz the divine will is free, and in particular whether it is contingent that God chooses the best, is unclear, since his pronouncements on the issue show the strain of accommodating contingency to divine necessity. If the divine attributes belong to God necessarily and infinite goodness entails choosing the best, then the divine being could not fail to choose the best, much in the same way in which God could not fail to know all that is knowable. However, in the *Theodicy*, Leibniz seemed quite ready to hold outright that God chooses the best contingently (*Theodicy* § 234, 282: GP VI, 256–57, 284–85; *On King* 14: GP VI, 413–14).[19] It is hard to see how he could maintain this position consistently without giving up the idea that moral attributes belong to God as necessarily as the metaphysical ones, and indeed some scholars have taken this interpretive option.[20] At the very least, one can safely conclude that on this issue Leibniz was less forward than Clarke, who flatly held that moral attributes belong to God contingently. However, these issues did not come up in the exchange with Clarke, who limited his critique to Leibniz's claim that the Principle of Sufficient Reason applies to the divine volition, which is therefore strictly determined.

In his treatment of free will, Leibniz made use of the Principle of Sufficient Reason. In one way, the requirement that every volition must have its reason amounts to the demand that volitions, like other mental events, be enmeshed in the causal web of the mind. Thus understood, a reason is a psychological cause, that is, given Leibniz's internalist theory of motivation, a conscious or unconscious perception of the good. It would then include a belief in an evaluative proposition and, in the case of creatures, confused perceptions about the apparent good. As Leibniz explained in the *New Essays*,

> volition is the effort or endeavour [*conatus*] to move towards what one finds good and away from what one finds bad, the endeavour

arising immediately out of one's awareness of those things. . . . There are other efforts, arising from insensible perceptions, which we are not aware of; I prefer to call these 'appetitions' rather than volitions, for one describes as 'voluntary' only actions one can be aware of and reflect upon when they arise from some consideration of good and bad. (NE II, 21, 5)

The other way in which the Principle of Sufficient Reason was used was with reference not to beliefs of evaluative propositions, but to the evaluative propositions themselves. For example, Leibniz told Clarke that if God were to choose between equally good alternatives he would act "contrary to . . . wisdom, as if he could operate without acting by reason" (Lz III, 7). In other words, a choice between indiscernible good options would have no reason in the sense that it could not be justified. At least in the case of God, the causal and justificatory sense of "reason" are equivalent. Leibniz rejected the existence of a "third realm" à la Frege, and consequently all propositions are nothing but divine thoughts. Therefore, since all divine decisions are perfectly justified, the actual thoughts that bring them about are the very propositions that justify them.[21] However, this does not apply to humans, since certainly many of the causal "reasons" affecting our choices are not justifying "reasons," although one might perhaps argue that they are the kind of reasons that would justify us if all our judgments were correct. Leibniz tended to be rather cavalier in the use of the word "reason," but generally it is clear from the context and the nature of the argumentation which use he had in mind.

3. The Correspondence

In his second letter, in the middle of an open attack on one of the basic tenets of Newtonianism, the thesis that Newtonian science provides conclusive evidence for a metaphysical view of the world supportive of religion, Leibniz argued that not Newton's confused metaphysics masquerading as science, but the Principle of Sufficient Reason, namely, that "nothing happens without there being a reason why it should be so rather than otherwise," is the great foundation of metaphysics and, to some extent, of physics (Lz II, 1). Clarke, who had himself used the principle in his version of the Cosmological Argument and in the refutation of Toland's claim that motion belongs to matter essentially, easily granted part of his interlocutor's point: "'Tis very true, that nothing is, without a sufficient reason why it is, and why it is thus rather than otherwise. And therefore, where there is no cause, there can be no effect" (Cl II, 1). However, much to the chagrin of Leibniz, who complained that his interlocutor had granted the principle in name only, Clarke proceeded to qualify it:

> But this sufficient reason is oft-times no other, than the mere will of God. For instance: why this particular system of matter, should be created in one particular place, and that in another particular place; when, (all place being absolutely indifferent to all matter,) it would have been exactly the same thing *vice versa*, supposing the two systems (or the particles) of matter to be alike; there can be no other reason, but the mere will of God. Which if it could in no case act without a predetermining cause, any more than a balance can move without a preponderating weight; this would tend to take away all power of choosing, and to introduce fatality. (Cl II, 1)

Clarke's reply determined the terrain on which the rest of the discussion on free will took place. His metaphysical views about space and time compelled him to hold that the divine decision concerning the spatio-temporal location of the world was taken in a state of equilibrium, one in which the available options are relevantly equivalent with respect to all the previous mental states of the subject. Here, Clarke was helped by his identification of free will with agent causation, because agent causation entails freedom of indifference, the view that volition is not fully determined causally by antecedent mental states, and freedom of indifference is a necessary, albeit not a sufficient, condition for choice in a state of equilibrium.[22] Leibniz objected both to freedom of indifference and to choice in a state of equilibrium.

3.1 Leibniz's Critique of Clarke

Much of the discussion in the correspondence revolved around choice in a state of equilibrium; however, since such a choice presupposes freedom of indifference, we shall start by considering Leibniz's arguments in the *Theodicy* against the latter and then discuss the former.

3.1.a Freedom of Indifference

Leibniz's points against freedom of indifference can be grouped under three headings: first, liberty of indifference is contrary to experience; second, it would be an imperfection to the subject having it; third, it conflicts with the Principle of Sufficient Reason. That Leibniz would be ready to argue from experience against liberty of indifference is surprising in light of the fact that other philosophers, including Clarke, had tried to ground liberty of indifference in our alleged experience of it. For example, Descartes had argued that since we have a strong internal feeling of liberty of indifference we can conclude that we are in fact endowed with such liberty.[23] Such a claim had not gone unchallenged, and Spinoza had argued that we think we enjoy liberty of indifference because we are not aware of the causes that determine us.[24] In effect, Leibniz agreed with the broad outlines of Spinoza's analysis, which he refined by arguing that we cannot have a reliable feeling of the alleged independence of the will because we cannot be conscious of all the imperceptible causes of our volitions. If a compass were endowed with consciousness, and liked to point North, it would believe it did so by its own agent-caused volition without being aware of the magnetic particles in it which determine its motion (*Theodicy* § 50, 299: GP VI, 130, 293–95; *On King* 23: GP VI, 426–28). In sum, negative existential claims based on experience and concerning the mind assume its transparency, which Leibniz rejected. Not only does experience fail to provide evidence for liberty of indifference, but at times it also provides some evidence against it. Upon scrutiny, we can often find out that even when we seem to have taken a decision against all reason and inclination, as if we were endowed with freedom of indifference, some desire or hidden inclination we did not notice at the time was the cause of our volition (*On King* 24–5: GP VI, 428–32). One might object that Leibniz cannot hold on the one hand that the determining causes of volition are minute perceptions and on the other that we can become aware of them. However, this objection would be misplaced. Certainly, we cannot be aware of a minute perception when we have it, otherwise it would not be minute; but Leibniz did not claim that we cannot in principle become aware that in the past we had such and such minute perception (NE preface, 54).[25]

According to Leibniz, liberty of indifference not only does not agree with all the evidence provided by experience, but were we endowed with it, we would be rendered more imperfect because we would act without reason (*Theodicy* § 313–15: GP VI, 302–3). In particular, it cannot possibly be attributed to God (Lz III, 7). Clarke did not directly answer this objection in the correspondence; however, in the fifth reply, he repeated the distinction he had already drawn in *A Demonstration* between the cause of volition, which is to be found in the active principle essentially belonging to the soul, and the reason for the volition, which consists in the evaluative judgment (Cl V, 1–20). A few months later, in his critique of Collins's work on freedom of the will, Clarke rhetorically asked:

> By *what clear* and *distinct Ideas* can any Man perceive, that an *Indifferency* as to *Power*, (that is, an *equal Physical Power* either of *acting* or of *forbearing to act;*) and an *Indifferency* as to *Inclination*, (that is, an *equal Approbation* or *Liking* of *one thing* or of *the contrary;*) is *one and the same Thing*? . . . The Author always [supposes] that if a Man is not determined as *necessarily and irresistibly*, as a *Weight* determines the Motion of a *Balance;* then he can *in no Degree* be influenced by, nor have *any Regard* to, any *Motives* or *Reasons of Action* whatsoever, but must be *totally indifferent* to all Action alike. (W IV, 724)[26]

In sum, Collins, and presumably by implication Leibniz, confused reasons and causes.

From lack of causal influence from previous mental states one cannot directly, that is, without adding substantive metaphysical premises, infer lack of motivation based on reasons, be they good or bad. Nor is it obvious that when we explain somebody's decisions on the basis of his reasons we assume that the decision was part of a causal web that included his mental states. For example, if somebody tells me "I decided to walk quickly because I did not want to be late," it is not obvious that I make any assumptions about what caused his decision. Certainly, I must assume the existence of some link between his beliefs about punctuality and the time, and his decision to hurry, otherwise his claim that his desire to be on time was the reason why he hastened his pace would be false; however, whether the link is causal is left open. Of course, one might wonder how one's evaluation affects one's will. Clarke was silent on this issue, but presumably his position was that the relation between evaluation and volition is both noncausal and primitive, that is, ultimately unexplainable. To be sure, he did say that the evaluative judgment is the "occasion" for the action of the will (W IV, 723). However, this was mere handwaving. If God were the actual cause of our volition and evaluation were the mere occasional cause, then according to Clarke's theory we would not be free. These considerations lead us to Leibniz's last and more powerful objection against freedom of indifference.

According to Leibniz, liberty of indifference conflicts with the Principle of Sufficient Reason because ultimately it entails that volitions are uncaused:

Holding that a determination comes from a full indifference which is absolutely indetermined is holding that it comes naturally from nothing. One assumes that God does not give this determination; it does not have a source in the soul, or in the body, or in the circumstances . . . and yet here it appears and exists without preparation, without anything predisposing it, without an angel, or even God himself, being able to see or make anyone see how it exists. And not only does it arise from nothing, but it arises on its own. (*Theodicy* § 320: GP VI, 306)[27]

Of course it would be open to Clarke to argue that Leibniz was asking for what cannot be had, namely, the event that causes the substance to cause the volition. Nothing causes the soul to will and there is no change in the soul that causes the soul to will: in this respect, the soul is an unmoved mover.[28]

However, Leibniz had a powerful objection to this view. In his critique of King's *De Origine Mali*, he pointed out that the later Scholastics, in "the age of Chimeras" introduced liberty of indifference,

as if nothing would give us an inclination when we do not apperceive it distinctly, and as if an effect could be without causes when these causes are imperceptible. It is a bit like those who have denied insensible corpuscles because they could not see them. But as modern philosophers have changed the opinions of the Schools by showing in accordance with the laws of corporeal nature that a body could not be put into motion but by the movement of another body pushing it, similarly one must conclude that our souls (in virtue of the laws of spiritual nature) would not be moved but by the reasons of the good and the bad . . . some philosophers . . . have pulled out of their alembics the inexplicable notion of a choice independent of everything. . . . But this notion itself falls immediately in one of the greatest difficulties by offending against the great principle of reasoning which makes us always suppose that nothing happens without some cause or sufficient reason. Since the Schools often forgot to apply this great principle by admitting some primitive occult qualities, it is not surprising that this fiction of vague indifference has found support. (*On King* 3: GP VI, 401–3)[29]

In other words, as he pointed out in the *New Essays*, the positing of a faculty or principle requires an explanation of what it "consists in and how it is exercised" (NE II,10, 2). But since the supporters of liberty of indifference were neither ready nor able to provide such an explanation, their position was hopelessly obscurantist because it relied on an occult power (e.g., Clarke's active principle) to cause volitions, which Leibniz thought could be causally explained on the basis of previous conscious and unconscious mental states. In a way then, Clarke's psychology suffered from the same basic methodological defect as his physics: in both, Clarke was ultimately unable to free himself from the bondage of the Schools and allowed occult powers such as universal gravitation and an active principle of choice. Clarke, then, had rejected the defensible Scholastic doctrines about divine immensity and eternity and accepted the indefensible ones about the will.

If the alleged free power from which the action flows is not determined by objects, Leibniz claimed, then it must operate on the basis of "a disposition to act, otherwise anything could come from anything, *quidvis ex quovis*, and there would be nothing so absurd one could not suppose" (*On King* 20: GP VI, 421–22). But having a disposition to act, that is, being in such a mental state that upon certain stimuli one will act in a certain way, takes away liberty of indifference. Consequently, Clarke's acceptance of liberty of indifference ultimately destroys the very possibility of a science of the mind, which had already been put in jeopardy by his inability to recognize the parallel role of corpuscles in physics and minute perceptions in psychology.[30]

The point can be expanded by considering Leibniz's critique of the notion of "mere will," which Clarke used to explain how an agent chooses in a state of equilibrium. Leibniz claimed that in addition to being unworthy of God, a mere will could not exist, since its notion is incompatible with the definition of will (Lz IV, 2). Leibniz did not elaborate, but presumably what he had in mind was the sort of definition of volition one can see in the *New Essays*: "volition is the effort or endeavour [conatus] to move towards what one finds good and away from what one finds bad, the endeavour arising immediately out of one's awareness of those things" (NE II, 21, 5). Clarke, of course, did not know the *New Essays*, but he did manage to understand Leibniz's point and attempted to meet it, albeit briefly. He replied that an agent is a being capable of originating action "sometimes upon the view of strong motives, sometimes upon weak ones, and sometimes where things are absolutely indifferent" (Cl IV, 1–2). Clarke did not develop the point, preferring instead to accuse his opponent of fatalism, and Leibniz, probably realizing that his interlocutor would not be moved by appeals to a notion of the will he did not accept, dropped the issue.

This outcome was most unfortunate, since a discussion on the nature of the will could have led to an open confrontation on the theory of motivation. Leibniz was a determinist and an internalist who believed that volition is causally determined by our perception of the good; for him, volition is essentially linked to evaluation. Clarke rejected both determinism and internalism. Evaluation and volition are not casually linked; nor could there be a law-like connection between them, since law-like connections are incompatible with the capacity to have acted differently in the libertarian sense. In effect, Clarke's radical agent causation theory entails the rejection of externalism as well, if by "externalism" one means the view that volition is lawfully linked to a mental item different from evaluation, such as Locke's uneasiness.[31] Ultimately, if one takes the view that science deals with laws, as Leibniz saw, Clarke's view leads to the conclusion that no science of volition, and hence of human action, can be given.

3.1.b Choice in a State of Equilibrium

Leibniz's objections against choice in a state of equilibrium often paralleled those launched against liberty of indifference; however, while the former are often best understood as involving primarily a reference to volitions occurring without any reason in the sense of being irrational, the latter, as we saw, are best understood as involving a reference to volitions occurring without a reason in the sense of being uncaused. In the correspondence, Leibniz produced three main arguments against the possibility of choice in a state of equilibrium.

First, Leibniz correctly pointed out that choice in a state of equilibrium entails liberty of indifference, and as we saw, liberty of indifference is to be rejected (Lz III, 7; *Theodicy* § 48: GP VI, 129). Clarke's reply was in effect a counterattack: denying that God can choose in a state of equilibrium entails denying that he is an agent and maintaining that "he must needs (as it were mechanically) be always determined by things extrinsic" (Cl III, 7–8). Of course, Leibniz strongly denied that God is determined by external things and he prudently did not take up Clarke's remarks about having a mechanical model of divine volition (Lz IV, 20). However, as we shall see, the issue of Leibniz's mechanical analogies came up later in the correspondence.[32]

Second, a choice by mere will in a state of equilibrium would be contrary to divine wisdom because it would involve acting without reason. For example, if at creation God were to choose between two parts of space or two moments of time in which to place the world, then his choice would be groundless, since no reason could be given for it (Lz III, 7). Such a God would be a God in name only, and those who think otherwise are not careful in attributing to God only what is proper (Lz IV,18). In his replies, Clarke moved away, at least rhetorically, from the claim that God can act by mere will by dissolving it into two others. On the one hand, as we shall see later, he turned it into the claim that divine volition is not caused by divine evaluation, otherwise God would not be free. On the other, he turned it into the claim that even in a state of equilibrium divine volition need not be groundless. At times, Clarke contented himself with merely claiming without argument that even in a state of equilibrium there may be "very good reasons to act" (Cl IV,1–2). However, at other times he strengthened his position by pointing out that once God decided to create the world, he had to place it somewhere, and consequently his antecedent decision gave him ground to choose one of the admittedly indiscernible parts of space as the place of the world (Cl IV, 18).[33]

Clarke's admission that divine choice is not groundless even in a state of equilibrium, prompted Leibniz to argue that his opponent's position was incoherent at worst and indefensible at best. Saying that the mind may have

> good reason to act, when it has no motives, and when things are absolutely indifferent . . . is a manifest contradiction. For if the mind has good reasons for taking the part it takes, then the things are not indifferent to the mind. And to affirm that the mind will act, when it has reason to act, even though the ways of acting were absolutely indifferent . . . is to speak again very superficially. . . . For a man never has a sufficient reason to act, when he has not also a sufficient reason to act in a certain particular manner; every action being individual, and not general, nor abstract from its circumstances, but always needing some particular way of being put in execution. Wherefore, when there is a sufficient reason to do any particular thing, there is also a sufficient reason to do it in a certain particular manner; and consequently, several manners of doing are not indifferent. As often as a man has sufficient reasons for a single action, he has also sufficient reasons for all its requisites. (Lz V, 16–17)

Here Leibniz presented his interlocutor with a double-barrelled argument. If Clarke held that when in a state of equilibrium one can have a reason to choose on the basis of two options equivalent by hypothesis, then his view was incoherent. If he claimed that the reason came from some antecedent consideration, he was disregarding the fact that the actual choice for which this alleged antecedent reason existed had to be the choice of an individual action. For example, the actual choice that brought about the placement of the world in one of an infinity of indistinguishable places had to be the choice of one place and consequently something about that place must have provided a reason for choosing it, contrary to the hypothesis.

Leibniz's argument, such as it is, lacks the force to attack Clarke's position successfully. Leibniz is certainly right in claiming that every action is individual, but his claim is hardly relevant to the issue at hand. No doubt a person in the situation of Buridan's ass who has reasonably chosen eating over not eating must eat first one of the two dates A and B in front of him; but one need not have any reason to eat A over B in order to have a reason to eat A or B, and the transition from having a reason to eat A or B to having one to eat A over B (or vice versa) can be brought about, as Bayle suggested, by "the lot or chance."[34]

Perhaps sensing that his argument was not as strong as required, Leibniz referred Clarke to another part of the letter where he made a much stronger point. Humans may decide to do something and then be

> perplexed about means, ways, places and circumstances. But God never takes a resolution about the ends, without resolving at the same time about the means, and all the circumstances. Nay, I have shown in my *Theodicy*, that properly speaking, there is but one decree for the whole universe, whereby God decided to bring it out of possibility into existence. And therefore God will not choose a cube without choosing its place at the same time; and he will never choose among indiscernibles. (Lz V, 66)

Presumably, then, divine omniscience prevents God from having a reason to choose A or B without having either a reason to choose A or a reason to choose B. Nor is divine omniscience compatible with choosing by lot, since God would know the outcome beforehand and consequently could not be in a state of indifference with respect to A and B, contrary to the hypothesis.[35] Hence, even an implicit attribution of such capacities to God entails a preposterous view of the knowing powers of the divine being. In sum, Clarke's views were incoherent, or confused the abstract with the concrete, or were demeaning of God's perfection.

Leibniz's point was dialectically very powerful. For Clarke, as for Leibniz, omniscience is a metaphysical attribute of God, and

Leibniz managed to mount a strong case for the view that the triad divine omniscience, divine wisdom (which demands that God always acts with good reason), and divine choice in a state of equilibrium is inconsistent. Giving up divine omniscience amounts to accepting the ignorant Socinian God; giving up divine wisdom involves making God morally imperfect; giving up divine choice in a state of equilibrium entails giving up, among other things, absolute space and time. The choice, then, was either Clarke's god and religion or Newtonian metaphysics. Worse, to the extent that it was driven by the belief in absolute space and time, Clarke's theology was inadequate for the ends of religion and morality. Unfortunately, Clarke's reply in his final letter did not address these issues and merely repeated his position (Cl V, 1–20,124–30).

Leibniz's third argument against choice in a state of equilibrium hinged on the claim that the Identity of the Indiscernibles assures us that a condition of true equilibrium could not be given unless God were to perform a miracle (Lz IV, 4; V, 25). While the Principle of Sufficient Reason denies that a mind in a state of equilibrium could act, the Identity of Indiscernibles denies that a state of equilibrium occurs.[36] Consequently, barring divine intervention, the case of Buridan's ass cannot obtain, since

> the universe could not be bisected by a plane passing through the middle of the ass cut vertically along its length in such a way that everything on one side would be equal and similar to everything on the other as an ellipse . . . can be bisected in this way by any straight line passing through the center. For, neither the parts of the universe, nor the viscera of the animal are similar or equally situated on the two sides of this vertical plane. Consequently, there will always be things in the ass and outside it which would determine it to go toward one side rather than the other, although they would not appear to us. (*Theodicy* § 49: GP VI, 129–30)

Clarke rejected the Identity of Indiscernibles and consequently did not allow Leibniz's argument to get off the ground. Leibniz complained about Clarke's refusal to grant him the principle, and there is little doubt that he was dialectically justified, since the one obvious argument for choice in a state of equilibrium is to infer a lack of relevant difference among possible options from a lack of any difference among them. But of course the Identity of Indiscernibles cripples this argument by flatly denying its premise. However, Leibniz's recriminations were hardly justified beyond the dialectical level. For Parkinson has quite reasonably argued that the Identity of Indiscernibles does not entail that a state of equilibrium never obtains, because even if any two alternatives are discernible, it does not follow that they are discernible in the aspects relevant to the choice. For example, suppose an ass were to choose between two stacks of hay A and B, and that A is nearer than B to the spire of Salisbury Cathedral; one would be hard pressed to find the relevance of the difference.[37]

It might be replied that any difference could be relevant to one's choice, and the point could be reinforced by noting that for Leibniz each soul represents everything and that everything is related to everything else. But aside from the fact that Clarke would not have accepted it, even this suggestion would not be sufficient to save Leibniz's argument because it cannot guarantee that the resulting motives causing the decision are not equivalent. The motivating force arising from the fact that bundle A is closer to the spire of the Cathedral than bundle B might be equivalent to that generated by the fact that B is closer than A to the center of mass of Alkaid. Of course, the same point can be made with respect to merely intrinsic qualities of A and B. That Leibniz did not realize this is even more surprising in light of Bayle's example of the ass between a measure of oats and a pail of water, which "act equally on its organs."[38]

However, at times Leibniz seemed ready to give a different reading of the relevance of the Identity of Indiscernibles to the issue of whether a state of equilibrium like that of Buridan's ass can obtain. The Identity of Indiscernibles guarantees that "the case of perfect equilibrium is impossible, since the universe cannot be halved in such a way that the impressions of one side and the other are equivalent" (*Theodicy* § 307: GP VI, 299). Here, Leibniz could perhaps be understood as claiming that the impressions of the two haystacks cannot have the same motivating force. However, if this is what he had in mind, I think he was wrong. If the Identity of Indiscernibles were to preclude two sets of impressions from having the same motivating force, it would also preclude two weights from having the same weight and keeping a balance in equilibrium. Leibniz's claims about the relevance of the Identity of Indiscernibles to the case of Buridan's ass were just mistaken.

3.2 Clarke's Critique of Leibniz

While Leibniz's criticisms of Clarke tended to revolve around the Principle of Sufficient Reason, Clarke's criticisms of Leibniz tended to hinge on the issue of necessitarianism. One group of arguments, which we shall consider in the last chapter, tried to link Leibniz's views on divine volition to the position that matter is uncreated and spatio-temporally infinite. Here we shall look at Clarke's broader charge that the denial of divine liberty of indifference ultimately leads to "fatality" (Cl II,1). Presumably, what he had in mind is that if the divine will were causally determined by the divine understanding, God could not but produce what he did. Furthermore, lacking agent causation, God could not communicate it to us, who would presumably act on the basis of our last evaluative judgment, which, as we saw, Clarke was ready to admit is necessitated by events. Leibniz reacted by distinguishing two types of fatality, an acceptable type stemming from divine choice of the good and an unacceptable one stemming from, "a blind fatality of necessity, void of all wisdom and choice" (Lz II, 8). Clarke showed dissatisfaction with Leibniz's distinction and kept renewing the charge that Leibniz's views lead to "universal necessity and fate" (Cl IV, 1–2). In spite of the reference to necessity, the point was the same as before. As much as Leibniz was intent on distinguishing various senses of the term "necessity," so much Clarke was ready to use it as a blanket term. To be sure, he told Leibniz that "necessity in philosophical questions, always signifies absolute necessity," but clearly his idea of what was absolutely necessary was quite generous (Cl V, 1–20). For example, discussing the issue of free will, he claimed that a stone falls necessarily and consequently cannot be an agent, and that a balance moved by weights is subject to "absolute necessity" (WB 548; Cl V,1–20). But clearly he did not think that the stone's falling or a balance's tipping are necessary in the same sense in which, say, God's existence is, since both depend on divine will. For Clarke, the phrase "absolute necessity," when used in connection to free will, referred to what Leibniz felicitously called *"necessité machinale"*, the prime example of which is given by the deterministic mechanical behavior of a clock (GP VII, 333–34). If *per impossibile* a clock could have intelligence, it would still not be a subject of morality because it would have no freedom (W III, 905).

The repeated charges of introducing fate and necessity clearly touched a raw nerve in Leibniz, who was not new to this sort of criticism. This partially explains the impatient tone of Leibniz's last letter:

> He [Clarke] often endeavors to impute to me necessity and fatality; though perhaps no one has better and more fully explained, than I have done in my *Theodicy*, the true difference between liberty, con-

tingency, spontaneity, on the one side; and absolute necessity, chance, coaction, on the other. I know not yet, whether the author does this, because he will do it, whatever I may say; or whether he does it, (supposing him sincere in those imputations,) because he has not yet duly considered my opinions. I shall soon find what I am to think of it, and I shall take my measures accordingly. (Lz V, 2)

There is little doubt that Leibniz's impatience was justified. He was a compatibilist determinist, and determinism, whether ultimately defensible or not, is certainly distinct from necessitarianism, as his letter to Coste discussed above makes abundantly clear. Given the sensitivity of the topic, one must admit that Clarke's accusations were both ill taken and tendentious.

Leibniz continued by contrasting absolute with hypothetical necessity and metaphysical with moral necessity. God's creation of the best possible world is governed by moral necessity which, unlike metaphysical necessity, does not preclude that the actual world could have not existed (Lz V, 4, 7). That Clarke could not see this was an indication that he had confused moral and metaphysical necessity, the actual will of God, determined by the laws of wisdom, and the power of God, determined by the laws of metaphysics (Lz V, 79). Consequently, he had eliminated moral necessity in order to eliminate metaphysical necessity from the divine choice. Hypothetical necessity, Leibniz claimed, "is that, which the supposition or hypothesis of God's foresight and pre-ordination lays upon future contingents" (Lz V, 5). This sort of necessity must be admitted, lest one deny with the Socinians divine foreknowledge and providence.

Moreover, Leibniz told Clarke, hypothetical necessity does not endanger liberty, since

> God, being moved by his supreme reason to choose, among many series of things or worlds possible, that, in which free creatures should take such or such resolutions, though not without his concourse; has thereby rendered their occurrence certain and determined once for all; without derogating thereby from the liberty of those creatures: that simple decree of choice, not at all changing, but only actualizing their free natures, which he saw in his ideas. (Lz V, 6)

In the light of these explanations, the term "hypothetical necessity" is somewhat of a misnomer. Leibniz often employed it in connection with the necessity of the consequence ("Necessarily, if P then Q"), which he generally contrasted with absolute necessity ("Necessarily,

Q"; or "if P, then necessarily Q") (*De Rerum Originatione Radicali*:
GP VII, 303=L 487; to Coste, 19 December 1707: GP III, 400). But
this seems hardly what he was trying to convey to Clarke, since in
his letter to Coste he had pointed out both that divine foreknowledge
and providence do not require that the link between events, for example, previous mental states and volitions, be logically necessary,
and that such a link would destroy freedom. If one makes the reasonable assumption that Leibniz was trying to present his views in
ways acceptable to his interlocutor, one can conclude that in effect
he was pointing out that divine choice, like all free choice, is contingent and that his determinism was the minimum requirement
needed for divine foreknowledge and providence, which only a Socinian would deny and which Clarke had clearly accepted in *A Demonstration*. As far as fatality was concerned, Leibniz trotted out his
distinction among Muslim, Stoic and Christian fate (Lz V, 13).

Clarke was not impressed with the barrage of Leibnizian dis-
tinctions and prudently decided to glide over the issue of Socinianism. The only important issue, he replied, "is whether the
immediate physical cause or principle of action be indeed in him
whom we call the agent; or whether it be some other reason sufficient, which is the real cause of the action, by operating upon the
agent, and making him to be, not indeed an agent, but a mere pa-
tient" (Cl V,1–20). From Clarke's libertarian position, the only thing
that really mattered was agent causation, and denying it was falling
into necessity and fate. For a libertarian, I have free will only if I
truly and unqualifiedly could have done otherwise than I did, without the compatibilist qualification of "if I had so willed." But then,
any sort of law-like connection between previous mental states and
volition, be it logical, metaphysical or natural, involves the denial
of freedom because breaking any of these laws is simply beyond my
power. Clearly, the libertarian Clarke and the compatibilist Leibniz
had opposing basic intuitions on the nature of free will. What seemed
an unmitigated disaster to Clarke, namely, the causation of volitions
by previous mental states, was taken to be a necessary requirement
by Leibniz; conversely, what seemed an irrational and obscurantist
move to Leibniz, namely, the introduction of a principle of volition
springing into action on its own, was seen as perfectly justified by
Clarke.

In his last letter, almost as an afterthought, Clarke claimed that
Leibniz's theory is incoherent. Leibniz claimed to have shown in the
Theodicy that our will does not always exactly follow the practical
understanding because it may have or find a reason to suspend its

resolution till a further examination (Lz V,11). What Leibniz had in mind is not altogether clear. Obviously he was not advocating Locke's view that often we have a power to refrain from acting even when all the determining conditions are in place, since he criticized it. Locke had a libertarian streak, which was absent in Leibniz.[39] Presumably, Leibniz was trying to separate himself from the Spinozistic and Hobbesian position that the last judgment of the understanding either is volition or its final and decisive cause. Clarke objected that the reasons responsible for suspending one's resolutions are part of the last judgment of the understanding (Cl V, 1–20). Clearly, Clarke's point was correct, if by "reason" one means "rational considerations." However, what Leibniz had in mind was probably the following passage:

> whatever perception of the good one has, the effort of acting after the judgment, which in my opinion constitutes the essence of the will, must be distinguished from it. So, since it takes some time to bring this effort to completion, it may be suspended or even changed by a new perception or inclination which interposes itself, derails the spirit and at times makes it approve of a contrary judgment. (*Theodicy* § 311: GP VI, 300–301)

Leibniz's reasons may be passions or inclinations, and consequently Clarke's objection missed the mark, although it pointed out the rather cavalier way in which Leibniz used the word "reason."

Throughout the correspondence, Clarke characterized Leibniz's position in terms of an analogy: his interlocutor, he claimed, had a mechanical model for the processes leading to volition in which the motives played the role weights play in a balance. But a balance is completely passive, and therefore subject to necessity because its behavior is fully determined by external factors, such as the weights (Cl V, 1–20; IV,1–2; II,1; III, 7–8). Leibniz had confused the power of the mind to act with impressions and motives, and the final result was that a Leibnizian agent would be like a balance endowed with perception (Cl V, 1–20).

Undoubtedly, Clarke's insistence on the balance analogy did capture a central feature of Leibniz's analysis. Leibniz was clearly fond of making use of mechanical examples to illustrate his views on the will, and he compared the processes leading to choice to the operations of a compass, a balance, a fluid under pressure inside a vessel, or, at a more abstract level, a composition of forces (Lz V, 3; *Theodicy* § 325: GP VI, 309; NE II, 21, 40). Some of these examples did not escape Clarke's attention, who put them in section 3 of the

appendix to his edition of the correspondence and referred to them
at every possible occasion in his marginal notes to the text. Moreover, Clarke viewed Leibniz's claim that Buridan's ass, or God,
would not act in a state of equilibrium as a further clear indication
that mechanical systems did provide the model of Leibnizian free
agents, and consequently, Leibniz's pronouncements on the
wretched beast, which he shared with Spinoza, found their way in
section 4 of the appendix as well.[40] The inability of Leibniz's God to
act in a state of equilibrium was taken by Clarke as a sign that such
a god was not a self-determining originator of action and was moved
by extrinsic factors, outside causes (Cl III, 7–8; V, 1–20).

Leibniz's reply to the accusation that he was engaged in a quasi-
mechanical analysis of the processes leading to volition, which confused active minds and passive balances, had two components. First,
he claimed that since the Principle of Sufficient Reason applies both
to actions and passions, the fact that minds are active and balances
passive is irrelevant (Lz V,14). Events, be they actions or passions,
must have causes. That Clarke could not see this, was a clear indication of his deep misunderstanding of the Principle of Sufficient
Reason. Second, Leibniz argued that the balance analogy had been
misconstrued by Clarke, since

> motives do not act upon the mind, as weights do upon a balance;
> but 'tis rather the mind that acts by virtue of the motives, which
> are dispositions to act. And therefore to pretend, as the author does
> here, that the mind prefers sometimes weak motives to strong ones,
> and even that it prefers that which is indifferent before motives:
> this, I say, is to divide the mind from motives, as if they were with-
> out the mind, as the weight is distinct from the balance; and as if
> the mind had, beside motives, other dispositions to act, by virtue
> of which it could reject or accept the motives. (Lz V,15)[41]

So, not he, but Clarke was in fact thinking of the mind as a balance.
The balance analogy held in the sense that the motives, like the
weights, are causes; but the motives are not external to the mind
like the weights are to the balance. Clarke's misunderstanding of the
Principle of Sufficient Reason had in effect led him to disregard the
good aspect of the analogy and to operate, albeit unawares, with the
bad one.

In his final letter, Clarke partially addressed Leibniz's charge and
managed to provide a condensed account of his views:

> The motive, or thing considered as in view, is something extrinsic
> to the mind: the impression made upon the mind by that motive,

is the perceptive quality, in which the mind is passive: the doing of any thing, upon and after, or in consequence of, that perception; this is the power of self-motion or action: which in all animate agents, is spontaneity; and, in moral agents, is what we properly call liberty. (Cl V, 1–20)

Clarke's own admission that motives are external to the mind seem to justify Leibniz's criticism. However, by "motive" Clarke and Leibniz meant two different things. For Clarke, motives are evaluative propositions; for Leibniz, they include "not only the reasons, but also the inclinations arising from the passions, or other preceding impressions" (Lz V, 15). Leibnizian motives look much more like Clarkean impressions, that is, beliefs about evaluative propositions. But Clarke never dreamt of saying that impressions are not in the mind, although, of course, he denied they play any causal role in volition. However, insofar as Leibniz's criticism was directed at the lack of explanation for the link between Clarkean impressions and volitions, it was justified.

Clarke's critique of Leibniz's mechanical examples was linked to his critique of Leibnizian physics. For Leibniz, human activity does not impart new force to the body, since the quantity of force in the universe is constant (Lz IV, 33). But for Clarke, activity involves the generation of new force; if humans could not generate new force, they would not be principles of action and would rather be like clocks (Cl IV, 33; V, 92–95). So, Leibniz's wrong physical views were further evidence that he had done away with morality because, as we saw, for Clarke an intelligent clock would not be a moral subject.

On the topic of freedom of the will Leibniz and Clarke failed to reach any agreement. In retrospective, this is hardly surprising, given the contentious climate in which the exchange occurred and the importance both philosophers attributed to the topic. However, significant as they were, these were not the only factors, since the confrontation on free will was connected to other equally important issues. For Leibniz, Clarke's libertarian views were associated both directly and indirectly with a diminished view of God. His readiness to allow divine choice in a state of equilibrium made God an irrational being whose blueprint of the world is incomplete. But such a God, who "lives from day to day," would be like that of the Socinians (Lz II, 9). Clarke's libertarian views were also a precondition for the belief in absolute space and time, whose essential ties to God had led to the immersion of the divinity into the world and to its transformation into an *intelligentia mundana*. Moreover, Clarke's insistence in agent causation, by reintroducing occult powers, destroyed the very possibility of a science of the mind, which the admission of minute perceptions had finally made possible. Clarke's psychology, then, was as obscurantist as his physics full of occult attractive and repulsive powers.

In Clarke's eyes, Leibniz's determinism was destructive of all he stood for both in philosophy and in theology. Leibniz's determinist theory of the will transformed volitions into paramechanical events, thus depriving God and us of agency, freedom, and moral capacity, turned the divinity into a being unworthy of worship, and ultimately engendered necessitarianism. Clarke's suspicions that Leibniz had deprived us of freedom were increased by Leibniz's denial that we impart new force to our bodies. Of course, according to Leibniz's preestablished harmony the body, without alteration of the universal quantity of force, does exactly what it would do if the mind were to move it. But, as we saw in the chapter on the soul, Clarke thought that preestablished harmony was not merely a fairy tale, but also bore the germs of materialism. Worse, as we shall see in the chapter on miracles, in the editions of *A Demonstration* published after the controversy with Leibniz, in the middle of his attack on Hobbes's views on free will, Clarke associated the Hobbist hypothesis, that all matter would perceive if it had the appropriate sense organs, with Leibniz's claim that all matter "acts," that action is "characteristic of substances," and that every substance is "naturally endowed with perception." Leibniz's wrong view of nature as a great clock had expanded to include the human and the divine minds: the end of Leibnizianism was naturalism.

4

SPACE & TIME

On the topic of space and time, Clarke and Leibniz were in direct opposition. To be sure, they agreed on the topological features of space and time, but their agreement ended there. For Clarke, space and time are properties of God which share in the necessary existence of the divinity; for Leibniz, they are relations and mere *entia rationis*, like mathematical entities. In previous chapters we considered Leibniz's theological objection to Clarke's view of space and time. Here we shall concentrate mainly on the nontheological arguments used by Clarke and Leibniz. We shall consider first Clarke's and Leibniz's views and then their correspondence.

1. Clarke

On the issue of space and time, there is no *locus classicus* in Clarke comparable to Newton's "De gravitatione" or the scholium on space and time. Much of his views are expressed in the midst of others regarding different topics, for example, the proof for the existence of God or the extension of the soul, to which they are ancillary. The picture that emerges, however, is virtually identical to Newton's, to whose views he often referred. Hence, in the following I occasionally supplement Clarke's views with Newton's.

According to Clarke, the ideas of space and time are the two "first and most obvious simple Ideas, that every Man has in his Mind" (W II, 752).[1] Like many of the philosophers who investigated the nature of space and time, he tended to produce arguments with regard to space, leaving the reader to infer that parallel arguments could be drawn with respect to time. In *A Demonstration* he explained that while matter can be thought of as nonexisting, space exists necessarily because "to suppose *any part of Space removed*, is to suppose it removed *from* and *out* of itself: And to suppose the *Whole* to be *taken away*, is supposing it to be *taken away from itself*, that is, to be *taken away* while it *still remains*: Which is a *Contradiction in Terms*" (WB 528).[2] Although space is not sensible, Clarke rejected its identification with nothingness because nothing has no properties, while space has some, for example, quantity and dimensions (WB 528; W II, 752–53; III, 794; Cl V, 46 n.).[3] One might add other properties that he certainly accepted, such as homogeneity, immutability, and continuity.[4] Space, then, is an entity in which things are, and not the mere absence of matter, as at least some of the ancient atomists seem to have thought.[5] One might insist with Berkeley that the properties usually attributed to empty space, such as infinity, immovability, insensibility, indivisibility, lack of internal differentiation, are merely negative, as the negative prefixes suggest, and that consequently empty space is a mere nothing.[6] But Newton resisted this sort of argument by claiming that the allegedly negative properties of space are not negative at all: infinity, for example, is a positive quality because the notion of limit is negative and the denial of limit is therefore positive, in spite of grammar.[7]

Clarke, like Leibniz, denied that space is an aggregate of its parts (WB 537; Cl IV, 11–12). Since he believed that space and time are divine properties, he had theological reasons for holding this view; however, Newton had also reasons of a different sort. In a series of manuscripts drafted around 1692–93, he denied that space is composed of parts because

> there is no least in it, no small or great or greatest, nor are there more parts in the whole of space than in any place which the smallest body occupies. In each of its points it is like itself and uniform nor does it truly have parts but mathematical points, that is everywhere infinite in number and nothing in magnitude. For it is a single being, most simple and most perfect in its kind.[8]

The passage is rather confusing because on the one hand space is supposed to have no smallest part, and on the other dimensionless points are supposed to be its parts. Presumably, what Newton meant is that space has no smallest dimensional part. However, clearly Newton here was grappling with the problem of the composition of the continuum, namely how continuous extended space could be composed of unextended points.

Like Newton, Clarke adopted the view that space is necessarily infinite because "to set *Bounds* to Space, is to suppose it *bounded* by something which itself *takes up Space*; and That's *a Contradiction*: or else that 'this *bounded by Nothing*, and then the Idea of *That Nothing* will *still* be *Space*: Which is another Contradiction" (W II, 753).[9] What Clarke had in mind here is rather unclear. He seemed to think that what has a boundary must be bounded by something else. If so, the argument was not well taken because a sphere, for example, has a boundary which stems from its own nature, not by the presence of something external bounding it: one needn't think of space in analogy to a gas kept in place by the walls of a vessel. Perhaps, however, he had in mind Archyta's powerfully intuitive argument, which Locke had recently repeated, that one could in principle stretch one's hand out of any edge allegedly bounding space, and therefore that space is infinite. If so, the argument counters the objection that one cannot in principle stretch anything into nothing by stating, albeit without argument, that the alleged nothing bounding space in reality is more space.[10]

Whether for Clarke, and for Newton, space is penetrable is unclear. Clarke seems silent on the topic, and while in "De gravitatione" Newton did assume the penetrability of space, in *Principia* he did claim that the place of a body "is internal, and in the whole body," which intimates that space penetrates bodies.[11] If he did change his mind, then he joined More and Raphson, who for theological reasons denied that space, an attribute of God, could be penetrated.[12] That space is impenetrable would sit well with Clarke's view that absolute space has an essential and invariable structure, which belongs to it independently of the bodies in it and which is not altered by their presence.[13] We can infer then that any possible world must conform to it, since creatures must be in space and God cannot alter essences because his power is limited to the metaphysically possible. The same is true of time, which "flows equably" independently of anything in it. Creatures occupy an absolute position in space and time which we may or may not be able to establish because we have no direct access to absolute space and time. Such position is privileged in the sense that the true spatio-temporal relations among creatures are completely parasitic upon the spatio-temporal relations of the spatio-temporal locations they occupy.

The introduction of absolute space, allegedly demanded by Newtonian physics, offered Clarke an immediate philosophical advantage in the fight against Spinoza, a declared target of the Boyle
Lectures. For it showed that the Cartesian identification of extension
with matter, which had made possible Spinoza's excesses, was
wrong, a consequence that was not lost on Bayle and was insisted
upon by Maclaurin.[14] Of course the existence of absolute space introduced a new difficulty, that of its relation to God, but, as we saw,
Clarke and Newton thought they had solved it by claiming that
space and time are attributes of God or the result of divine existence.

2. *Leibniz*

Leibniz's views on space, and presumably time, underwent major
shifts during his philosophical career. At one time, probably during
his atomistic period, he believed in the existence of absolute space.[15]
And even later, when he had renounced absolute space and had come
to view space and time as relational, he still considered them well-
founded phenomena, on a par with bodies.[16] However, around the
turn of the century his views coalesced around the following ideas.

Space and time are, respectively, the order of coexistence and the
order of succession of creatures. As such, they are relations (NE II,
13, 17; *Remarques sur les Ojections de M. Foucher*: GP IV, 491–92;
568–69; to Schulenburg, 17 May 1698: GM VII, 242). They are to be
distinguished from extension and duration, which are real properties
of creatures (*Entretien de Philarete et d'Ariste*: GP VI, 584); they, by
contrast, are mere "beings of reason," and as such ideal things like
numbers.

Since space and time are continua, they are subject to the traditional paradox of composition, namely, of how they can result
from the addition of extensionless points and durationless instants.
Leibniz became convinced that the paradox, as space and time are
concerned, could be resolved only by denying that they are real beings composed of their parts (To Tolomei, 17 December 1705: GP
VII, 467; NE II, 17, 3). His solution centers around the distinction
between resolution into notions, composition out of parts, and divisibility into parts (To De Volder, 19 January 1706: GP II, 282–83;
to Bourguet, 5 August 1715: GP III, 583; *Remarques sur les Ojections
de M. Foucher*: GP IV, 491–92).

Space and time are wholes that are presupposed by their parts
much in the same way in which a proper fraction presupposes the

unity without which it cannot be understood. The unity is not made up of its proper fractions: rather, they are the result of divisions in it (GP III, 622; to Sophie, 30 November 1701: GP VII, 562). Hence, space and time are not composed of their parts, nor are their notions resolvable into those of their parts. They are, however, divisible into parts, but not into points and instants, which are not parts but extremities or *termini* of potential parts (NE II, 14, 10).[17] As continua, space and time are homogeneous, without any differentiation or variety. Hence, they have no actual parts and the isomorphism between their potential parts guarantees their infinite divisibility and multipliableness (To Des Bosses, 14 February 1706: GP II, 300; to Des Bosses, 31 July 1709: GP II, 379; to Sophie, 30 November 1701: GP VII, 563).[18] By contrast, in spite of appearances, both matter and the duration of creatures are, like motion, discontinuous (to Sophie, 30 November 1701: GP VII, 564).[19]

2.1 Space

In his third letter Leibniz told Clarke that "space denotes, in terms of possibility, an order of things which exist at the same time, considered as existing together, without entering into their manner of existing" (Lz III,4). Although this account made clear Leibniz's opposition to absolute space, it certainly fell short of offering more than an inchoate account of his own view. However, under pressure from his interlocutor, he finally explained the three steps by which "men come to form to themselves the notion of space" (Lz V, 47).

Leibniz's phrase makes it clear that his claim that space is the order of coexistence is not be understood merely as establishing an identity in the way in which, say, we claim that water is H_2O, without an eye to the epistemological order of the two terms of the identity. His concerns are also epistemological, and perhaps psychological as well: objects and their distance relations are epistemologically and psychologically prior to space. Leibniz's enterprise, then, is a type of reduction: space is reduced to objects and their distance relations in the same way in which, say, tables and chairs are reduced to sense data in phenomenalism, or rational numbers to the epistemologically and psychologically prior natural numbers.

Leibniz's first step seems very unpromising: "[Men] consider that many things exist at once and they observe in them a certain order of co-existence, according to which the relation of one thing to another is more or less simple. This order is their situation or distance" (Lz V, 47). Here, Leibniz would seem already to presuppose the notion of space; if space is an order of coexistence, not much is gained in saying that we form the notion of space by observing an order of coexistence among objects. However, as we shall see, the order of coexistence we notice initially is not space because it is not as yet abstracted from the objects in that order.

The second step involves the construction of the notion of "same place": "When it happens that one of those coexistent things changes its relation to a multitude of others, which do not change their relation among themselves; and that another thing, newly come, acquires the same relation to the others, as the former had; we then say, it is come into the place of the former" (Lz V, 47). However, we do not stop at the consideration of the positions bodies actually occupy or have occupied, but consider also "that relation which any other co-existent would have to this, or which any other co-existent would have to any other, if it had not changed, or if it had changed any otherwise." (Lz V, 47). The point here is that we employ counterfactuals by considering, for example, that body A could have been in place of body B and that body D could have been between A and B, where nothing is now. Now two bodies having the same relation of situation with respect to others assumed as fixed, have the same place. The final step is to consider all the places together: "that which comprehends all those places, is called space" (Lz V,47).

Leibniz's point can be paraphrased as follows. If bodies $X_1, \ldots X_n$ preserve their relations of distance and two other bodies A and B are such that at time t_1 A has or could have relation of distance R with $X_1, \ldots X_n$ and at time t_2 B has or could have a relation Q which is quantitatively identical with R, A having lost R, then B at t_2 occupies the same place P as A at t_1.[20] Space is "that which comprehends all . . . places." Hence, from possible relations of distance among bodies one constructs places, and from places space.[21]

What Leibniz meant by the last phrase is unclear. Presumably, he did not mean that space is that *in* (in a spatial sense of "in") which places are under pain of circularity, and in fact later in the paragraph he said that "space is that which results from places taken together" (Lz V,47). Even so, some obscurity remains. One might be tempted to hold that Leibniz is best understood as saying that space is the set of all places. The point could be supported by noticing that for Leibniz space is an ideal thing, like numbers, and certainly sets are ideal things. But then it would be unclear why in the same section he insisted on the ideality of place as evidence of the ideality of space, for if space is a set, then the ontological status of its members would not matter: a set of brick houses is as ideal as a set of numbers.

Alternatively, one might argue that he had in mind something akin to the notion of aggregate in that some of the properties of the members brush off on the whole; an aggregate of bricks is heavy because the bricks are. Unfortunately, although this approach explains the appeal to the ideality of place, it involves the problem that an aggregate is the paradigm of a totality posterior to its parts while space is prior to its parts.

In the remainder of section 47 of his fifth letter, Leibniz went to some lengths to show that space thus constructed must be, as he put it, an "ideal thing." He drew a sharp distinction between place P and the relations R and Q:

> two different subjects, as A and B, cannot have precisely the same individual affection; it being impossible, that the same individual accident should be in two subjects, or pass from one subject to another. But the mind not contented with an agreement, looks for an identity, for something which should be truly the same; and conceives it as being outside the subjects: and this is what we call *place* and *space*. But this can only be an ideal thing; containing a certain order, wherein the mind conceives the application of relations. (Lz V, 47)

Space, then, is ultimately abstracted from the creatures and the relations of distance from which it is constructed. The situation is analogous to that obtaining in a genealogical tree in which one abstracts from the concrete individuals (Joe, Peg, Jim) and therefore from the actual family relations (the actual individual filial relation between Peg and Jim) out of which the tree is constructed. What one is left with is a tree, a mathematical entity whose structure is sufficiently rich to accommodate that of the family relations conceived in abstraction from their *relata* and *a fortiori* that of the actual family relations (I said "sufficiently rich" rather than "isomorphic" because, as we shall see momentarily, the structure of space and that of matter are not isomorphic: the former is continuous and the latter discrete. But what is discrete can be mapped on what is continuous). Since the abstraction from concrete individuals and their relations renders space and time ideal, they can be continuous entities. As Leibniz told Bayle, space "relates not only to what actually is but also to anything which could be put in its place, just as numbers are indifferent to the things which can be enumerated. This inclusion of the possible with the existent makes a continuity which is uniform and indifferent to any division" (*Response aux reflections . . . de M. Bayle*: GP IV, 568=L 583). When counterfactuals are used and bodies have become variables, mere place holders, we obtain what Leibniz called "abstract space" (Lz V, 104).

In thinking about Leibnizian space one must then distinguish three notions, from the more general to the less general; the first two are part of the very notion of space; the third, while occurring in the construction of space, is left behind, as it were. The first notion is the general definition of space as the order of coexistence: any space in any possible world satisfies this definition because at this level of generality all spaces are the same. The second is the definition of space as the order of coexistences. The space being defined here is "abstract space," and not all spaces in all possible worlds are the same because the metric grounding the relations of coexistence among bodies may differ from world to world. For example, the relations of distance among two-dimensional things on a spherical surface are different from those among two-dimensional things on a flat one (NE II, 13, 3). However, as long as two worlds have the same metric, then their spaces will be the same, that is, the concepts constructed at the end of Leibniz's account will be the same. The third notion is that of the order of coexistents, namely the actual order of coexistence among bodies, counterfactuals aside. This notion is a mere step in the construction of that of space, not a part of the end product, or so I have argued.[22]

To what extent Leibniz's account in his last letter is merely a fuller rendition of his previous inchoate account or a significant departure from them is unclear. If space, "that which results from places taken together," is the collection or even the set of places, it is hard to see how it can be the order of coexistence. For one thing, order is a relationship, but a collection is not, although admittedly its members' places are obtained from relationships of distance among creatures. Perhaps, as we noted, Leibniz had in mind some construction whereby the whole would acquire some of the characteristics of its members, so that since places are relations, the result of their grouping (space) would be as well. But here Leibniz does not help us: if I am right, we know his wishes but not how to satisfy them. In effect, then, Leibniz's claim that space is "relative" means two things: that the notion of space presupposes that of creature, and that space is a relation. To be sure, one could reasonably argue that the latter claim entails the former, but given the obscurity surrounding the latter there seem to be little hope of understanding the issue fully. The same holds for time.

Leibniz did not explain whether space can be given where no body is or, more, has ever been. At times he seemed to imply a negative answer. When accused of holding, like the Cartesians, that matter and space are one and the same thing, he replied "I do not say that matter and space are the same thing. I only say that there is no space where there is no matter, and that space itself is not an absolute reality" (Lz V, 62). Such a tight link between matter and space sits rather well with Leibniz's notorious denial of the vacuum and of extramundane space. Furthermore, Leibniz's definition of "sameness of place" does make an essential use of the notion of body. The point can be reinforced by noticing that this is how Clarke interpreted Leibniz's claim (Cl V, 26–32). However, Clarke was bent on showing that Leibniz made matter necessarily infinite and eternal as space is, and consequently his interpretation should not be accepted uncritically. Rather, for the following two reasons, Leibniz is best understood as saying that space is given only if matter is given (the construction of space requires spatial relations among objects), not that space and matter must be, as it were, coextended.

First, Leibniz did hold that a vacuum is metaphysically possible (NE II, 13, 21; 14, 24; to Bourguet, 22 March 1714: GP III, 565). Moreover, since he claimed that the vacuum among bodies and extramundane space "differ only as the more or less," he was also committed to the possibility of extramundane space (Lz IV, 7). Of course, as the actual world is infinitely extended and the parts of matter are contiguous, neither the vacuum nor extramundane space are given. But they could be given, and consequently it must be possible to have unoccupied places. That this was Leibniz's considered view can be reinforced by his statement to Clarke that space "does not depend on such and such a situation of bodies; but it is that order which renders bodies capable of being situated" (Lz IV, 41; NE II, 4, 5; 13, 17; 14, 26). The same, Leibniz continued, is true of time.[23]

Second, as continua, space and time are homogeneous and therefore infinitely divisible. A yard of space can be divided in half, and since each half is homogeneous to the whole, it too can be divided in half, and so on. But by the same token, Leibniz claimed, a quantity of space can be doubled, and since each double is homogeneous to its half, it too can be doubled. Hence, space can be extended *ad infinitum*. The same holds for time (*Initia Rerum Mathematicarum Metaphysica*: GM VII, 22; to Des Bosses, 14 February 1706: GP II, 300; NE II, 17, 3). In effect, then, space and time are potentially infinite in the sense of being greater than any assignable magnitude (to Des Bosses, 11 March 1706: GP II, 304). God's wisdom has brought about that our world's extension is potentially infinite (nothing is actually infinite in extension) (Lz III, 9; *De Ipsa*

Natura § 11: GP IV, 510–11=L 503–4). However, in a world that is materially finite, empty space (and time) must be given.

One might object that the admission of space (and time) beyond the confines of the world produces the same difficulties Leibniz found with Clarke's theory, namely that God would have no reason to place the world in one set of spatio-temporal coordinates than another. But such objection would be misguided, for space and time are not ontologically prior to the universe: they are mere *entia rationis*. Asking whether empty space or time can be given is not asking an ontological but a conceptual question, very much like whether the series of natural numbers can be extended to infinity even if the world is finite.

One might propose a third reason for the separation of matter and space. Space is continuous while matter is discrete (To De Volder, 11 October 1705: GP II, 278; 19 January 1706: GP II, 282–83; to Sophie, November 1705: GP VII, 562–63). Consequently, matter cannot cover space much in the same way in which a blanket full of wholes cannot cover a bed: there must be empty parts of space corresponding to the holes of discontinuity in matter. The issue is complicated by the difficulty in understanding the relation between density and continuity in Leibniz's thought. One might be tempted to attribute to Leibniz the modern view that density is not a sufficient condition for continuity. Indeed, in some sense this attribution is not anachronistic, at least in so far as the density of rational numbers and the incommensurability of the side and the diagonal of the square, both known to Leibniz, are sufficient to see that there are points on the line (the paradigm of continuity) to which no rational numbers correspond.

There is, however, ample evidence that for Leibniz, dense quantities, namely such that between any two items there is a third, are continuous. For Leibniz,

> Continuous is a whole such that its co-integrating [cointegrantes] parts (i.e. such that taken together coincide with the whole) have something in common, and moreover such that if its parts are not redundant (i.e. they have no part in common, that is, their aggregate is equal to the whole) they have at least a term [terminum] in common. (*Specimen Geometriae Luciferae*: GM VII, 284)[24]

One can informally see that discrete sets do not satisfy the definition, but dense sets do. Consider the closed interval N=[1,2,3,4,5]. Then, the closed intervals [1,2,3] and [4,5] taken together make up N and yet they have nothing in common. Consider now R, the dense closed interval of rational numbers between 1 and 2, and two closed intervals A=[a_1, . .a_n] and B=[b_1, . . . b_n] contained in R such that together they make up R. Suppose now that A and B have nothing in common. Then, density requires that between a_n and b_1 there is a rational number, and therefore A and B together do not make up R, contrary to the hypothesis. Hence, density involves Leibnizian continuity. The point can be reinforced by Leibniz's claim to Des Bosses that density entails continuity: "if points are such that there are not two without an intermediate, then a continuous extension is given" (To Des Bosses, 29 May 1716: GP II, 515). Such a view should not surprise us. Under the plausible, if incorrect, assumption that "discrete" and "continuous" are mutually exclusive and exhaustive properties, being incompatible with discreteness (there must be at least an item for which there is a next one in a discrete series) density must entail continuity.

Since matter is discontinuous, it is not dense, although the parts of matter are contiguous in the Aristotelean sense that "their limits are together", that is, they touch (To Sophie, November 1705: GP VII, 561).[25] Suppose now two contiguous parts of matter AB and CD, with B and C touching. Then between the corresponding spatial points b and c there is an infinity of others to which no parts of matter correspond: the discrete structure of matter is too coarse to map onto that of space. So, there must be space where there is no matter. One might object that since each part of matter is infinitely divisible, density must apply to it in the sense that between any two points of matter there must be a third. But this would be wrong: between AB and CD there is no matter because B and C touch, and therefore their distance is zero.

While this argument does manage to separate matter and space, it also has the unpleasant consequence of making the void not merely possible but actual. The difficulty, of course, is that notoriously Leibniz denied that empty space exists. However a text suggests a way to remedy the problem. Leibniz told De Volder that "matter is not a *continuum* but an actually infinitely divided *discretum*, although no assignable part of space lacks matter" (To De Volder, 11 October 1705: GP II, 278). Leibniz did not elaborate, but the reference to assignable quantities, usually used in connection with infinitesimals, suggests the following.

The Leibnizian calculus requires that each point P of the geometrical line is surrounded by an infinite set, a cloud, of points unreachable by any process of division and lying at infinitesimal but different distances from P. Homogeneity, which is an essential characteristic of the continuum, transfers down to the infinitesimal level: the differential and the finite structure of the line are isomorphic, and within the infinitesimal level, one can operate on infinitesimal quantities as if they were ordinary ones.[26] Here at the infinitesimal level, there is no matter: in spite of the infinite actual divisions in matter, its structure indeed is too coarse to map onto one as fine as that of space. However, infinitesimal quantities, Leibniz held, are unassignable; they are, as he put it, zeros of which one can be greater than another. But under the reasonable assumption that the distance between b and c is zero (AB and CD touch), the part of space between them is unassignable. So, the discrepancy between space and matter is less than any given and only unassignable parts of space are void. The gap between discrete matter and continuous space is not a greater reason for denying their coextension than the difference between x and x+dx is for denying their equality.[27] Differently put, the discrepancy between ideal space and real matter is infinitesimal and therefore unassignable.

One might object, as Bernoulli did, that since matter is infinitely divided *in actu*, it must have infinitesimal parts (To Leibniz, 26 August 1698: GM III, 529). But Leibniz resisted the suggestion. Each of the parts of matter has a finite "ordinary" noninfinitesimal size (To Johann Bernoulli, 29 July 1698; September 1698: GM III, 524; 536). It would be different if there were an "infinitieth" part of matter, as it were; but such part is not given in spite of the fact that the division is given *in actu* (GM III, 536; to Johann Bernoulli, 30 September 1698: GM III, 541).[28]

2.2 Time

Time, for Leibniz, is the "order of existence of those things which are not simultaneous" (*Initia Rerum Matematicarum Metaphysica*: GM VII, 17=L 666). However, while Leibniz explained in some detail how to construct space out of spatial relations, he was not as forthcoming with respect to time. Luckily, since the issue is only marginal to the exchange with Clarke, we can be brief. Clearly, Leibniz thought that a procedure analogous to that employed in the case of space could be used in the case of time. All states of things, or events, can be ordered on the basis of the temporal relations of priority, posteriority, and simultaneity (*Initia Rerum Matematicarum Metaphysica*: GM VIII, 17=L 666). Presumably, starting with an actual event E as a reference point, all the events, including possible ones, which are at the same distance relation from E are simultaneous.

Temporal "places" are to be constructed out of the relation of simultaneity among events or states of things and taken together constitute time.[29] The final result is a structure endowed with a partial ordering in which an instant enjoys on its successors not only priority in time but also, as Leibniz rather mysteriously put it, in nature (To Bourguet, 5 August 1715: GP III, 582).

The attempt to construct time out of temporal relations among states of things might lead to the conclusion that Leibniz rejected the A-series (tensed) view of time or thought that A-statements are reducible to B-statements. The point can be reinforced by noticing that Leibniz's handling of time is "objective" in the sense that the subject of consciousness hardly plays a role in it, as one can easily see by comparing it with Saint Augustine's, and that the tensed view of time has occasionally been associated with the idiosyncrasies of human subjectivity.[30] Such a conclusion, however, would be hasty. As we shall see later, when trying to show that time is not a real existent, Leibniz at times seemed to adopt the tensed view that only the present instant, the "now," is real. Moreover, a relational view of time does not entail a nontensed view because the relations of priority and posteriority might themselves be analyzed in tensed terms, that is, in terms of past, present, and future.[31] Finally, a tensed view of time need not involve what one might call "subjective facts": the "now" glides along, one might argue, because of the very nature of time, independently of any subject, and in this respect it is therefore radically different from the "here". Differently put, the peculiarities of the "now" are not fully reducible to the fact that "now" is an indexical expression.

Many of the considerations we applied to space can be applied to time. Time is a continuous quantity and, consequently, has an infinitesimal structure to which, for example, we appeal when determining the instantaneous velocity or the acceleration of bodies. By contrast, duration, like motion, is discrete, resulting from a series of divine acts of preservation in a way analogous to that in which matter results from an aggregate of monads (To De Volder, 11 October 1705: GM II, 279; to Sophie, 31 October 1705: VII, 562, 564; *Monadology* § 47: GP VI, 614=L 647).[32] But Leibniz pointed out that the application of continuous structures like space and time to phenomena is justified because the difference is less than any given (To De Volder, 19 November 1706: GP II, 283=L 539). This suggests that, in spite of its discrete substratum, the duration of creatures, like motion, is infinitely divided, with a structure as fine as that of matter and that the parts of duration are contiguous as those of matter.

3. The Correspondence

3.1 Leibniz's Objections to Absolute Space and Time

Leibniz's attack against Clarke's view had two main components: one directly involved theological considerations; the other involved the use of the Principles of Sufficient Reason and of the Identity of Indiscernibles.

Leibniz's theological objections have already been discussed in the chapter on God, and consequently a brief summary will suffice. If absolute space and time existed, then either there would be something absolute and eternal besides God, or they would have to pertain to God's nature, with the result that God would have parts. Either way, the outcome would be theologically unacceptable. Clarke in effect restated the position he had put forth in the Boyle Lectures, namely, that space and time are properties of God, which however do not introduce parts in the divine being because space is essentially indivisible. Leibniz, quite reasonably, retorted that inseparable parts are still parts. As we saw, Clarke, and Newton, must have felt some discomfort with the way the relation between space and time and God had been handled in the correspondence; the outcome was the rather obscure *Avertissement* composed for Des Maizeaux's edition of the correspondence.

Leibniz's most famous critique of absolute space and time involved the Principle of Sufficient Reason and the Identity of Indiscernibles. He did not explain why, among the "many demonstrations" he claimed to have against absolute space and time, he advanced one based on the Principle of Sufficient Reason. His standard arguments against absolute space and time were based on his views of the continuum. The notion of absolute space as an infinite whole composed of parts, in contrast to a mere infinite aggregate (not a whole) like the world, is incoherent, presumably because it impinges on the basic theorem, which Leibniz in contrast to Galileo and others refused to relegate to the finite, that the whole is bigger than the part (NE II, 17, 3; GP I, 338–39). Moreover, space and time, as undifferentiated homogeneous wholes with mere potential parts, cannot exist because what is real and composed cannot but have actual divisions in it (NE II, 1, 2).

However, these arguments did not appear in the correspondence, probably because since Clarke had used the Principle of Sufficient Reason (or the causal version of it) in *A Demonstration*, the bulk of which amounts to a protracted version of the Cosmological Argument, Leibniz viewed the appeal to the Principle of Sufficient Reason as a good way to engage Clarke. So, in his third letter, Leibniz argued that if absolute space and time existed, then, since they are homogeneous, God's choice of where and when to create would be without reason, contravening the Principle of Sufficient Reason (Lz III, 5).[33] Worse, if absolute time existed, then it would be legitimate to ask why God did not create the world earlier. But since any two instants are indiscernible, no reason could be given for God's choice (Lz III, 6). So, either God does not create, or he creates before any assignable time (Lz IV, 15). But since the world does exist, the reader was left to infer that Clarke's view on time entails that the world is eternal, which although falling short of implying the independence of the world from God, was nevertheless a heterodox view. Presumably, an analogous point could be made with respect to space and the infinity of matter. And while Leibniz had no philosophical objections to the infinity and eternity of the world (he had a religious one to the latter), as we saw, Clarke had grave philosophical objections to both.

Clarke, consistent with his libertarian views, replied that if God had a reason for creating anything at all, his mere will would be sufficient to choose a set of spatio-temporal coordinates in which to place the world (Cl III, 2; 5). In effect, all that Clarke required is that the reasons determining the divine will do not do so causally. Leibniz, of course, disagreed, and the bulk of the debate, with a minor side-show we shall consider later, joined the discussion we have already considered in the chapter on free will. However, Clarke also attempted, unsuccessfully, to pin a heterodox position on Leibniz. "It is they," Clarke argued "who suppose matter and space to be the same who are bound to admit that the world is necessarily infinite and eternal because space is" (Cl IV,15). This was hardly Clarke at his best, since Leibniz denied both that matter and space are the same, although he admitted that they are inseparable like time and motion, and that space is eternal (Lz V, 62–63).[34]

More interestingly, Clarke also claimed that "the wisdom of God may have very good reasons for creating this world, at that particular time he did; and may have made other kinds of things before this material world began, and may make other kinds of things after this world is destroyed" (Cl IV,15). Unfortunately, Clarke did not develop the point, but what he said could be read as providing a scenario that would in effect answer Leibniz's charge that God would have no reason to create the world when he did. Suppose an infinite series of temporally finite worlds arranged in some significant way, for example, in order of increasing perfection. Then, at any time some world would exist and the absolute dates of our world would depend on its position in the series. So, God would have a reason to create our world when he did after all.

There is some evidence that Newton was not far from such a view. He wrote in his notes that "God . . . will be demonstrated to be more powerful, wiser, better and in every way more perfect from the eternal succession and infinite number of his works, than he would be from works merely finite. For God is known from his works." He did not elaborate the point, but barring the heterodox view that the world is eternal, a reasonable interpretation is that there has been an infinite succession of worlds.[35]

As he did elsewhere, Clarke also tried to use a modal argument against his opponent. If God had created the world "Millions of Ages sooner than he did," he would not have created the world sooner at all, if a relational theory of time were right (Cl III, 4). The point was reasonably well taken: either Leibniz showed that an earlier creation would be metaphysically impossible, or he had to concede that absolute time exists. Leibniz replied, as he did with the parallel example of the motion of the world, that Clarke's hypothesis of an earlier creation is "chimerical," and the debate moved along the lines we looked at in the parallel discussion of space (Lz IV, 15; Cl IV, 15; Lz V, 55–56; Cl V, 55–63). However, Leibniz also tried to explain how, compatibly with his view of time, one could make sense of the notion of an earlier creation. He appealed not to a transposition of the world as it is back in time, which on a relational theory would be impossible and would make his position inconsistent, but to an extension of it by adding events before the originally first one, while at the same time pointing out that such an extension would be a monster unworthy of divine architecture (Lz V, 56).[36] In his reply Clarke charged Leibniz with inconsistency for both admitting and rejecting the possibility of an earlier creation (Cl V, 55–63). The charge was, however, unjustified and based on a misreading of Leibniz's example.

However, part of Clarke's reply to Leibniz's charge that God would have no reason to place the world in one place rather than another consisted in a *tu quoque*: even with Leibniz's relational theory of space God would be unable to create three equal particles of matter because there would be no reason for placing them in one order rather than another (Cl III, 2). When Leibniz replied that this shows that God does not create three equal particles, Clarke finally showed his hand: if Leibniz's argument were correct, God could not create any matter at all. For, he continued, "the perfectly solid parts of all matter, if you take them of equal figure and dimension (which is always possible in supposition) are exactly alike; and therefore it would be perfectly indifferent if they were transposed in place" (Cl IV, 3–4). The implication was obvious: since matter exists and God cannot create it, it must exist necessarily.

Leibniz's answer was to point out that Clarke's supposition went against the Identity of Indiscernibles, which he inferred from the Principle of Sufficient Reason plus divine wisdom: two identical pieces of matter do not exist because if they did, God would act without reason in ordering them one way rather than another, and such a behavior would be incompatible with divine wisdom (Lz V, 21). So, although the Identity of Indiscernibles is not metaphysically necessary, we can rest assured that no two things are exactly alike and the identical atoms needed in Clarke's argument are but a chimera (Lz V, 25). One might argue on Clarke's behalf that all that he needs is the metaphysical possibility of his supposition, but this would be wrong, since Leibniz could then reply that God could create a world without identical atoms. In his last letter, Clarke claimed that his opponent had failed to show that the Identity of Indiscernibles is metaphysically necessary or even that creating identical pieces of matter would be unwise of God. He had, Clarke concluded, begged the question (Cl V, 21–25). However, Clarke's analysis of the exchange was unjustified. For the issue at hand was Clarke's *tu quoque* attack, as Leibniz had rightly pointed out, and in this respect it was Clarke who begged the question by assuming that there are identical atoms (Lz V, 21).

In a sheet composed with the fourth letter but which Leibniz did not send, he argued that time cannot be real because its parts cannot exist together (R 101). He presented the argument in his last letter: "how can a thing exist, whereof no part does ever exist? Nothing of time does ever exist, but instants; and an instant is not even itself a part of time" (Lz V, 49). Why any part of time is not real can be gathered from his remarks to Sophie, to whom he proposed the same argument, that it does not exist "whole and in all its parts" (To Sophie, 31 October 1705: GP VII, 564; *Specimen Dynamicum*: GM VI, 235=L 436).[37]

Clarke hastily rejected the argument as a "quibble upon words" without providing any analysis of it (Cl V, 49–51). Such a peremptory dismissal was, however, unjustified. That instants are not parts of time follows from Leibniz's solution to the problem of composition of the time continuum. Moreover, the argument itself has a long tradition and is based on the the prima facie plausible belief that only the present instant, the "now," is real: the past has gone out of existence, the future does not exist yet, and the existing present is but a durationless instant.[38] Nevertheless, one can understand Clarke's impatience given that Leibniz failed to appeal overtly to the "now." Furthermore, the argument is open to a retort. Instants are *termini* of temporal intervals as points are *termini* of spatial intervals. But since points are not real, so instants should not be. More broadly, it is hard to see how *termini* of the parts of an *ens rationis* can be more than *entia rationis*. Conversely, if instants are real, the stretches of time of which they are the termini must be real as well, as Aristotle noticed.[39] Perhaps, Leibniz had in mind the discrete but contiguous units of duration which make up the discontinuous existence of created things and provide the order of succession out of which time is constructed (To De'Volder, 11 October 1705: GP II, 279; to Sophie, 31 October 1705: GP VII, 564). But these units of duration are hardly instants of time.

3.2 Clarke's Arguments for Absolute Space and Time

3.2.a Buckets and Globes

What Newton intended to show with the bucket experiment and the globes thought experiment is not clear. For a long time the accepted view has been that he attempted to prove that absolute space exists because absolute circular motion is determinable by its effects. Often the corollary to this interpretation has been that the attempt failed.[40] However, perhaps the aim of the two experiments was to provide an illustration of cases in which absolute and relative motion can be distinguished once Newton's mechanics is accepted. While under the traditional interpretation the experiments play a foundational role with respect to Newton's physics, under the latter the roles are reversed. Be that as it may, there is little doubt that Clarke interpreted the bucket and globes experiments as showing the difference between "real motion, or a body's being carried from one part of space to another; and relative motion, which is merely a change of the order or situation of bodies with respect to each other," and therefore that absolute space exists (Cl IV, 13–14).[41]

To be sure, in his exchange with Collins, Clarke did deny the reality of circular motion. At any time, he claimed, a body contains only the "Determination to move in a certain straight Line"; however, when it meets with a "continual Resistance" it moves in a curve, and "every such curvilinear Motion . . . is but the Idea of a Number of successive Motions of a Body, never existent together; a pure *Ens Rationis*, or Operation of the Mind" (W III, 838). So, only rectilinear motion is ultimately real. This view seems to contradict, or at least run against the grain of, Clarke's statements to Leibniz. However, the difficulty can be mitigated by considering that in his answer to Collins, who had suggested that consciousness might be a type of motion, Clarke was under pressure to deny the possibility of the emergence of any new quality in motion: if thinking were a mere mode of motion, he told Collins, it would have to be a mode of *any* type of motion. Moreover, Clarke's denial of the reality of curvilinear motion is compatible with the claim that the water in the bucket has a "real" (i.e., absolute) motion in the sense that its droplets "really" try to move along the tangent and are "really" prevented from doing so by the walls of the bucket, which provide continual resistance; hence, the concavity of the water's surface reveals the water's "real" motion.

The idea that the effects of circular motion allow to distinguish between merely relative and absolute real motion was not original with the Newtonians nor, indeed, recent. It constituted the nerve of one of the most famous and powerful arguments for the claim that the earth does not rotate. If the earth, large as it is, were to rotate once every day, then the linear velocity at its surface would be so great that clouds and birds would always appear to move westward. Since no such phenomena occur, the earth does not rotate; rather, the heavens do and their motion does not cause clouds and birds to fall behind. As Newton pointed out in "De gravitatione," the merely relative rotation of the earth with respect to the heavens has no mechanical effects on it.[42]

However, as Leibniz told Burnett in 1697, by the publication of Newton's *Principia* both he and Huygens had stopped believing that the appearance of centrifugal forces in circular motion proves the existence of absolute motion (To Burnett, 18 May 1697: GP III, 205).[43] He was not convinced by the bucket experiment, and his first reaction was to doubt its accuracy.[44] What brought about Leibniz's change of heart is unclear, and although in his exchange with Huygens he spoke rather mysteriously of "reasons," he did not provide any detail (To Huygens, 22 June 1694: GM II, 185). However, elsewhere he was more forthcoming: since uniform rectilinear motion is relative and circular motion is reducible to uniform rectilinear motions, the latter is relative as well (*Dynamica de Potentia*: GM VI, 507–8).

According to Leibniz, all rectilinear uniform motions are relative because no observation allows to determine whether a body is in absolute rectilinear uniform motion or at rest. The point, Leibniz thought, can be extended to include collision: even if various bodies in apparently rectilinear uniform motion were to hit each other, observation would still not allow to determine which is in absolute motion, since their behavior is fully determined by their relative motion (and mass). In other words, in all these cases phenomena underdetermine the choice of an absolute frame of reference or, as Leibniz put it, various hypotheses are equivalent (*Dynamica de Potentia*: GM VI, 500).[45]

However, even granting Leibniz's point about the equivalence of hypotheses, one would be hard pressed in seeing why rectilinear uniform motion is relative. From the inability to determine which among several bodies is moving absolutely, it does not follow that none is. Worse, Newton would have felt justified in inferring that at least some of the bodies in question do move absolutely, since all the bodies that are absolutely at rest are at rest with respect to each other as well. However, Leibniz seemed ready to imply that none among adequate but incompatible empirically equivalent hypotheses can be a true description of reality. Discussing Descartes's view that motion is but change of position with respect to a circumambient body, he argued that "if there is nothing more in motion than this reciprocal change, it follows that there is no reason in nature to ascribe motion to one thing rather than to others. *The consequence of this will be that there is no real motion*" [emphasis mine] (*Animadversiones in partem generalem Principiorum Cartesianorum*: GP IV, 369=L 393).[46]

Leibniz did not explain why if no reason can be given for the motion of A rather than B it follows that neither moves, but one might suggest the following. The case is analogous to his account of Archimedes's axiom that if the weights suspended from the arms of a balance are equal, neither of the arms will move because no reason could be given for the motion of one arm rather than the other (Lz II, 1). Presumably, then, the principle at play here is the contrapositive of the Principle of Sufficient Reason: if there must be a reason why X occurs, then if no reason for X can be given, not-X is the case. Since the equivalence of hypothesis entails that no reason can be given why any given body has absolute rectilinear uniform motion, it follows that such absolute motion simply does not exist.[47]

However, the invocation of the Principle of Sufficient Reason is not sufficient to get what Leibniz needs; from the fact that neither a sufficient reason for the motion of body A nor one for the motion of body B can be given, it does not follow that no sufficient reason for the motion of body A or body B can be given. The situation is similar to that of Buridan's ass, who has no reason to eat haystack A and no reason to eat haystack B but has a very good reason (hunger) to eat A or B. What Leibniz can claim, however, is that there is no reason to say that rotational motion with observable centrifugal force is absolute, and this is sufficient to dismiss the bucket experiment, although not sufficient to establish that all motion is relative.

Leibniz's argument for the claim that all motions are composed of rectilinear uniform ones was quite general:

> All motion is *per se* rectilinear uniform. But all action in bodies consists in motion. Therefore, rectilinear motion cannot be inflected but by the impression [impressione] of another also rectilinear . . . and consequently the origin of curvilinear and non-uniform motion cannot be understood but as a composition of rectilinear uniform ones. (*Dynamica de Potentia*: GM VI, 502)[48]

Some of the impetus behind Leibniz's view probably came from his work in calculus, in which he viewed curves as polygons with infinitesimal sides: just as a curve is a polygon, so curved motion is made up of rectilinear motions. However, it is unlikely that Leibniz viewed the mathematical representation of a particular curvilinear motion as providing an insight into the actual trajectory of the body, because the choice of which polygon to use in the study of the curve depends on the mathematician.[49]

Not surprisingly, then, Leibniz produced a metaphysical argument to the effect that motion is per se rectilinear. Since motion, precisely understood, is unreal because it is a whole of noncoexisting parts, what is real in it is but "that momentary state which must consist of a force striving towards change" (*Specimen Dynamicum*: GM VI, 235=L 436). But every effort, he claimed, tends in a straight line, and consequently *per se* all motion is in straight lines (*Specimen Dynamicum*: GM VI, 252=L 449). Leibniz did not explain why every effort tends in a straight line. Probably, if challenged he would have invoked the Principle of Sufficient Reason: since in the absence of external influence no reason could be given for the effort to tend to the right rather than to the left of the rectilinear line, the effort will tend in a straight line. By the same token, the motion would be per se uniform. Or perhaps he would have defended the choice of the straight line by noting that since it constitutes the shortest path between two points, it provides the maximum determination (GM V, 146).

In his kinematic discussion of motion, Leibniz had claimed that "every curvilinear motion in a plane can be understood as composed of two rectilinear ones, of which one is uniform or of velocity increasing or decreasing according to a certain law." For example, he continued, Galileo had shown that the parabolic path of a projectile is the result of the composition of two motions, one rectilinear uniform and the other uniformly accelerated (*Dynamica de Potentia*: GM VI, 472). But he also thought that rectilinear uniformly accelerated motions could be broken into infinitesimal elements of rectilinear uniform motion by considering infinitesimal stretches of time. This sits well with Leibniz's dynamical ideas about the origin of curvilinear motion out of the impacts among bodies producing in each other infinitesimal impulses (*Illustratio Tentaminis de Motuum Coelestium Causis*: GM VI, 259; *Dynamica de Potentia*: GM VI, 509–10).[50]

From the premises that rectilinear uniform motions are relative and that curvilinear motions are actually composed of them, Leibniz inferred that the latter must be as relative as the former. The conclusion was reached with the added premise, which Leibniz considered obviously true, that if the composing motions are subject to the equivalence of hypothesis, the composed motions will be subject to it as well or, more broadly, that "of those things whose determinants cannot be distinguished, the determinates cannot be distinguished as well" (*Dynamica de Potentia*: GM VI, 507). So, all motion is by nature relative, and Newton's hopes of determining absolute rotation ill founded.

However, Leibniz's argument from the alleged relativity of rectilinear uniform motion to that of curvilinear motion bristles with difficulties. For one thing, the physical status of infinitesimal elements of motion used by Leibniz to reduce accelerated to uniform motion is questionable, given Leibniz's claims that there are no infinitesimals in nature. Moreover, the polygonal representation of curvilinear motion is hard to reconcile with the Principle of Continuity, which requires that a body cannot change direction instantaneously.[51] More generally, even granting the validity of Leibniz's inference from the alleged relativity of uniform rectilinear motion to that of curvilinear motion, the obvious reply open to a supporter of absolute rotational motion is that since the deformation of the surface of the water in the bucket shows that the rotation of the water is absolute, the uniform rectilinear motions, whatever they might be, allegedly composing the rotational one must be absolute as well. Leibniz could insist on the relativity of rectilinear uniform motion; but as we saw, his argument is not more convincing than that inferring the absolute rotation of the water from the deformation of its surface.

Many have thought that Leibniz's problems go well beyond his inability to reject absolute motion. For after telling Clarke that nothing in Newton's eighth definition of the *Principia* even began to prove the existence of absolute space, Leibniz made an apparently damaging concession:

> I grant that there is a difference between an absolute true motion of a body, and mere relative change of its situation with respect to another body. For when the immediate cause of the change is in the body, that body is truly in motion; and then the situation of other bodies, with respect to it, will be changed consequently, though the cause of that change be not in them. 'Tis true that, exactly speaking, there is not one body, that is perfectly and entirely at rest; but we frame an abstract notion of rest, by considering the thing mathematically. (Lz V, 53)

Not surprisingly, Clarke charged him with outright inconsistency by pointing out that since Leibniz admitted a distinction between absolute and relative motion, he de facto admitted the existence of absolute space (Cl V, 53). There is little doubt that Clarke's point was dialectically powerful, and indeed many commentators have agreed with him to some extent.[52] However, Leibniz's distinction between absolute and relative motion does not entail that the former can occur without the latter. Discussing Descartes's view of the nature of motion, Leibniz argued that if all there were to motion were change of relative position, then there would be no reason to ascribe motion to one body rather than to another, and consequently there would be no real motion. Therefore, Leibniz concluded, "in order to say that something is moving, we will require not only that it change its position with respect to other things but also that there be within itself a cause of change, a force, an action" (*Animadversiones in partem generalem Principiorum Cartesianorum*: GP IV, 369=L 393). The "concession" he made to Clarke is to be understood along the same lines. All motion is relative in the sense that it consists in change of relation among bodies. A single body in an empty universe would have no more motion than solidity. However, when the cause of the change of relation between, say bodies A and B is in A, then A's motion is not only relative, as all motion must be, but absolute as well. In other words, absolute motion is a subset of relative motion. In effect, Leibniz's "concession" was more than that; it was required by his own views about empirically equivalent theories and therefore occurs elsewhere as well. One might disapprove of Leibniz's confusing terminology, but he can hardly be charged with incoherence.[53]

3.2.b The Motion of the World

In his third letter, Clarke advanced a different objection against Leibniz's relational theory of space. Suppose, Clarke said, that God were to move the whole world in a straight line.[54] Then, if space were an order of coexistents, the world would remain in the same place, and if its motion were suddenly interrupted, it would not receive a jolt (Cl III, 4). Clarke clearly thought both of these consequences preposterous, presumably because the first was contrary to the hypothesis that God could move the universe, and the second to a reasonable extrapolation from experience. Leibniz responded by claiming that the supposition of the motion of the whole universe is "chimerical" for

> two states indiscernible from each other are the same state; and consequently, 'tis a change without change. Besides, there is neither rhyme nor reason in it. But God does nothing without reason; and 'tis impossible there should be any here. Besides, it would be *agendo nihil agere*, as I have just said, because of the indiscernibility. (Lz IV, 13)

In his fifth letter, Leibniz made his point more clearly: the motion of the world hypothesized by Clarke would not be observable, and when an alleged change is not observable, it does not occur (Lz V, 53). Both the hypotheses that the world is at rest and that it is in motion have no observable consequences, and therefore must be rejected. Clarke disagreed and repeatedly told Leibniz that if the world were suddenly stopped, there would be an observable jolt (Cl III, 4; IV, 13; V, 26–32). He did not elaborate, but he compared the motion of the world to that of a ship: in the same way in which a man shut in the cabin of a ship would notice a sudden acceleration of the ship, so would we if the world, supposing it in motion, were suddenly accelerated (Cl IV, 13).

However, Clarke's analogy was hardly well taken. When a ship is suddenly stopped, for example, by hitting a reef, all objects within it show a forward motion with respect to it because their motion has not undergone the sudden deceleration the motion of the ship has. That is, while the ship slows down, its cargo continues with the same velocity the ship had before hitting the reef. The jolt is the result of the relative motions of the various parts of the ship and of the ship and its cargo. This is perfectly compatible with Leibniz's views. But by hypothesis, such relative motion is not present in the case of the motion of the world as a whole. To have a case against Leibniz, Clarke must maintain that when literally everything undergoes the same deceleration and consequently there is no change in the relative motions of bodies (as Newton's sixth corollary to the laws of motion points out), there is still a jolt. So, there is no parity between the ship-example and the world-example: the world is not like a vessel with a cargo.[55] Indeed, Clarke's example was so ill taken that one could hardly believe that it would have won Newton's approval.

In his fifth letter, Clarke proposed a different type of motion by claiming that the world might rotate. Such a motion would generate a centrifugal force and consequently observable consequences, and yet it would be impossible in Leibniz's theory of space (Cl V, 26–32). He did not produce any argument to show that a centrifugal force would be present, but presumably he felt justified in extrapolating from observations about buckets or inferences about the earth. Of course, the jump from the effects of the earth's rotation to that of the universe as a whole is immense, but if the jump is allowed, Clarke's case becomes stronger than with his hypothesis of the rectilinear motion of the world, since the observable effect does not seem to depend on the relative motions of the parts. Of course, Leibniz's analysis of circular motion denies its absolute nature; indeed, given his account of rotation as involving circumambient medium pressure, the rotation of the world would be at least physically impossible. But, as we saw, Leibniz's attempts at showing the relativity of circular motion are not more convincing than Clarke's attempts at showing its absolute nature.

Typically, the debate over the motion of the universe took on theological overtones. Clarke argued that if the world is finite, then "it is by its nature moveable, for nothing which is finite is immovable." Hence, Leibniz's alleged denial that God could "have altered the time or place of the existence of matter" entails that the universe is essentially spatio-temporally infinite, which reduces everything to "necessity and fate" (Cl IV, 5–6). The context makes clear that by "moveable" Clarke meant 'could have been created at another time and in another place,' and it shows Clarke's misinterpretation of Leibniz's relational theory of space and time. However, in his reply Leibniz creatively chose to interpret "movable" as 'capable of being moved in space' and denied that everything finite is moveable, since the finite parts of space are not moveable, as Clarke himself put great effort in proving (Lz V, 31). In spite of its apparent dialectical aim, Leibniz's point was not well taken, and Clarke effectively replied by denying parity. The only reason why the finite parts of space are immovable is because they are parts of a whole that is infinite and necessary (Cl V, 26–32). Leibniz was more successful in arguing that the infinity of matter does not entail objectionable consequences, such as necessity and fate, since it depends on the divine will (Lz V, 30, 32, 73).

However, Leibniz's insistence on the role of the divine will inspired Clarke to pose a dilemma in his final letter. If Leibniz held that the world could be finite and moveable, then he de facto accepted that space is independent of matter and Clarke's position was vindicated. If, on the other hand, Leibniz held that the world is necessarily infinite and unmovable, then he embraced the view that the world is so independently of the divine will (Cl V, 73–75). But this position had dire consequences and reduced to the Cartesian view that the supposition of the finiteness of the world is contradictory, "Which if be true, it never was in the Power of God to Determine, the Quantity of Matter; and consequently he neither was the Creator of it, nor can Destroy it" (Cl V, 26–32). In sum, either Leibniz's position collapsed into Clarke's, or into a form of cryptoSpinozism.

Although Leibniz could reject the second horn of the dilemma, since he denied that the world is necessarily infinite, the first horn did manage to raise some interesting issues. To be sure, he denied the inference from finiteness to mobility, but Clarke was partially justified in that his interlocutor's terminology was rather unclear. Leibniz claimed that the supposition of the motion of the world is "chimerical" or "unreasonable and impracticable" (Lz IV, 13; V, 29, 52). Such terminology seemed to convey the view that God could make the world move although he decided not to. Leibniz would then be open to what one might call Clarke's "modal argument":

> My argument . . . for the notion of space being really independent upon body, is founded on the possibility of the material universe being finite and moveable: 'tis not enough therefore for this learned writer to reply, that he thinks it would not have been wise and reasonable for God to have made the material universe finite and moveable. (Cl V, 52)

However, Leibniz was probably innocent of the confusion Clarke charged him with. He clearly stated that his relational theory of space precluded the possibility of the motion of the world (Lz V, 29).

Mobility, he told Clarke, requires the possibility both of a change of situation with respect to other bodies and of the transition to a state discernible from the original one (Lz V, 31). In sum, mobility requires the possibility of an observable change of relation with other bodies. Leibniz's remarks about the unreasonableness of the hypothesis of world's motion must be understood contextually. Arguing against Clarke's hypothesis merely from a relational theory of space entails prejudging the issue and de facto precluding the possibility of discussion. Hence, Leibniz tried to show that Clarke's hypothesis is unwarranted. That he could not prove that the motion of the world is metaphysically impossible without appealing to his views on space is no indication either that such motion is metaphysically possible or that he conceded that it is.

3.2.c Relations are Not Quantities

In his third letter, Clarke charged that viewing space and time as an order or a relation is incompatible with the fact that they are, as he put it, "real quantities" (Cl III, 4). His prodding forced a rather reticent Leibniz to reply in his last letter:

> Order has its quantity; there is in it that which goes before and that which follows; there is distance or interval. Relative things have their quantity, as well as absolute ones. For instance, ratios or proportions in mathematics, have their quantity, and are measured by logarithms; and yet they are relations. And therefore, though time and space consist in relations, yet they have their quantity. (Lz V, 54)[56]

Leibniz's answer shows the tension between viewing space and time as the collections of all spatial and temporal places on one hand and as relations on the other. In effect, the first part of the answer could be read as stating that a metric can be applied to space and time, viewed as collections of spatial and temporal places, because of the relation of distance among their members. But this is hardly what Leibniz meant, as shown by the second part of the answer, which embarks on a piece of philosophy of mathematics in an attempt to demonstrate that relations, here exemplified by ratios, are bona fide quantities.

Clarke's reply to the second part of Leibniz's statement was of marginal interest to the discussion. He argued that Leibniz's appeal to ratios as quantitative relations was both irrelevant and mistaken. Irrelevant because spatio-temporal relations are different in kind from mathematical ratios. Mistaken, because proportions are not quantities anyway (Cl V, 54).[57]

However, Clarke's reply to the first part of Leibniz's statement was more significant. He claimed, as he had done previously with respect to time, that

> the distance, interval, or quantity of time and space wherein one thing follows another, is entirely a distinct thing from the situation or order and does not constitute any quantity of situation or order: the situation or order may be the same, when the quantity of time or space intervening is very different. (Cl V, 54)[58]

We do not know, of course, what Leibniz would have replied, but we can make an educated guess by looking at his answer to the analogous charge with respect to time that Clarke made in his fourth letter. If the intervening time is different, for example, greater, Leibniz said, "there will be more successive and like states interposed; and if be less, there will be fewer; seeing that there is no vacuum, nor condensation, or penetration (if I may so speak), in times any more than in places" (Lz V, 105).

Clarke viewed this reply as saying that time is both the order of succession and the sum of the intervals between events, and dismissed it as contradictory (Cl V, 104–6). His charge, however, was unjustified. In effect, Leibniz can be read as saying that a change in interval among temporal events alters the order of succession as well because more, or fewer, possible states of creatures will be interposed. Since space and time involve not only the actual but, as we saw, the possible, they are continua, and the distance between any two points is given by the simplest path between them, a straight line in the case of spatial points (*Initia Rerum Mathematicarum Metaphysica*. GM VII, 17=L 666–67). So, if events A and B in that temporal order are given, with T the set of instants between them, and the time between them is stretched, then the new set U of instants between them properly includes T, and the order of succession, namely, the collection of temporal "places," is different from the original one.

Clarke and Leibniz disagreed both on the nature and the ontological status of space and time. For Clarke, space and time are necessarily existent divine properties; for Leibniz they are relational *entia rationis*. Leibniz argued against the claim that rotation can show when absolute motion occurs by trying to reduce all motion to rectilinear uniform motion and argued that since the latter is relative the former must be relative as well. When Clarke appealed to the possibility of the motion of the universe as a whole, he reasonably declared Clarke's hypothesis "chimerical" because such motion would be unobservable in principle even within Clarke's philosophical and scientific framework. Not only did Leibniz deny any value to Clarke's arguments for absolute space and time, but, as we saw in the chapters on God and free will, he thought that they lead to a diminished view of God.

Clarke judged Leibniz's attempt at a relational theory of space and time hopeless, in particular because he thought that it could not account for their quantitative nature. However, he also viewed (wrongly) Leibniz's arguments against the possibility of motion of the whole universe as leading to the conclusion that the world is not only infinite, a view Leibniz accepted, but necessarily so. But since he believed that if God cannot determine the quantity of matter he is not its creator, he concluded that Leibniz's objection to his argument for absolute space and time entails that matter exists necessarily. So, while Newtonianism had achieved the separation of space and matter, thus destroying their Spinozistic (but ultimately Cartesian) identification, Leibniz effectively if not intentionally had substituted the necessarily existent space and time with a necessarily existent matter, which, to make things worse, as we shall see in the next chapter, is essentially active and sentient.

5

MIRACLES & NATURE

In one of the most tense moments of the exchange with Clarke, answering the accusation of having removed God from the world, Leibniz curtly told his interlocutor that he had explained the continual dependence of creation on God better than any other:

> But, says the author, *this is all that I contended for*. To this I answer: *your humble servant for that, sir*. Our dispute consists in many other things. The question is, whether God does not act in the most regular and most perfect manner? Whether his machine is liable to disorders, which he is obliged to mend by extraordinary means? Whether the will of God can act without reason? Whether space is an absolute being? Also concerning the nature of miracles; and many such things, which make a wide difference between us. (Lz III, 16)

At first sight, the reference to miracles as one of the main issues of the correspondence may seem odd. When considering miracles and the seventeenth century, one is likely to think about Spinoza's impassioned attempt to prove that they are impossible.[1] Indeed, one may even think of miracles as belonging to an odd and antiquated frame of thought in fundamental antithesis with the new worldview brought about by modern science and soon to be swept away. However, this view would be wrong. Many of the philosopher-scientists who directly brought about the scientific revolution or like Clarke were closely associated with it, did believe in miracles and engaged in debates concerning their possibility and their evidential role in support of Christianity. Furthermore, in both Leibniz and Clarke the topic of miracles was connected with significant metaphysical issues concerning the power of creatures and the nature of natural laws. On these Clarke and Leibniz disagreed deeply, and consequently to a good extent the issue of miracles became a rallying cry for a deeper confrontation. In this chapter, we look first at Clarke's and Leibniz's views on miracles in works preceding their exchange, and then at the correspondence itself.

1. *Clarke*

Since Clarke was a divine, it is not surprising that the motivations behind his interest in miracles were mainly apologetic. However, it would be a mistake to attribute it merely to his theological training. Like Glanville, Sprat, Boyle, and Locke, he belonged to that group of English intellectuals associated with the Royal Society who thought that miracles could be used as evidence for the claim that Christianity is the true religion.[2] He wrote at a time when, in England, the controversy about miracles was intense between the deists, who doubted or even denied the very possibility of miracles or at least their evidential role in favor of Christianity, and more orthodox religious thinkers. Not surprisingly, in 1705 Clarke devoted a whole section of his *Discourse* to the defense of the view that miracles are possible and capable of providing very strong evidence, amounting in fact to moral certainty, for Christianity.

According to Clarke,

> the true *Definition* of a *Miracle*, in the *Theological* Sense of the Word, is this; that it is work effected in a manner *unusual*, or different from the common and regular Method of Providence, by the interposition either of God himself, or of some Intelligent Agent superior to Man, for the Proof or Evidence of some particular Doctrine, or in attestation to the Authority of some particular Person. (WN 701)

Armed with this definition, Clarke tried to achieve his apologetic ends with an argument that had both a historical and a philosophical component. The former attempted to show that we are justified in believing that the miracles described in the *Scriptures* really occurred, and that consequently the belief in the divine commission of Christ is justified. However, since the philosophical content of this part of Clarke's argumentation is negligible, we can put it aside. The latter tried to show that the basic causal structure of nature is compatible with the occurrence of miracles.

Clarke was well aware that the historical component of his defense of the evidential role of miracles would be worthless unless one could reject the view that miracles are impossible in principle. This "obstinate Prejudice," Clarke claimed, is held by "Modern Deists" who, noticing that nature is regular and constant and that certain causes produce certain effects according to "fixed Laws and Rules," come to the conclusion that "there are in *Matter* certain *Laws* or *Powers* the Result of which is that which they call the *Course of Nature*; which they think is impossible to be changed or altered, and consequently that there can be no such things as *Miracles*" (WN 698). Prima facie, it is difficult to see why Clarke worried about this allegedly deist view. Certainly, even in a physical world ruled by metaphysically necessary laws, events can have unusual causes, for example, by being brought about by invisible agents. Presumably then, when Clarke claimed that miracles are "effected in manner unusual, or different from the common and regular Method of Providence," he meant that the causes of a miracle are not subsumable under the laws of nature; consequently, if the natural laws are unbreakable and all pervasive, as the deist view claims, then miracles are impossible.

The deistic view, Clarke argued, is completely wrong because

All things *Done* in the World, are done either immediately by God himself, or by *created Intelligent Beings*: *Matter* being evidently not at all capable of any *Laws or Powers* whatsoever, any more than it is capable of Intelligence; excepting only this *One Negative Power*, that every part of it will, of itself, always and necessarily continue in that State, whether of *Rest or Motion*, wherein it at present is. So that all those things which we commonly say are the Effects of the *Natural Powers of Matter*, and *Laws of Motion*; of *Gravitation, Attraction*, or the like; are indeed (if we will speak strictly and properly) the Effects of *God's* acting upon Matter continually and every moment, either immediately by himself, or mediately by some created intelligent Beings. Consequently, there is no such thing, as what Men commonly call the *Course of Nature* or the *Power of Nature*. The Course of Nature truly and properly speaking is nothing else but the *Will of God* producing certain Effects in a continued, regular, constant and uniform Manner which

... being in every Moment perfectly *Arbitrary*, is as easy to be altered at any time, as to be *preserved*. (WN 697–98)

So, the possibility of miracles, and ultimately the strongest evidence for the divine commission of Christ, is for Clarke linked—indeed it depends upon—a form of theological voluntarism and the denial of the activity of matter.

Clarke's theological voluntarism was moderate if compared to the extreme views of Descartes, since necessary and moral laws are independent of the divine will and even the *potentia dei absoluta* is limited to what is logically possible. Nor is the divine will inscrutable, if that entails that divine attributes and powers are absolutely different from the human ones: as we saw in the chapter on God, they have the same nature and differ only in degree. Moreover, the "arbitrariness" of God's will is not to be construed as irrationality; rather, the divine will infallibly follows his necessarily correct judgment, and consequently God always acts on the basis of rules of "uniformity and proportion." However, true to his libertarian position, Clarke held that the will, in God as in us, is not causally determined by the understanding, and therefore the rules governing the *potentia dei ordinata*, a subset of which are the laws of nature, are freely self-imposed and not the result of the necessarily correct divine understanding: they are a manifestation of God's moral, and therefore free, attributes, not of God's metaphysical, and therefore necessary, ones.[3]

Clarke did not explain why matter is not capable of "any Laws or Powers" but the negative power of inertia, and the inchoate argument he provided seems to involve a confusion between prescriptive and descriptive, civil and natural law. That he had in mind the prescriptive sense of law is evidenced by another passage against the deists in which he repeated that "dull and lifeless Matter is utterly incapable of obeying any Law, or being indued with any Powers" (WN 698; 601). The confusion is rather surprising in light of the distinction of the two senses of law in Suarez.[4] Perhaps, however, far from being guilty of the confusion, Clarke was trying to charge the deists with it. If matter is inert and without powers, then the operations of the world cannot be explained by appealing to descriptive laws depicting the operations of alleged material powers, and any appeal to normative laws would be utterly misplaced with respect to brute and unintelligent matter.[5] The laws of nature, properly understood, are not the laws of matter, but those of the divine will.

In the passage quoted above, Clarke attributed to matter merely the "negative power" of inertia. But in the same passage he also seemed ready to embrace the radical view that matter never has any causal power in itself by claiming that what is done in the world is done by spirits and that the very laws of motion are the result of continuous divine or angelic activity on bodies (WN 697–98). He repeated the same point elsewhere. Since "Matter is utterly uncapable of obeying any Laws, the very original Laws of Motion themselves cannot continue to take Place, but by something Superiour to Matter, *continually* exerting on it a certain Force or Power, according to such certain and determinate Laws" (WN 601). But if matter follows the laws of motion just insofar as spirits act on it, one is left to wonder whether matter per se, albeit in motion, has any causal efficacy.[6]

However, he criticized Malebranche and LeClerc for holding that a body can move only insofar as God positively wills it to move; on the contrary, he claimed, if God were to cease to will anything specific about a body, if it were at rest, it would remain at rest, and if it were in motion, it would remain in motion.[7] Similarly, he argued that that since gravitation is not proportional to "the Surfaces of Bodies, (by which alone they can act one upon another)," but to their masses, it must be produced by "a Force or Power entirely different from that by which Matter acts on Matter," which implicitly recognizes that matter can act on matter by impulse (WN 601). Nevertheless, it is fair to say that for Clarke the causal activity of bodies is rather minute, since what he took to be basic forces in nature, for example, gravitation and repulsive forces, are the result of continual spiritual activity (W III, 847, 904; Cl V, 107–9).

What Clarke steadfastly maintained is that matter has neither an essential nor an accidental power of self-motion. The first claim was very common among early modern philosophers and was held not only a fortiori by Occasionalists like Malebranche and Sturm, but also by thinkers of different persuasion like Descartes, Locke, and Boyle. In fact, even Gassendi, who had upheld the notion of a *materia actuosa* by claiming that atoms have in internal corporeal principle of action, had fallen short of claiming that they possess it essentially.[8]

Clarke's second claim, however, was more controversial. To be sure, most early modern mechanists programmatically attempted to substitute a nature made of inert particles for the living nature of Renaissance philosophy, but the attempt soon ran into great difficulties. Strict mechanism proved inadequate to explain phenomena like exothermic reactions (When gunpowder is ignited, where does the explosive motion come from?) or the spring of the air (Why does a deflated ballon expand in a vacuum tube?). In order to explain such phenomena, mechanism was altered by philosopher-scientists like Boyle, Charleton, Petty, and Newton to include particles variously endowed with powers of motion, attraction, and repulsion.[9]

Clarke's position on the issue was quite radical: the various non-mechanical powers particles are endowed with are the result of direct divine or spiritual activity. This explains his reaction to Toland's revival in the *Letters to Serena* of the claim that matter is essentially endowed with "autokynesis," to use Toland's word.[10] In the fifth letter, Toland had argued at length that motion is essential to matter because matter is endowed with an essential motive force. The issue was particularly charged because in spite of the critique of Spinoza in the fourth letter, Toland had been taken by some to revive Spinozism by adding to it the thesis that motion is essential to matter. For, it was pointed out, the sum of his criticisms of Spinoza amounted to the accusation of not allowing that thesis.[11] Worse, Toland had the temerity to support his views by quoting the explanation of inertia in the third definition of the *Principia*, in which Newton had noted that bodies that are vulgarly taken to be at rest are at times in motion.

Therefore Clarke, whose Boyle Lectures explicitly aimed at confuting Spinoza and Hobbes, devoted a section of his argument against the allegedly Cartesian and Spinozistic view that matter is a necessary being, to the refutation of the claim, explicitly attributed to Toland, that matter is essentially active. If motion were essential to matter, then every piece of matter would either tend to move in one determinate direction, or in all directions. However,

> A *Tendency* to move some *one* determinate way, cannot be essential to any Particle of Matter, but must arise from some External Cause; because there is nothing in the pretended necessary Nature of any Particle, to determine its Motion necessarily and essentially *one way* rather than *another*. And a *Tendency* or *Conatus* equally to move *every way* at once, is either an absolute Contradiction, or at least could produce nothing in Matter, but an Eternal *Rest* of all and every one of its Parts. (WB 531)

Nor could one hold that only some matter has an essential tendency to move, since not only would the previous objection still apply, but one would make an essential quality not universal, which is absurd (WB 531; W IV, 717).

Not only was the notion of a *materia actuosa* demonstrably

wrong, but the idea that matter is passive, with the concomitant view that God constantly operates on it by implementing his will in accordance with principles of wisdom, sits well with Clarke's and Newton's view of God as the Lord God, the *Pantocrator*.[12] Of course, after creation the Lord God could imbue matter with power and let it go, as it were; after all, such transmission of power had taken place with respect to us, since God had given us the power of liberty or free will (WB 559). But Clarke could not bring himself to accept active matter because he thought of it as a prelude to atheism, for, as we noticed in the chapter on God, Clarke believed that denying God's continuous direct intervention in nature in effect amounts to eliminating him.

Given his account of the powers of nature, Clarke could then conclude that, in spite of the fact that God acts on the basis of "rules of uniformity and proportion," miracles are possible; that since all that is consistent is "equally and alike easy to be done" both with respect to divine power and to "the Nature of things themselves," miracles should not be distinguished from ordinary events on the basis of their alleged greater intrinsic difficulty, but rather on the basis of their unusualness, that is, of their being exceptions to the constant and uniform manner of God's acting"; that, as far as we know, they can be be worked by created spirits, since we do not know which powers God chose to communicate (WN 696–98).

2. *Leibniz*

While Clarke's reflections on the nature of miracles were motivated by apologetic purposes, Leibniz's seem to have been more strictly philosophical in nature. Whereas Clarke was primarily interested in miracles in an ontological sense, that is, in showing that they have in fact occurred, and his philosophical comments are ancillary to his overall apologetic intentions, Leibniz was primarily interested in miracles in a methodological sense, that is, in criticizing models of reality he thought required unnecessary divine intervention or were ultimately unintelligible. In fact, prior to his exchange with Clarke, Leibniz showed a tendency to talk about miracles mostly when involved in the critique of Malebranche and Occasionalism, and, to a lesser extent, of Locke.

Leibniz gave two accounts of what a miracle is. The first made use of the idea of the force inherent in creatures. While he was ready to concede that in the popular sense a miracle is just a rare and wonderful thing, he also insisted that "in the philosophical sense [a miracle is] that which exceeds the power of created beings" (*Eclaircissement des difficultés que M. Bayle a trouvées. . . .*: GP IV, 520=L 494). As one would expect, this notion of miracle was especially used by Leibniz against Occasionalism, which he thought, systematically underestimated the power and activity of creatures. Leibniz's second account of miracles made use of two related notions, namely, the intelligibility by a finite mind and the order of nature: "a miracle is a divine action which transcends human knowledge; or more strictly which transcends the knowledge of creatures, or [vel] in which God acts beyond the order of nature"(C 508). Leibniz tended to invoke this notion of miracle in conjunction with his critique of Locke's claim that matter might think or that matter might act at a distance, both of which he found unintelligible.

Malebranche's Occasionalism, Leibniz told Arnauld in 1687, is a perpetual miracle (To Arnauld, 30 April 1687: GP II, 92).[13] *Prima facie*, this criticism appears both odd and misguided. Odd because, if anything, Malebranche was accused of not leaving enough room for miracles in his system.[14] Misguided because Leibniz's point could be, and has been, taken to consist of the claim that Malebranche introduced God's particular volitions without any reason. For example, every time I will to move my arm, Leibniz's Malebranche would be saying, God produces a particular volition whose effect is that my arm moves in the appropriate way. If this were the whole point of the criticism, then Malebranche could simply note that it is an *ignoratio elenchi*, since he did not hold that God's particular volitions are needed every time I decide to move my arm. On the contrary, Malebranche did point out that the relations between the soul and the body are governed by God's general volitions. That is, God set once and for all what motions would correspond to what volitions by instituting general laws of nature. If not, Malebranche would be the first to hold that the relation between the soul and the body is a perpetual miracle, since according to him "an effect, whether usual or unusual, if not produced by God in consequence of his general laws . . . is a miracle."[15] Of course, the same point holds for any two items of which one is the occasional cause of the other.

However, the nerve of Leibniz's criticism lay elsewhere. To Bayle's accusation of having misunderstood Occasionalism by saddling it with the view that God affects the mind-body relation on the basis of particular volitions, like a *deus ex machina*, Leibniz replied that he agreed that the occasionalist God acts through general volitions, but, he continued,

that does not suffice to remove the miracles . . . if we take this term
. . . in the philosophical sense of that which exceeds the power of
created beings. It is not enough to say that God has made a general
law, for besides the decree there is also necessary a natural means
of carrying it out, that is, all that happens must also be explained
through the nature which God gives to things. The laws of nature
are not so arbitrary and so indifferent as people imagine. (*Eclaircissement des difficultés que M. Bayle a trouvées.* . . . GP IV 520=L
494)[16]

Leibniz clarified the point that the laws of nature must be embedded
in creatures, as it were, in *De Ipsa Natura*. For Malebranche, he
claimed, God's volitions, even general ones, are "bestowed upon
things only as an *extrinsic denomination*" (*De Ipsa Natura* § 5: GP
IV, 506=L 500). In other words, the power implicit in the divine will
remains of necessity external to creatures, so that their source of
activity is outside them. But this, Leibniz continued, is unacceptable
for several reasons. First, since there must be a connection, mediate
or immediate, between cause and effect, if God's volitions imparted
no lasting power in things, then God's decisions would have to be
constantly renewed. But this, Leibniz maintained, does not conform
to divine greatness (*De Ipsa Natura* § 6: GP IV, 507=500–501). Second, maintaining that God cannot give power to things because they
are intrinsically inert is detracting from God's greatness (*De Ipsa
Natura* § 8: GP IV, 508=L 501–502). Third, and more important,
since "the substance of things itself consists in the force of acting
and being acted upon" and "their internal nature is no different from
the force of acting and suffering," it is unreasonable to hold that a
thing can persist without any force or power (*De Ipsa Natura* § 8–9:
GP IV, 508–9=L 501–2). Indeed, such a view, Leibniz continued,
would ultimately lead to Spinozism by making God the only substance, since God would be the only agent (*De Ipsa Natura* § 8, 15:
GP IV, 508; 515=L 501–2; 506–7). Finally, if the human soul strictly
speaking did not act and did not even bring about its own thoughts,
then there would be no human freedom, God would be the cause of
evil, and it would contradict the data of our immediate experience
(*De Ipsa Natura* § 10: GP IV, 509=L 502).

Leibniz's last two reasons for rejecting Malebranche's view are
of special interest. In pointing out that Malebranche seemed unable
to find room for free will because according to Occasionalism the
soul is unable to produce its own thoughts, Leibniz was of course
arguing from his view that freedom requires spontaneity, that is, true
causation on the side of the free agent (To Lady Masham, September

1704: GP III, 364). But he also managed to score a dialectical point, since notoriously, Malebranche's treatment of the issue of human freedom is problematic.[17] Of greater significance is Leibniz's other reason for rejecting Occasionalism, namely, the alleged inadequacy of the notion of substance embedded in it. Since for Leibniz being active belongs to the very notion of substance, Malebranche's created substances turn out to be very thin indeed. Not surprisingly, Leibniz complained that Malebranche's substances looked dangerously like accidents.[18]

After telling Bayle that for Malebranche the laws of nature are extrinsic to creatures and criticizing that view, Leibniz concluded that "the laws of nature are not so arbitrary and so indifferent as people think" (*Eclaircissement des difficultés que M. Bayle a trouvées* . . . : GP IV 520=L 494, quoted above). This comment was not a mere afterthought. Rather, there is evidence that Leibniz thought of it as directly connected to his previous criticism of Malebranche. In a note serving as answer to the Occasionalist Lamy's claim that miracles are merely exceptions to God's general and ordinary laws, Leibniz wrote:

> In reasoning in this way, one lacks a proper sense of what a miracle is. For following this idea, the laws of nature would be arbitrary, and those that God would have willed to establish would be the nature of things, just as exceptions to them would be miracles. Consequently, the natural and the miraculous would not differ in themselves, but only by the extrinsic denomination [denominatione extrinseca] taken from the antecedents and the consequents. For, that which would be preceded and followed by similar events would be natural, and that which would not, would be a miracle. But it must be known that not every sort of rule or law is appropriate to constitute a law of nature, and that there is an essential difference between the natural and the miraculous, so that if God acted continually in a certain manner, he would bring about perpetual miracles. For example, if God had established that a planet must always go on its own in a line curved like an ellipse, without adding anything explicable that caused or maintained this elliptical movement, I say that God would have established a perpetual miracle and that it could not be said that the planet proceeded thus in virtue of its own nature or following natural laws, since it is not possible to explain this, nor to provide a reason for such a phenomenon. (*Addition à l'Explication du Systeme nouveau* . . . , GP IV, 587–88)

If the natural laws are extrinsic to the creatures following them, then there is nothing *in creatures* that makes a set of laws better, that is, more appropriate and explicable, than another. If Jupiter is constantly pushed around, or even worse, recreated at every instant by God, there is nothing in it that makes its elliptical orbit around the sun more appropriate than, say, a circular one. That is, in relation to the whole cosmos it may be better that Jupiter follows an elliptic trajectory, but there is nothing in Jupiter itself which justifies or grounds it. In this respect, Leibniz was extending to the Occasionalist view of the laws of nature the same sort of criticism he was launching against the Cartesian and Lockean views of the relation between bodily and mental states. Consider the way in which, say, Descartes would account for the fact that when I prick my finger I feel pain. For him there is nothing in pain itself which connects it with tissue damage. Of course, one can come up with a general reason why God so chose by making reference to the role of pain in the general economy of survival. But for Leibniz this account, though correct, would only be partial. For he held that because of its very constitution, pain expresses tissue damage in a way that other mental states do not (NE II, 8,13). For Leibniz, there is more harmony and connection in the world than Descartes, Occasionalism, or Locke allowed for.

Leibniz's claim that natural laws are embedded in things as their nature might seem to commit him to the unwelcome position that they are the same in all possible worlds, since it may seem reasonable to attribute to him the view that the natures of things are the same in all possible worlds. For example, if the laws of mechanics are at one with the nature of material things, then, in all the worlds in which there is matter, these laws must be the same.[19] Moreover, since for Leibniz truths depending merely on the essences of things are eternal truths independent of God's will, if one somewhat plausibly identifies the natures of things with their essences, then the laws of nature become as metaphysically necessary as the laws of geometry. Indeed, Leibniz might seem to have faced a dilemma: if he grounded the laws of nature in the nature of things, then he would end up with necessary laws, like Descartes and Spinoza before him; if he did not ground the laws of nature in the natures of things, then he would end up with laws that are mere extrinsic denominations, as, according to him, Malebranche's are.

However, in reality Leibniz was not bound to accept the argument leading to the view that the laws of nature are necessary. He pointed out that the natures of things depend on God's will, which shows that he was at least prepared to reject the identification of the natures of things with their essences.[20] Although he did not seem to

develop the point, it is likely that he had in mind something similar
to Malebranche's attempt to link divine volitions to the essences of
things while at the same time safeguarding the freedom of the divine
choice. For Malebranche, bodies are essentially not only extended,
but impenetrable' as well. Hence, it is metaphysically impossible for
two colliding bodies to merge. However, this impossibility does not
deprive God of the choice among different laws of impact; it merely
limits the array of choices. In other words, God can still choose
among all the laws that are compatible with the impenetrability of
bodies.[21] Leibniz could follow an analogous line of reasoning. The
essences of things delimit, but do not determine, the natures of
things, leaving God free to impose the general volitions he wants
and thereby determine what the natures of things are. More precisely, Leibniz could argue the following. Consider the essence E of
a thing. It is given in God's understanding independently of the divine will and it determines the set S of predicates, which are modifications in the attributes in the essence. For example, if the attribute
of extension is contained in E, then "being round" would belong to
S. God can associate to the essence E natures grounded in the predicates belonging to S. In other words, while the essence of a thing
includes all its necessary attributes, its nature goes beyond this, to
include all those properties that are modifications in the essential
attributes and in virtue of which the thing embodies and brings
about the natural laws God has chosen. For example, consider the
essence of matter; God could associate with it a nature based on
modifications generating Descartes's rules of motion or modifications generating the actual rules of motion.[22]

Leibniz's second account of miracles consisted in the claim that
they are in principle unintelligible to created minds and beyond the
order of nature. Prima facie, Leibniz's association of intelligibility
and natural order may seem confusing, since at times he talked as if
literally everything, random events included, must belong to some
order.[23] But elsewhere he made clear that when invoking the idea of
order in relation to miracles, what he had in mind was a more re-
stricted notion of order. For he claimed that "since nothing can happen which is not according to order, it can be said that miracles are
as much subject to order as are natural operations and that the latter
are called natural because they conform to certain subordinate maxims which we call the nature of things" (*Discourse on Metaphysics*
§ 7: GP IV, 432=L 306–7). It seems clear that in addition to the most
inclusive notion of order according to which every logically consistent set of events is orderly, Leibniz used at least another, and

stricter, notion of order. He appealed to it in reference to the laws of nature, which are subordinate maxims, or divine volitions, that are embedded in things themselves as their natures. Since the nature of a thing is grounded in the predicates that are modifications in the attributes of the essence of that thing, the laws of nature are intelligible, that is, in principle comprehensible by rational creatures. Moreover, they are chosen by God because of their simplicity and fruitfulness (*Discourse on Metaphysics* § 5: GP IV, 429–30=L 305).

In spite of the absence of official and workable criteria for lack of intelligibility, Leibniz often associated miracles with the introduction of nonmodal qualities, namely, qualities that could not be construed as modifications in the attributes of their subject (NE preface, 61–68). This is not surprising, for while it is not clear that for him lack of intelligibility can always be explained on the basis of the introduction of nonmodal qualities, it is clear that he held that nonmodal qualities, such as nonmechanical gravity, are always unintelligible (NE IV, 3, 6).

Leibniz's fundamental reason for regarding nonmodal qualities as unintelligible had to do with the notion of inherence, that is, the relation linking a quality to its subject. In September 1712, he told Des Bosses: "I do not see . . . how we can explain intelligibly what it is to be or to inhere in a subject, except by considering that which inheres a mode or state of a subject" (GP II, 459=L 606). Leibniz did not explain what he found unacceptable in the nonmodal notion of inherence, but I believe that we can understand what he had in mind by considering Berkeley's own attack on the notion of matter as a mere substratum of qualities. Those who talk about an unspecified substratum supporting accidents, Berkeley noted, clearly speak metaphorically. But certainly it is not enough to say that a substratum supports its qualities, for "supports" conjures up images of pillars or walls supporting ceilings, and it could hardly be maintained that the relation between a quality and its substance is of this sort.[24]

Leibniz's concrete utilization of the connection between nonmodal qualities and miracles is especially visible in his critique of Locke's suggestion that matter might think. According to Locke, although it is metaphysically impossible for matter to produce thought, God could superadd thought to matter.[25] It is true that such a superaddition would be unintelligible, but in effect, Locke seemed to say, the world is full of such things. For we know that God superadds life to appropriately disposed systems of matter, and the "judicious Mr. Newton's incomparable book" shows that God does the same with the capacity of matter to gravitate toward matter, although how this might come about Locke confessed to find unintelligible.[26] However, in Leibniz's opinion, Locke's position was not stated with sufficient care because it failed to make an adequate distinction between the ordinary and the miraculous course of nature. According to Leibniz, since thought cannot be a modification of matter, as Locke himself seemed to admit implicitly by claiming that matter cannot possibly produce thought, it cannot belong to it without a miraculous intervention because "within the order of nature (miracles apart) it is not at God's arbitrary discretion to attach this or that quality haphazardly to substances. He will never give them any . . . which cannot arise from their nature as explicable modifications" (NE preface, 66).[27] Of course, the same point applies to universal gravity (NE preface, 66).

At times, Leibniz was even ready to imply that Locke had failed to grasp the technical subtleties entailed by the notion of superaddition. In June 1704, he explained to Lady Masham that if God wants to superadd thought to matter, he must "not only give matter the capacity to think, but he must also maintain it continually by the same miracle, since this capacity has no root [racine], unless God gives matter a new nature" (GP III, 356). But of course, giving a new nature to matter would make Locke's point idle. So, when Locke talked about thinking matter, he faced, unawares, the same difficulty Malebranche faced all the time. Leibniz developed the point in the *New Essays*. Superaddition involves "a kind of supernatural elevating of things, as in the claim of some theologians that hell-fire burns separated souls; which leaves open the question of whether it would be the fire which was acting, rather than God acting in place of the fire and producing the same effect" (NE IV, 3, 6). So, it is not sufficient to say that God can superadd thought to matter without explaining who does the thinking, since if it is God who performs the operation of thinking, it is not clear in which sense one could even say that matter could think.

Not only did Leibniz think that he had diagnosed Locke's error in the confusion between the ordinary and the miraculous course of nature, but he also thought he knew its philosophical aetiology. In the preface to the *New Essays*, he took care to highlight for the reader some of the points Locke had made to Stillingfleet on the issue of thinking matter. Locke claimed that the general idea of substance is the same everywhere, and that consequently God is not more at pains in joining it to extension and thought than to extension and motion (NE preface, 62; 64–65).[28] It is because substance was understood by Locke as a mere substratum in isolation from its attributes, that he maintained that it is indifferent to the qualities it may receive.[29] And with this general philosophical background, unable to discriminate between modal and nonmodal qualities, it became easy to believe that matter might think just in the same way in which it might, and indeed does, move.

In Leibniz's eyes, then, ultimately both Malebranche and Locke failed to distinguish appropriately between what is miraculous and what is not because they both had inadequate notions of substance. Malebranche deprived created substances of all power and made every action divine, thus making it miraculous. The outcome was a system that not only destroyed human freedom and diminished the status of God, but also ran the risk of rendering nature unintelligible and of opening the door to Spinoza's one-substance metaphysics. Locke, by isolating the notion of substance from that of attributes, made it possible to view qualities as nonmodal. But nonmodal qualities are linked to their subjects unintelligibly and hence, according to Leibniz, miraculously. The outcome was a system which, in his judgment, opened the way to an unintelligible view of nature by allowing action at a distance, and also to a materialist view of the soul by being unable to explain that matter might, if at all, think only miraculously.[30]

3. The Controversy

In October 1715, Leibniz received from Rémond a set of letters by Conti that detailed the situation in England concerning the controversy between Leibniz and the Newtonians (GP III, 653–56). By then, the dispute on the issue of the priority in the invention of calculus had extended to physics and metaphysics. Conti reported that the Royal Society had published an extract of the *Commercium Epistolicum* with an account of it that also contained comments about Newton's and Leibniz's natural philosophies.[31] While Newton's philosophy was "experimental," Leibniz's was "conjectural"; while Newton did not decide on the nature of the cause of heaviness, Leibniz claimed that it is mechanical; while Newton held that the basic particles of matter are intrinsically hard, Leibniz claimed that they are hard because of conspiring motions; while Newton was agnostic on whether the bodies of animals are in principle fully understandable in mechanical terms, Leibniz used the notion of preestablished harmony. Finally, Conti concluded, according to the anonymous account Newton claims that "God is *Omnipresens* but not as the soul in the body. Mr. Leibniz calls God *Intelligentia Supramundana*, from which it follows, it is claimed, that God cannot do anything in bodies but by Miracle. He is violently attacked on the term 'Miracle' " (GP III, 655).

Conti's report was probably the reason that Leibniz introduced the issue of miracles at the end of the very first letter that opened the controversy with Clarke. The Newtonian God intervenes from time to time to mend the machine of the world. But, Leibniz claimed, "when God makes miracles, it is not in order to supply the wants of nature, but those of grace. To think otherwise, would be to have a very mean notion of the wisdom and power of God" (Lz I). Clarke did not react immediately to Leibniz's criticism. Indeed, in his first reply the issue of miracles was not even mentioned. Probably Clarke, whose interest in miracles, as we saw, was fundamentally in the fact of their occurrence and its evidential support of Christianity, did not want to engage in a discussion on their nature. But Leibniz was not ready to let go: he concluded his second letter with what amounts to an attempt to corner Clarke through the methodological use of the notion of miracle. For, Leibniz said,

> if God is obliged to mend the course of nature from time to time, it must be done either supernaturally or naturally. If it be done supernaturally, we must have recourse to miracles, in order to explain natural things: which is reducing an hypothesis ad absurdum: for, every thing may be easily accounted for by miracles. But if it be done naturally, then God will not be *intelligentia supramundana*: he will be comprehended under the nature of things; that is, he will be the soul of the world. (Lz II, 12)[32]

Clearly, Leibniz had made the issue of miracles a central part of his criticism, and in fact, during the month of December, he brought it up in his correspondence with both Conti and Bernoulli (NC VI, 251=R 41; GM III, 952). Clarke's reaction started the dispute on miracles, which was to continue, rather acrimoniously, for the rest of the exchange.

Throughout the correspondence, Clarke in effect kept repeating two points implied in his definition of miracle in the *Discourse*: first, that since there is no intrinsic difference between what is miraculous and what is natural, the notion of miracle is merely relative to us; second, that a miracle must be unusual (Cl II, 12). Both of these views, Leibniz found strongly objectionable. He attempted to link Clarke's view that the distinction between miraculous and natural events is not intrinsic but merely relative to us, with the position that God is the soul of the world. He claimed that if Clarke were right, then

> at the bottom, every thing will be either equally natural, or equally miraculous. Will divines like the former, or philosophers the latter? Will not this doctrine, moreover, make God the soul of the world if all operations are natural, like those of our souls upon our bodies? And so God will be a part of nature. (Lz V, 110–11)

Leibniz's conclusion that for Clarke all things are equally natural or equally miraculous is substantially correct. Indeed, in the *Discourse* Clarke himself had made a similar point by claiming that all things that do not imply a contradiction are not only with respect to divine power, but also with "respect to the *Nature of the Things themselves* absolutely speaking . . . are *equally and alike easy* to be done" (WN 696–97).

However, Leibniz's argument, if there was really one, linking Clarke's views to the thesis that God is the soul of the world is far from clear. Clarke denied that God is the soul of the world because, among other things, the world does not act on God while the body acts on the soul, at least in the vulgar idea of their relation. To be sure, Leibniz's point rests on God's activity on the world, not on his alleged passivity or lack thereof, and if the claim that divine operations are natural entails that they are analogous to those of the soul on the body, then one could reasonably suspect that for Clarke, God is the soul of the world. But it is hard to see why Clarke should accept the first entailment, given his views of miracles.

In an early draft, Leibniz had put forth the same criticism, but through a different route. Creation, he had claimed, is a truly miraculous event the very nature of which sets it apart from all others. But Clarke cannot admit such a distinction, and consequently God would not be the creator, but at most the governor, and ultimately the soul, of the world (R 174). But this argument as well looks quite problematic. To be sure, Clarke could not say that creation is set apart from all other events in the way Leibniz wanted, but this certainly does not entail that he denied creation altogether. On the contrary, he repeatedly claimed that God created the world (Cl I, 4; IV, 30). It looks as if Leibniz searched for an argument leading from Clarke's views on miracles to unorthodox conclusions without finding one, and consequently resorted to rhetorical questions and innuendos. All Leibniz could reasonably argue for is that Clarke's views on miracles as events per se not different from nonmiraculous ones is compatible, indeed sits quite well, with the view that God is the soul of the world. But perhaps this is all Leibniz wanted to claim, since he was antecedently convinced that Newton's philosophy entails, or at least prepares the way for, the view that God is the soul of the world (Lz I; II, 10; IV, 34; V, 82, 86, 111; to Johann Bernoulli, 7 June 1716: GM III, 963). Moreover, showing that Clarke's position on miracles sat well with such a heretical view carried considerable strategical force. Clarke chose not to answer Leibniz's criticism and merely repeated that neither he nor Newton ever held that God is the soul of the world (Cl V, 83–91).

Since Clarke maintained that the notion of miracle, when duly unpacked, is found to be relative to human beliefs, it is not surprising that he saw an essential connection between being miraculous and being unusual. He told Leibniz that if something "be usual . . . 'tis no miracle, whether it be effected immediately by God himself, or mediately by any created power: but if it be unusual . . . 'tis equally a miracle, whether it be effected immediately by God himself, or mediately by any invisible power (Cl III, 17).[33] Not unreasonably, Leibniz took Clarke to hold that rarity is at least a sufficient condition for the miraculous, and counteracted by pointing out that if Clarke were right, then monsters would be miracles (Lz IV, 43). Clarke's reply consisted in claiming that unusualness is not a sufficient but a necessary condition for the miraculous, and that many unusual things such as eclipses, madness in men, and monstrous births are merely "the irregular and more rare effect of usual causes" (Cl IV, 43). In effect, then, in step with his definition of miracle in the *Discourse*, Clarke's claim entails that miracles must not only be rare, but also have unusual causes, that is, they must not be subsumable under the laws of nature, that is, God's general will.

Clarke's position, then, was more strict than Malebranche's, since not only must miracles be the result of divine particular volitions, but they must also be rare. Indeed, Clarke's position was even more strict than indicated in the correspondence. For in his official definition of miracle in the *Discourse*, Clarke claimed that miracles come about for the attestation of somebody's religious authority. This added a third necessary condition for miracles in addition to unusual causation and rarity. Nor was this third condition incidental. On the contrary, it was the direct result of Clarke's fundamental interest in miracles as the only reasonable ground on which to believe in Christ's divine commission. Furthermore, it shaped the requirement of rarity, since only what is unusual can excite the admiration necessary for the miracle to perform its religious function. But in effect, the context of the debate with Leibniz precluded

Clarke from bringing up this third condition, since Leibniz's use of the notion of miracle was methodological, and consequently many of the religious overtones of Clarke's account of miracles were irrelevant to the discussion.

In the same way in which Clarke had mixed success in defending his view that miracles are rare events not intrinsically different from natural ones, he had mixed success in attacking his opponent's denial of that view. It was not for lack of trying. Indeed, in his fifth reply, Clarke went as far as attempting to saddle Leibniz with the view that God is not a perfect unity. For, he claimed, if there is a difference between what is miraculous and what is not "absolutely, and with regard to God," then one should admit two "different and really distinct" powers in God. If one rejects, he continued, this conclusion, then one must hold either that the notion of miracle is relative to us, or that a miracle is what is done directly by God and what is nonmiraculous is what is done by secondary causes. But, Clarke concluded, Leibniz's attack of his views shows that his opponent rejects the former position; and by admitting that angels can perform miracles Leibniz shows that he rejects the latter as well (Cl V, 110–16).

Clarke's appeal to the unity of God is rather surprising, given that his views of divine unity and simplicity were looser than Leibniz's and given that his views on free will require that the will and the understanding be distinct, the former being free and the other fully determined. Presumably, then, his point was that Leibniz's theory entails the denial of the unity of divine power. However, it is far from clear why Leibniz should accept that admitting a difference in re and with respect to God between miracles and natural events entails admitting a real distinction within divine omnipotence. Since the one divine power is infinite, it is sufficient to bring about both effects that require an infinite power and effects that do not. If a distinction there is, it would have to be located in the divine will in that a miracle involves a will to change the set course of nature. But neither does a will to change involve a change of will, nor does the subsumption of the laws of nature (God's general volitions embedded, as it were, in creatures) and miracles (God's particular volitions) under the general plan of the world involve a distinction in re in the divine will.

Perhaps inflamed by polemical ardor, Clarke also was not very careful in using the notion of miracle consistently with his own claim that miracles must be rare, which had been indicated by his attempt to attack Leibniz's preestablished harmony with the claim

that it is miraculous (Cl IV, 31).[34] Of course, Leibniz did reply that
Clarke, in charging that preestablished harmony is miraculous, was
contradicting himself, since in Leibniz's system it cannot be considered an unusual phenomenon (Lz V, 109). Clarke, probably realizing
his mistake, did not respond.

However, Clarke did manage to make a dialectically effective
point against his interlocutor. Leibniz's position that miracles need
not be rare but must exceed the powers of creatures, left him open
to the rebuttal that then "for a man to walk on the water, or for the
motion of the sun or the earth to be stopped, is no miracle; since
none of these things require infinite power to effect them" (Cl III,
17).[35] Obviously, in the midst of a controversy with many theological
overtones, for which he was mainly responsible, Leibniz wanted to
maintain that scriptural miracles like those cleverly mentioned by
Clarke were bona fide miracles. Consequently, he felt compelled to
distinguish between higher and lower level miracles: "It may be said
that the angel, who carried Habakkuk through the air, and he who
troubled the waters of the pool of Bethesda, worked a miracle. But
it was not a miracle of the highest order; for it may be explained by
the natural powers of angels, which surpass those of man" (Lz V,
117). Similarly, an angel could make a man walk on water, although
there are some miracles, for example, creating and annihilating,
which only God can perform (Lz IV, 44). Clarke's reaction was stern:
he chastised Leibniz for his apparent turnabout and went as far as
accusing him of outright inconsistency (Cl V, 117).

One can see the sort of problems facing Leibniz's view by noticing that it had no ready way to make room for angelic miracles. Of
course, Leibniz could argue that although an angel could make a man
walk on water or perhaps make the earth stand still, nevertheless
walking on water and standing still exceed the natural powers of
man and earth, respectively, and consequently they are bona fide
full-fledged miracles. However, some reflection shows that this line
of defense is full of difficulties. If the acquisition of a property ex-
ceeding the natural powers of its subject were miraculous, then the
trivial flying of a stone I threw in the air would be miraculous, since
flying is certainly beyond the natural powers of stones. Of course, in
throwing the stone I did not exceed my natural powers, but, we are
told, neither did the angel who made Habakkuk fly. Leibniz, for
whom usualness is irrelevant to the nature of miracles, overcame
the risk of rendering them trivial by demanding that they be performed by divine infinite power. Consequently, angelic miracles are
such only by courtesy, as it were.[36]

By the end of November 1715, Leibniz had read those works by Clarke that Caroline had sent to him and had probably been struck by some of the similarities between Clarke's and Malebranche's views about the laws of nature.[37] For, as we saw, at times Clarke seemed almost ready to hold that, aside from the actions of living organisms, matter is active only insofar as constantly acted upon by angels operating in accordance with divine instructions (WN 601, 698). And even in his less radical statements, he clearly put forth the point that the majority of the effects of bodies are brought about by spirits acting on them (WN 601). Of course, for Clarke, but not for Malebranche, not only God, but also immaterial entities like angels, and human and animal souls act on matter. But this disagreement does not change the fact that for both philosophers the laws governing bodies are extrinsic denominations, and that miracles, to the extent that they are exceptions to these laws, are viewed as mere deviations from God's general volitions.

Evidence for this claim can be gathered from an early version of Leibniz's third letter, in which, after stating that what is supernatural exceeds all the powers of creatures, he continued by starting to draw a comparison between Clarke and some followers of Malebranche: "il ne faut point l'imaginer avec quelques Malbranchistes, que naturel est . . ." (R 57). Leibniz did not finish the sentence, perhaps because he did not want to provide Clarke with indirect support from Malebranche. However, the version he sent to Clarke does sufficiently convey the point, already made against Malebranche and Lamy, that what is natural must be within the power of created beings:

> There is an infinite difference [between the natural and the supernatural]; but it plainly appears, it has not been duly considered. That which is supernatural, exceeds all the powers of creatures. I shall give an instance, which I have often made use of with good success. If God would cause a body to move free in the aether round about a certain fixed centre, without any other creature acting upon it: I say, it could not be done without a miracle; since it cannot be explained by the nature of bodies. For, a free body does naturally recede from a curve in the tangent. And therefore I maintain, that the attraction of bodies, properly so called, is a miraculous thing, since it cannot be explained by the nature of bodies. (Lz III, 17)[38]

The reference to gravitation being unexplicable by reference to the nature of bodies would seem to suggest that in Leibniz's eyes not only had Clarke fallen into Malebranche's error of making natural laws extrinsic to bodies, but he also had fallen into a variant of Locke's error by allowing nonmechanical, that is, nonmodal and unintelligible, qualities in bodies. Such a view would seem reinforced by Clarke's apparent agreement with Locke on some issues concerning substance; for example, Ferguson has pointed out that there are similarities between Locke's views and Clarke's claim that we do not know the substance or essence of anything (WB 538).[39] The point can be strengthened by noting that for Clarke, as for Locke, substance and essence are two different things and that at times he seemed ready to accept the notion, as he put it, of "substance in general capable of thinking and numberless unknown properties besides" (WB 581 n. a, 563). So, Clarke allowed substance in general, something equivalent to the naked Lockean substratum Leibniz had criticized in the Preface of the *New Essays*, to be the subject of predication (WB 555).

One might resist the comparison by noting that Clarke, but not Locke, felt justified in arguing very passionately that matter cannot think; but this objection would be misplaced. For, although we do not know what matter is, that is, we do not know its essence, Clarke pointed out to Collins that we know enough to say that it is not only necessarily divisible, but, being constituted by *partes extra partes*, also of necessity actually divided (W III, 761). Consequently, he inferred, matter cannot be the subject of inherence of consciousness, which is an essentially unitary, and hence indivisible, power. Had Locke agreed that divisibility is incompatible with consciousness, this argument would have won his approval.

However, in spite of all these similarities between Locke's and Clarke's views, Leibniz did not launch against the latter the same attack he had launched against the former. The reason may be that Leibniz deemed the evidence that Clarke had a Lockean view of substance inconclusive. In the Preface to *A Discourse*, Clarke told William Caroll, who had written what Clarke judged a scurrilous pamphlet against *A Demonstration*, that since the attributes of God and those of matter are incompatible with each other, the substances to which they belong must be different (WB 582).[40] But this claim could be read as to render it incompatible with the view that substance is the same everywhere if one assumes, as the context seems to warrant, that Clarke's point was not merely that a substance cannot have incompatible qualities.

Given Clarke's views on the laws of nature, one can see how Leibniz could understand the philosophical genesis of Clarke's position on gravitation as a development of dangerous tendencies present in Malebranche's system. For, if it is God and other spirits who are the true, extrinsic, and continually acting causes of the activity of bodies, then there is nothing in bodies themselves to explain why they should behave in accordance with the laws of mechanism and influence each other only by impulse rather than in accordance with nonmechanical laws. Universal gravitation, which in Malebranche and Lamy was a mere dangerous possibility, in Clarke and Newton had become a reality. In sum, the view that, with respect to the "Nature of things themselves," all that can possibly happen to creatures is "equally and alike easy to be done," that is, the view that nature is indifferent to the course of nature that Clarke had used to show the possibility of miracles, prepares the way for such monsters as Newtonian gravitation (WN 696). Moreover, to the extent that Leibniz was convinced that Clarke viewed substances as Lockean substrata, he *may* have thought that from a Clarkeian perspective there is no reason *in rebus* that God should restrict the natural laws to those explainable on the basis of modal qualities. If he did, then Leibniz's analysis was that Clarke's support of universal gravity, like his view on miracles, was philosophically grounded on a combination of both Malebranche's and Locke's errors.

Of course, Clarke was not impressed by Leibniz's claim that there is an infinite distance between natural and miraculous operations because the latter, but not the former, stem from "the laws that God has given to creatures, which have been given the ability to follow through their natures" (Lz V, 112). He tended to associate the view that nature constitutes a self-contained system with the theories espoused by those deists who deny the role of providence (Cl I, 4; WN 600–602). Moreover, there is some evidence that he considered Leibniz's view on nature, with the concomitant thesis that matter is never at rest, as a form of crypto-Hobbesianism. For, in the editions of *A Demonstration of the Being and Attributes of God* published after the controversy with Leibniz, he twice associated the Hobbesian hypothesis that all matter would perceive if it had the appropriate organs of sense, with Leibniz's claims about the activity of nature and matter, and preestablished harmony, and referred the reader to sections 2 and 11 of the appendix to his edition of the correspondence (WB 546; 562).

Although Clarke did not provide any explanation for the attribution to Leibniz of Hobbes's view, an examination of the appendix can help to get an idea of what he had in mind. Section 2 of the appendix contains a list of passages dealing with the concepts of nature and action. Two are especially relevant: "to act, is the characteristic of substances," and "every part of matter is, by its form, continually acting."[41] In addition, many other passages from section 2 contain the claim that matter, at times characterized as "corporeal substance," is active. In sum, it looks as if Clarke became convinced that for Leibniz, bodies are substances, although in order to be so, they need some inadequately specified "principle" that supposedly is "superior to the (common) notion of matter, . . . active, and . . . vital," as other passages in the same section show. Section 11 of the appendix is overall devoted to preestablished harmony, but its first passage says that "every single substance is naturally endowed with perception."[42] So, it looks very much as if Clarke took Leibniz to hold that bodies are substances and consequently do or could perceive. Significantly, throughout the first passage of section 11, Clarke kept mistranslating Leibniz's text by writing "single substance" instead of "simple substance," which, barring devious plans on his side, reinforces the conclusion that he believed that for Leibniz bodies are substances.

The same point can be made by considering Clarke's reaction to Leibniz's view that motive force is *vis viva* and not quantity of motion, as Clarke believed. In 1724, Clarke published an article in the *Philosophical Transactions* in which he tried to show that motive force is quantity of motion by using essentially metaphysical arguments. The reason Leibniz disagreed, Clarke noted, is that for him there is "some Living Soul essentially belonging to every Particle of Matter," and the extra element of velocity which *vis viva* has over quantity of motion is attributable to such soul (W IV, 738).[43] Ultimately then, Clarke took Leibniz to hold that every part of matter is ensouled and, at least potentially, capable of consciousness. Clarke's interpretation, however, is wrong. For although Leibniz held that "nature is full of life," he explicitly denied that a stone or any non-organic body is ensouled or that every portion of matter is animated (*Principles of Nature and Grace* § 1: GP VI, 539=L 586). Only organic bodies qualify as corporeal substances (To Bierling,12 August 1711: GP VII, 501).[44]

Clarke's primary interest in miracles centered around proving that their occurrence provides evidence for the truth of Christianity. He tried to show their possibility by appealing to a system that emphasizes the role of a libertarian divine will and direct divine intervention in the ordinary course of nature, denies activity to matter, and claims that the basic forces that keep the world together are the effect of continual spiritual activity. As a result, properly speaking, natural laws govern the divine will not matter, to which they are therefore extrinsic. By contrast, Leibniz's interest in miracles centered around their use against models of reality that made natural laws extrinsic to the nature of bodies. Such models, he thought, would lead to a diminished view of God and, by being associated with incorrect views on substance, could open the door to Spinozism or to a materialist view of the mind.

In the correspondence, Clarke's and Leibniz's contrasting views came into overt conflict in the midst of often acrimonious and belligerent exchanges. In Clarke's eyes, Leibniz's misunderstanding of the nature of miracles was grounded in a view of nature which, by emphasizing its active powers, led to the materialism of free thinkers or at least provided them with philosophical weapons. Of course, Leibniz could reply that the active powers to be found in nature have been implanted by God, but such an answer would hardly satisfy Clarke, who viewed Leibniz's denial of contra-causal freedom as evidence that Leibniz's God was a necessary agent, that is, no agent at all. In Leibniz's eyes, Clarke's mistaken ideas on miracles were based in a view which, by emphasizing the passivity of nature and the role of a contra-causal divine will, led, or could lead, to a diminished view of God and ultimately to irreligion. And although he certainly could not charge Clarke with a materialist view of the mind, as we saw in the chapter on God, he was ready to charge him with the view that God is the world-soul. Ironically then, Clarke, who had denied to matter any power but inertia, had ended up by making the world something similar to a divine animal.

6

MATTER & FORCE

Given the metaphysical and theological ground on which Leibniz had decided to mount his last attack against Newtonianism, physical issues played an ancillary role, and consequently those which the disputants perceived more directly tied to the positions they wanted to press received the earliest and greatest attention. Leibniz kept attacking Newtonian gravitation as miraculous or occult and the view that the quantity of force in matter is decreasing as leading to a debased notion of God. Similarly, Clarke criticized Leibniz's claim, that the quantity of matter is infinite and its force conserved, as conducive to the effective expulsion of God from the universe. Other issues, such as the existence of atoms and the void, arose when Caroline attended some experiments conducted by Newton at court. However, in spite of their almost accidental entrance into the correspondence, these issues too had significant ties to Leibniz's and Clarke's metaphysical views and therefore ended up receiving a good degree of attention. The first part of this chapter is on matter and deals with quantity of matter, atoms, and the vacuum; the second part, on force, deals with the measure of motive force, inertia, and gravity.

1. *Matter*

1.1 *Quantity of Matter*

In his first letter, Leibniz claimed that Newtonianism did, or could, contribute to the weakening of natural religion. Such a remark must have been particularly galling to Clarke, whose whole philosophical orientation was to strengthen natural religion with the help of Newton's physics. Clarke viewed Spinoza and Hobbes as atheist materialists; not surprisingly he replied that "Mathematical Philosophy," that is, Newtonianism, alone could prove that matter is "the smallest and most inconsiderable part of the Universe" (Cl I, 1). Clarke did not elaborate, but presumably he had in mind Newtonian arguments (of which more later) to the effect that resistance to motion in fluids is directly proportional to their density—that is, quantity of matter per unit of volume, an argument that found its place in the last (1728) edition of *A Demonstration* published during Clarke's life (WB 532). His reply started a confrontation on the issue of the spatio-temporal extension of the physical universe, which continued to the end of the correspondence. Clarke tried to show that Leibniz's views entail that matter is necessarily eternal and infinite, and therefore endowed with necessary existence. We considered an argument based on Leibniz's denial of the mobility of the universe in the chapter on space and time. Here, we study Clarke's reaction to Leibniz's claim that divine wisdom produces an infinite extension of matter.

Leibniz kept repeating that the more creatures there are, the greater is the opportunity for the exercise of divine wisdom. Hence, since the infinite extension of matter does not limit the perfection of anything else, no "possible reason" could be found for not creating it (Lz III, 9; IV, 21–23). Clarke resisted the argument by claiming that God can exercise his wisdom on spiritual creatures, and that at any rate the finite quantity of matter constituting the universe is exactly what is needed for this world to be as God intended it to be (Cl III, 9). Of course, Leibniz disagreed, presumably in part because of his rejection of disembodied creatures, but also because Clarke's point is immaterial, the issue being not whether the present quantity of matter is exactly what is needed to fulfill the divine design but whether the divine design requires an infinite quantity of matter (NE preface, 58).

However, in his fourth reply, Clarke changed tactics by attacking not only Leibniz's argument but his position as well: "That God cannot limit the quantity of matter, is an assertion of too great consequence, to be admitted without proof. If he cannot limit the duration of it either, then the material world is both infinite and eternal necessarily, and independently upon God" (Cl IV, 21). This time, Clarke went to the heart of the issue. Leibniz complained of having been misunderstood. First, he argued, his position does not entail that matter is infinite necessarily and independently of God's will; on the contrary, it is the divine will, guided by the Principle of the Best, which brings about a world with an infinite quantity of matter (Lz V, 73–74). Leibniz's complaint was reasonable, but one can appreciate the motivations and the reasons behind Clarke's charge. As we saw, he was bothered by what he perceived as Leibniz's hylozoistic views of matter and its similarity to Toland's view that matter is essentially active. More important, if God's choices are brought about by reason-causes, as Leibniz had argued in the parallel discussion on free will, and "no possible reason" (Leibniz's words!) could be given for limiting the quantity of matter, then whether matter is infinite or not is not up to God. That this was really Leibniz's view received further support from his claim that Descartes's thesis that matter is unlimited had not been refuted, for as Clarke did not fail to point out, Descartes had held that it is contradictory to suppose that the world is finite. But if God could not alter the quantity of matter, then he could not be its creator. And if God did not create matter, then matter exists necessarily (Cl V, 26–32).[1]

Leibniz's second reason for complaint was Clarke's move from spatial to temporal infinity. Not unreasonably, Clarke may have thought that the Principle of the Best, with its corollary, the more matter the better, would lead to temporal as well as to spatial infinity. Leibniz presented two arguments to deny the parity between spatial and temporal infinity. First, if one assumes that the universe is increasing in perfection at a uniform rate, then its age must be finite, otherwise its perfection would be infinite now (Lz V, 73–74). Why the increase in perfection should be at a uniform rate rather than at a rate R decreasing fast enough to avoid the infinite perfection of the world even after an infinite amount of time has elapsed, Leibniz did not explain. However, he did believe that divine wisdom requires that the world increase in perfection beyond any given level. This eliminates the possibility that the perfection of the world increases at rate R, although one might object that the world could follow rate R and then, for example, now, follow a different rate leading to unlimited perfection, rejecting the requirement that the rate of increase in perfection be uniform.

Leibniz's second argument was less successful. He claimed that "the world's having a beginning, does not derogate from the infinity

of its duration *a parte post*; but bounds of the universe would derogate from the infinity of its extension. And therefore it is more reasonable to admit a beginning of the world than to admit any bounds
of it" (Lz V, 74). He did not argue for the disanalogy of spatial and
temporal boundaries with respect to infinity, and one immediate
objection is that a world bound on one side could be just as exten-
sionally infinite as one having a temporal beginning can be dura-
tionally infinite. Consequently, if Leibniz was ready to deny spatial
boundaries to the world, he should have done the same with respect
to temporal boundaries. However, Leibniz had a fall-back position,
for he reminded Clarke that the eternity of the world is perfectly
compatible with its dependence on God (Lz V, 75). He had tradition
on his side, and Clarke himself had made the same point in *A Demonstration*, but Clarke was perfectly justified in charging him with
an *ignoratio elenchi* (Cl V, 73–75; WB 536).[2] For the issue at hand
was whether the spatio-temporal infinity of matter depends on the
divine will, not whether matter is actually spatio-temporally infinite.

1.2 Atoms

Although Clarke held that matter is necessarily composed of *partes
extra partes*, this being the fundamental reason that it cannot possibly think, like other Newtonians he was an atomist in the sense
of believing in the existence of particles that only divine power could
break. Newton had apparently intended to include statements favorable to atomism in the first edition of *Principia* but had given up,
perhaps for theological reasons. But by 1706 he had been much more
forthcoming, and in query 23 of the *Optice* he had clearly stated his
view:

> it seems very probable to me, that God . . . at the beginning created
> matter so that its original particles . . . were firm, hard, impenetra-
> ble, inert, moveable, of such sizes and figures, with such other prop-
> erties, and in such number and quantity with respect to the space
> in which they would move, as most conducive to the end for which
> he created them. (NO 343)

These atomic particles have no pores and their parts are held together by an attractive power that makes them naturally unbreakable, immensely hard, and therefore endowed with minimal or no
elasticity, a fact that renders them unable to rebound when hitting
each other (NO 341–42).[3]
Leibniz had often argued against atoms and in his second letter

had compared Newton's "Mathematical principles of philosophy" with those of Democritus, Epicurus, and Hobbes, adding that the only difference was in the admission of immaterial souls, which the former accepted and the latter denied (Lz II, 1).[4] In spite of Hobbes's mention, the accusation was rather bland, amounting at most to the charge of Gassendism, and although as early as December 1715 Leibniz had told Conti that atoms and the void are the result of narrow philosophical views, his first objection to atomism in the correspondence was indirect (NC VI, 252=R 42). Clarke had countered Leibniz's criticism of absolute space by arguing that even in a relational space God would have no reason to place three equal particles A, B, and C in that order rather than in the reverse one (Cl III, 2). Leibniz agreed and inferred from this that God does not create equal particles, that is, atoms (Lz IV, 3; V, 21; to Caroline, 2 June 1716: KLC 112= R 78).

However, it was in a *post scriptum* to a letter to Caroline that Leibniz openly attacked atomism. Caroline had witnessed some experiments in pneumatics that had been interpreted as establishing the existence of vacuum (To Leibniz, 15 May 1716: KLC 93=R 67). So, she told Leibniz that she was now attracted to the hypothesis of the void and asked him to put her in the right road. Since the existence of the void and that of atoms usually have been connected, Leibniz's answer involved a full-fledged attack against atomism. To be sure, he was not unqualifiedly opposed to them. In 1714 he told Remond that "the philosophy of Gassendi" could be used to introduce students to physics if they were told that atoms and the void were but convenient hypotheses to be dismissed at a rigorous level of explanation (GP III, 619=L 657). But he was also clearly opposed to any claim that atoms really exist, and in 1712 he told Hartsoeker that the appeal to their primitive firmness or solidity was totally unjustified and on a par with that to gravitation or nonmechanical primitive qualities (GP III, 532). Solidity, Leibniz thought, must be explained on the basis of motion because only motion diversifies matter (To Huygens, 11 April 1692: GM II, 136; *Dynamica de Potentia*: GM VI, 509).

Moreover, Leibniz saw a link between the relativity of motion, the nature of solidity and the plenum. Since all motion is rectilinear uniform or the result of the composition of rectilinear uniform motions, circular motion is the result of tangential rectilinear uniform motion and rectilinear accelerated motion, itself to be resolved into infinitesimal elements of uniform motion, toward the center of rotation resulting from the pressure of the surrounding medium. So, the parts of a rotating solid disk begin to escape with rectilinear uniform motion along the tangent but are repelled toward the center of rotation by the impact with the surrounding particles. Consequently, the solidity of the disk is to be explained on the basis of circumambient medium pressure. If the solidity of the disk were intrinsic, then some circular motion would not result from rectilinear uniform ones. For example, if two diametrically opposite points of the disk were pushed with equal force in opposite directions, the disk would rotate and the curvilinear motion of its particles could be understood as resulting from its solidity and not from the dynamical composition of rectilinear uniform motions, that is, the impacts among bodies in rectilinear uniform motion (*Dynamica de Potentia*: GM VI, 508–9; *Specimen Dynamicum*: GM VI, 252–53 = L 449). Furthermore, from the fact that every body has some degree of solidity, Leibniz inferred the plenum, since a body in a vacuum would have no solidity at all (*Dynamica de Potentia*: GM VI, 511).

Leibniz's argument to Caroline, however, was different and in keeping with the theological tone of the correspondence. As he had told Bernoulli a few years earlier, the Principle of the Best embodying divine wisdom requires that the world contain as much variety as possible compatibly with the simplicity of covering laws. Hence, matter is heterogeneous, and therefore no two particles are identical. Further, each particle is subdivided into parts, and consequently there are no ultimate particles. In sum, there are no atoms (To Caroline, 12 May 1716: R 76–77; to Johann Bernoulli, 23 February 1699: GM III, 565; to Hartsoeker, 30 October 1710: GP III, 507; Lz, V, 22).[5] Clarke was little moved by Leibniz's appeal to the Principle of the Best, and replied by attempting a *reductio* of Leibniz's position. Either there are poreless particles, in which case the parts of such particles "taken of equal figure and dimension (which is always possible in supposition)" are indiscernible atoms; or,

> if there be no such perfectly solid particles, then there is no matter at all in the universe. For, the further the divisions and subdivisions of the parts of any body is carried, before you arrive at parts perfectly solid and without pores; the greater is the proportion of pores to solid matter in that body. If therefore, carrying on the division *in infinitum*, you never arrive at parts perfectly solid and without pores; it will follow that all bodies consist of pores only, without any matter at all: which is a manifest absurdity. (Cl IV, *post scriptum*)

The argument tries to infer the existence not merely of poreless solid particles, but of indiscernible parts of matter, both of which

Leibniz rejected, and is probably quite old since a simplified version of it seems to be attributed to Empedocles or Leucippus by Aristotle.[6] It also impressed Voltaire, who in his *Elements of Newton's Philosophy*, in effect interpreted it thusly. Suppose a body A is half matter and half pores; then, by subtracting from it half its apparent matter, we find that there is in it only half as much matter as it would seem prima facie. Suppose now that this half is itself half matter and half pores and that the same ratio holds independently of the size of the particles considered. Then, one can set up an infinitely decreasing series S in which each term is subtracted from the previous so as to indicate the quantity of matter actually present in A:

$$1 - \tfrac{1}{2} - \tfrac{1}{4} - \ldots \tfrac{1}{2^n} - \ldots.$$

As n gets bigger, the amount of actual matter in A gets smaller, and if n is infinitely large, that is, if A is infinitely divided, then since the series converges to 0 there is no matter left. Hence, A is not infinitely divided, and therefore there must be undivided, that is, poreless, particles of matter.[7]

Leibniz did not answer Clarke's argument (which shows that the argument was probably composed after Clarke had sent his fourth reply), but some objections come to mind. The argument works only if S converges to 0, and this occurs only if the terms of the series do not become too small too fast. Voltaire made sure of this by claiming that the ratio between matter and pores in any body is extremely small, and although Clarke was silent on the issue, we have no reason to doubt that he would have concurred. However, even with this added premise, the argument suffers from at least three problems. First, at best it can conclude that there must be poreless parts of matter, not that there must be poreless particles. For example, a body as porous as Swiss cheese that is not solid but has some solid (poreless) parts would satisfy the argument's conclusion. This, however, need not be a serious drawback. As we saw, for Clarke matter is composed of *partes extra partes*, and an atom is just a conglomerate the parts of which are held together by forces that cannot be naturally overcome. What the argument adds is that such parts must fully touch, so that among them there is no void, a view Clarke shared with Newton (NO *quaestio* 23, 336). However, as we saw, this was all Clarke claimed: no atom, in his view, need be a separate individual particle. That most atoms are physically separate from each other follows not from this argument, but from that for the vacuum.

The second objection stems directly from the first; if matter is composed of *partes extra partes* kept together by attractive forces, then the argument cannot show that these parts are identical so that atoms, or their parts, are indiscernible. Of course, the conclusion of the argument is compatible with the indiscernibility of atoms, but compatibility is not entailment. Even so, the objection affects only half of the stated aims of Carke's argument. The final objection, however, is more serious. Plenists like Leibniz hold that the pores of a body are not empty but filled with subtle matter, the pores of which are themselves filled with an even subtler matter, and so on to infinity. Clarke thought that this objection was misplaced, and in an addition to his 1717 edition claimed that: "the argument is the same with regard to the matter of which any particular species of bodies is composed, whether its pores be supposed empty, or always full of extraneous matter" (Cl IV, *errata*). But one can hardly see the force of Clarke's reply: if each pore, no matter how small, is full of matter, there is no vacuum and the argument cannot even get off the ground. Ultimately, then, Clarke's argument rests on that for the vacuum.

1.3 The Vacuum

The issue of intramundane vacuum came up rather late in the correspondence and, like the debate about atoms, was occasioned by Caroline's attendance at some pneumatic experiments conducted by Newton (To Leibniz, 15 May 1716: KLC 93=R 67). It was only partially connected to the issue of absolute space, since the existence of absolute space is compatible with that of an all-pervading ether, like the one Newton periodically considered.[8] To be sure, Leibniz thought that the very same arguments which show that extramundane space does not exist also show that intramundane space does not exist since they differ only in quantity (Lz III, 7). But historically the two had not always been conjoined. The ancient Stoics had a plenist world suspended in an infinite empty space, and their view had been reproposed by some seventeenth-century Aristotelians.[9] Moreover, while the issue of extramundane space was essentially metaphysical and had clear theological overtones, that of intramundane vacuum had become at least partially experimental after the work of Torricelli, Pascal, van Guerike, and Boyle.

Leibniz told Caroline that in the vacuum tube only the crass parts of matter are absent (2 June 1716: R 78–79). As he wrote to Clarke, an allegedly "exhausted receiver" is like a box with holes, filled with fish, and immersed in water; when the fish are removed, the box is still filled with water; analogously, when the air is removed, the vacuum tube is still filled with subtle matter (Lz V, 34).

This was a standard plenist interpretation of the various vacuum experiments, and not surprisingly Clarke had a reply:

> In an exhausted receiver, though rays of light, and perhaps some other matter, be there in an exceeding small quantity; yet the want of resistance plainly shows, that the greatest part of that space is void of matter. For subtleness or fineness of matter, cannot be the cause of want of resistance. Quicksilver is as subtle, and consists of as fine parts and as fluid, as water; and yet makes more than ten times the resistance: which resistance arises therefore from the quantity, and not the grossness of matter. (Cl IV, 7)

In effect, Clarke turned the discussion from what happens in a vacuum tube to how to explain the varying degrees of resistance to motion in a medium. Certainly the tenacity or viscosity of the medium plays an important role, but in the case of equally fluid media, the difference in resistance is due to the different quantity of matter per unit of space, that is, to their different densities. Hence, given two equally viscous fluids, that which offers less resistance to a body moving in it has the greater amount of pores. Therefore, intramundane vacua exist.

Probably, the idea behind Clarke's reply came from the general scholium in *Principia*, book 2, section 6, on "the motion and resistance of pendulous bodies."[10] Newton had performed an experiment to determine that mass is proportional to weight, and consequently that the fluid matter which, as he had pointed out in the first definition of *Principia*, some thought filled the bodies' pores has no effect on it. He had compared the oscillations of a pendulum with a wooden bob alternatively empty or filled with a piece of metal. If some ethereal fluid pervading the pores of bodies provides any sensible resistance to the motion of the pendulum, the presence or absence of the piece of metal should affect the oscillations. Since the pendulum behaves virtually identically with or without the piece of metal, Newton concluded that the resistance of the ethereal fluid is at best imperceptible and that all the resistance comes from air. He expressed the hope that the experiment would be repeated with greater precision, "since the demonstration of a vacuum depends thereon" (NP II, 6, general scholium, 456). The reference to the vacuum was not lost on Leibniz, who commented that Newton doubted the existence of an ethereal fluid.[11] The scholium also described other experiments to determine the resistance of mediums by pendulums oscillating in them. In particular, Newton had a pendulum oscillate in water and quicksilver and noticed that the ratio of the resistances they offer is the same as that of their densities. After repeating the experiment with some other fluids, he had concluded that this is "an accurate enough" rule (NP II, 6, general scholium, 459–60). Clearly, Clarke explained the experiment by claiming that other things being equal, resistance is given by the density of the medium.

Leibniz replied that "it is not so much the quantity of matter, as its difficulty of giving place, that makes resistance." For example, he continued, floating timber has less heavy matter than water and yet it offers more resistance (Lz V, 34). In effect this was a compressed statement of his views on motion in a medium which he had expressed at greater length in "Schediasma de Resistentia Medii," published in *Acta Eruditorum* in January 1689. There he had distinguished two types of resistance, absolute and respective. The former results from the viscosity of the medium, "as if the parts of broken filament were to be tangled together by the motion of the moving body." The latter "arises from the density of the medium" (understood as the ratio of heavy to light particles per unit of volume) and is due to the force spent by the penetrating body in displacing the heavy particles of the medium (GM VI, 136).[12] Then, both absolute and respective resistance result from the difficulty of giving place by the parts of the medium.

To some extent Newton would have agreed. He too held that part, albeit a small one, of the resistance of the medium is due to its viscosity and part to its density (NP II, 6, general scholium, 459–60). As we saw, he also agreed that the density of a body is not proportional to the absolute quantity of matter in a unit of volume, but to that of the grosser matter because the fluid matter occupying the body's pores is excluded. But while Newton did not show any tendency to an official commitment to such fluid matter prior to 1717, Leibniz made it a central part of his physics. So, Leibniz told Clarke that although quicksilver is fourteen times heavier than water, it does not contain more matter absolutely, if one considers both its own matter, which is heavy, and the fine weightless matter passing through its pores. For, he continued,

> both quicksilver and water are masses of heavy matter, full of pores, through which there passes a great deal of matter void of heaviness and which makes no sensible resistance; such as is probably that of the rays of light, and other insensible fluids; and especially that which is itself the cause of the gravity of gross bodies. (Lz V, 35)

This weightless, resistanceless fluid producing weight must be present because, Leibniz did not fail to point out again, Newtonian gravitation is an occult quality (Lz V, 35). In effect, then, his analysis was that Clarke's argument for the void was partially based on his belief in the occult quality of gravitation.

Clarke disagreed. The argument, he wrote, deals not with gravity but with resistance, "which must be proportionable to the quantity of matter, whether the matter had any gravity or no." "Otherwise— he added in footnote—what makes the body of the earth more difficult to be moved, even the same way that its gravity tends, than the smallest ball?" (Cl V, 33–35). Clarke's reply is not perspicuous, but presumably he intended to criticize Leibniz's references to heavy matter. The earth has greater inertia than a small ball because it has greater mass, and this is true whether the two are gravitating or not. The point is that mass, and therefore density, need not be understood in terms of weight because two bodies have the same density if their inertias are proportional to their volumes. Clarke's remark was justified in pointing out that mass is independent of weight, and Leibniz's repeated reference to heavy matter was rather unfortunate. But, as we saw, in denying that the subtle matter filling a body's pores is part of that body's mass, Leibniz was in agreement with Newton's official views. Clarke, unlike Newton, might have been ready to do away with the ether unambiguously and fully, but his argument failed to show that Leibniz was wrong even within the official, if not perhaps the true, Newtonian framework.

As for the issue of viscosity, Clarke reasonably pointed out that he had chosen quicksilver and water because they have the same degree of fluidity. So, Leibniz's appeal to "the difficulty of giving place" was irrelevant. To be sure, Clarke's comment was only partially justified, since for Leibniz "the difficulty of giving place" was linked not only to viscosity, but to density as well. But Clarke was right in claiming that with viscosity out of the way the issue reverted to density.

2. Force

2.1 Motive Force

As we saw in the discussion of the relation between the divinity and the world, the topic of force had a substantive theological dimension for both Leibniz and Clarke, with the former arguing that the periodic divine interventions required for the smooth working of the machine of the world involve a diminished view of God, and the latter welcoming such interventions as signs of the divine rule and presence in the world. However, the topic of force had also a nontheological, or better, a less directly theological, aspect, which we consider here.

When Leibniz claimed that the alleged diminution of force in the world reflects badly on divine perfection, Clarke retorted that it is due to the dependency of creatures (Lz III, 13; Cl III, 13–14). Leibniz replied by asking rhetorically how such a defect could result from the dependency of creatures, and Clarke told him that the loss of motion is not a defect but the natural result of the inertia of matter (Lz IV, 39; Cl IV, 39). Leibniz disagreed:

> That inertia, alleged here by him, mentioned by Kepler, repeated by Cartesius in his letters and made use of by me in my *Theodicy*, in order to give a notion and at the same time an example of the natural imperfection of creatures; has no other effect, than to make the velocities diminish, when the quantities of matter are increased: but this is without any diminution of the forces. (Lz V, 102)

Of course in a sense Leibniz was right: no motion is lost because of inertia per se. But Clarke had in mind a more complex situation: inertia causes "solid and perfectly hard bodies, void of elasticity" to lose motion (Cl V, 100–102).

Clarke's point highlighted the tension between atomism and the conservation of motive force in the seventeenth century.[13] By the third part of the century, after the work of Wallis and Mariotte, it became clear that only elastic bodies can rebound and therefore that the traditional view of atoms as poreless, perfectly hard, inelastic bodies entails that atoms hitting each other do not rebound, and that in general bodies rebound in proportion to their elasticity (NO *quaestio* 23, 342). Of course, the entailment could be blocked by endowing atoms with an intrinsic motive force, as Gassendi and perhaps some ancient atomists had done, but as we saw, Clarke was wedded to the idea of a passive matter. Moreover, since experiment shows that composite bodies are at best only partially elastic, Newton could reasonably conclude that every time two bodies collide, some amount of motion is lost (NO *quaestio* 23, 342). In addition, the viscosity of fluids and the friction among bodies, both reducible to the interaction among atoms, lead to the same conclusion, that in the mechanical machine of the universe motion is constantly being lost and that its replenishment requires the operation of some presumably nonmechanical "active principles" (NO *quaestio* 23, 342–43).

Leibniz agreed with Newton and Clarke that hard bodies do not rebound because they are not elastic. For, he claimed, not only Mariotte's experiments show it, but the Law of Continuity demands that in impact a body must bend before it rebounds, otherwise there would be an instantaneous transition from a degree of motion in one direction to a degree of motion in another without passing through the intermediate degrees. However, the Law of Continuity demands also what Newton did not concede, namely, that no body can come to an instantaneous stop without passing through the intermediate degrees of velocity (*Specimen Dynamicum*: GM VI, 248=L 446–47). From this Leibniz inferred that all bodies must have some degree of elasticity, which is possible only if each is permeated by some fluid, whose components are themselves permeated by a subtler fluid. Consequently, there are no atoms, no perfectly hard bodies, no most subtle fluid, and so all matter is infinitely divided (*Specimen Dynamicum*: GM VI, 249=L 447). As for the empirical evidence that in impact some motion seems to be lost, Leibniz claimed that it is simply transferred to the infinite parts of the impacting bodies.

Law of Continuity aside, which Newton and Clarke did not accept, atomism led to the rejection of the mechanical conservation of force. The continuous workings of the world's machine requires assuming, as Newton put it in query 23 of the 1706 *Optice*, that atoms have not only a *vis inertiae*, but are moved by "active principles, such as that of gravity, and that which causes fermentation, and the cohesion of bodies" (NO 343–44). As we saw, Clarke tended to appeal to spiritual activity on the side of God and creatures to replenish the decaying motive force in the world. When we move our bodies we introject new force in the world, and spiritual activity is present in cases of apparent action at a distance. Newton had more complex and confusing ideas. He did agree with Clarke that we give new force to our bodies when we move them and he did not seem to have any principled objection to considering the divine will a cause for apparent action at a distance, although he was also ready to entertain more exotic models involving light or even alchemic forces (NO *quaestio* 23, 343).[14] Atomism, then, led to the admission of direct divine intervention, that is, to miracles or to the world-soul, or to the introduction of nonmechanical, and in Leibniz's view occult, qualities.

Clarke and Leibniz not only disagreed on whether motive force is conserved, but also on what it is: Clarke and Newton, following Descartes, identified it with quantity of motion (mv), Leibniz with *vis viva* (mv^2). The controversy on the nature of motive force started in 1686, when Leibniz published the *Brevis Demonstratio*, a work he kept referring to in his later years, in which he proposed a coun-

terexample to the Cartesian identification of motive force with
quantity of motion. The counterexample was based on two principles. First, that a body falling from a height H acquires exactly the
same force needed to raise it to H again. Second, that the force needed
to raise a body B_1 weighing 1 pound to a height of 4 feet is equal to
that needed to raise a body B_2 weighing 4 pounds to a height of 1
foot. Both principles, Leibniz later argued, follow from the equality
between cause and effect (*Dynamica de Potentia*: GM VI, 439, 445).
Now Galileo had shown that the distances crossed by falling bodies
are proportional to the squares of their final velocities. So, if B_1 falls
from a height four times that of B_2, B_1's final velocity is double that
of B_2. Hence, B_1's quantity of motion is half that of B_2. But by the
second principle B_1 and B_2 have the same force; consequently, force
is not quantity of motion (*Brevis Demonstratio*: GM VI, 117–18=L
296).

Although in the *Brevis Demonstratio* Leibniz did not state that
motive force is *vis viva*, he did so later. The second principle in effect
entails that the forces are "proportional, jointly, to the bodies . . .
and to the height which produces their velocity or from which their
velocities can be acquired" (GM VI, 119=L 298). But, since the
height is proportional to the square of the final velocity, a body's
moving force is given by mv^2. Cartesian and Newtonian opponents
argued that not the height from which a body falls, but the time of
acceleration is proportional to its motive force. But since the time
of acceleration is proportional to the final velocity, motive force is
given by mv.

While it is unclear whether there were significant physical issues
at stake, the philosophical issues were important.[15] As we saw, theological considerations led Leibniz to the conclusion that motive
force is conserved. Moreover, the equivalence of cause and effect
entails, he argued, that the force in the universe is constant because
the universe is a closed system (*Dynamica de Potentia*: GM VI, 440).
But already in January 1680 he wrote to Filippi that "the ablest people in France and England" acknowledged that quantity of motion
is not constant in the world because it is not conserved in impact
(GP IV, 286). Hence, he was led to conclude that motive force is not
quantity of motion. Nor could it be vectorial quantity of motion. To
be sure, this quantity is conserved in impact if the system of reference is the common center of gravity of the bodies involved. But
given its vectorial quality, it can be nil even if all the bodies involved
are actually moving. Hence, it cannot be a measure of force (*Essay
de Dynamique*: GM VI, 216–17). *Vis viva*, by contrast, is both scalar

and conserved. Certainly, in actual impacts some *vis viva* seems lost, but that is only because some of it is transferred to the fluids ultimately constituting the impacting bodies.

In 1690, replying to criticism from the Abbé Catelan, Leibniz ventured the view that the philosophical root of the erroneous belief that quantity of motion is conserved is the Scholastic prejudice that motion is a "real and absolute entity" distributed among bodies much in the same way in which salt is distributed among various quantities of water. No surprise, then, that such a thing could not augment or diminish but by miracle. But in reality motion consists in a relation, and strictly speaking has no more existence than those quantities like time, the parts of which cannot exist together. What is real and absolute is motive force, "i.e., that state of things from which motion arises," and therefore motive force is not naturally altered (*De Causa Gravitatis*: GM VI, 202).

Clarke might have agreed with some of Leibniz's analysis. As we saw in the chapter on space and time, he held that circular motion is an *ens rationis* because its component rectilinear motions do not coexist (W III, 838); but what is measured both in quantity of motion and *vis viva* is instantaneous motion, and therefore whether motion through a determinate time is a whole of actually coexisting parts or not is irrelevant to the issue. Where Clarke really disagreed with Leibniz was on whether motion is by nature relative; but obviously the belief in the absolute reality of motion did not lead Clarke and Newton to the belief in the conservation of its quantity since, as we saw, they felt justified in holding that motion is lost in inelastic impact. One might perhaps argue that the belief in the absolute loss of a real entity does violence to the principle of equality between cause and effect, and consequently charge Clarke, who was ready to invoke the proportionality of the effect to its cause in the philosophical demonstration that motive force is mv, with inconsistency (W IV, 737–40). But metaphysical principles like the equality of cause and effect are notoriously hard to apply. Moreover, that the effect must be equal to the cause, or its weaker consequence that there can be nothing in the effect that is not in the cause, do not entail that every event must have an effect. Furthermore, one must remember that Clarke's theological views were best served by denying that motive force is conserved in the world because this opened the way for direct divine recharging of the system.

In a note composed around 1695, after a defense of the proportionality of force and distance of acceleration and the identification of force with *vis viva*, Leibniz claimed that the ultimate reason of the identification is that motion is not "something absolute and real in itself" (GM VI, 123=L 301). Leibniz explained in the *Specimen Dynamicum* that "there is nothing real in motion itself except that momentaneous state which must consist of a force striving towards change. Whatever is in corporeal nature besides the object of geometry, or extension, must be reduced to this force" (GM VI, 235=L 436). The details are rather unclear. Leibniz distinguished derivative active force into *vis mortua*, associated with the tendency of bodies to begin motion, as in a stretched spring that begins to recoil, and *vis viva*, associated with actual motion. *Vis viva* arises "from an infinite number of continuous impressions" of *vis mortua*, which would seem to suggest that *vis viva* is the integral of *vis mortua* over time (*Specimen Dynamicum*: GM VI, 238=L 438). But then *vis viva* would be proportional to velocity, not to the square of velocity. Elsewhere, however, Lebniz claimed that if the infinitesimal "solicitation" to motion associated with *vis mortua* is represented by the differential dx, then velocity is the ordinary quantity x, and the determination of motion associated with *vis viva* is $\int x dx$, that is, x^2 (To De Volder, no date: GP II, 156). Details aside, it seems clear that part of of the reason why *vis viva* plays a basic role in the phenomenal world is that although it must not be confused with the primitive force constituting substance, it is nevertheless a derivative force, "a modification or result of primitive force" (To De Volder, 20 June 1703: GP II, 251; GP IV, 390; *De Prima Philosophiae Emendatione*: GP IV, 469–70). It is, then, the physical manifestation of primitive force, and as such not the result of motion but its cause (*De Causa Gravitatis*: GM VI, 202).[16]

The appeal to supraphysical entities, which was clear in some of Leibniz's published works (e.g., *De primae philosophiae emendatione, et de Notione Substatiae*, which appeared in *Acta Eruditorum* in 1694) was not lost on Clarke. In 1728, he published an article in the *Philosophical Transactions* attempting to show that force is quantity of motion on the basis of considerations drawn from the equality of cause and effect, the same principle from which Leibniz had tried to infer that motive force is *vis viva*. There are two aspects to a moving body, he claimed, mass and velocity; and since motive force arises from them and the effect must be proportional to its cause, motive force must be mv. Hence, "If the Force were as the Square of the Velocity, all that Part of the Force, which was above the Proportion of the Velocity, would arise either out of Nothing, or (according to Mr. Leibnitz's Philosophy) out of some living Soul essentially belonging to every Particle of Matter" (W IV, 738). Here again we see Clarke's deep misgivings about Leibniz's alleged hylo-zoism, which the term "*living* force" did nothing to alleviate (W IV, 740). Leibniz's wrong physical views, then, were ultimately linked to his crypto-Hobbesianism and the materialist views of Toland and Collins.

2.2 Inertia

The topic of inertia emerged rather late in the correspondence and was brought about by Clarke's claim that the loss of motive force in the world is due to the inertia of matter (Cl IV, 39). As we saw, Leibniz disagreed, and Clarke took the opportunity to attack Leib-niz's view of inertia as pre-Cartesian and utterly preposterous in the age of Newton. Like Newton, he understood Leibniz as adopting Ke-pler's view of inertia as a natural resistance to motion, which causes bodies to have a natural tendency to rest (Cl V, 99 n. a).[17] To make sure that the accusation stuck, Clarke added a whole section in the appendix to his edition of the correspondence with quotations seem-ingly supporting it.[18] However, several reasons militate against Clarke's interpretation.

In one of the allegedly incriminating passages, as well as else-where, Leibniz did say that a body in motion does not by itself lose it (*Theodicy* § 30: GP VI, 119–20; *De Ipsa Natura* § 11: GP IV, 510–11=L 503–4; GM VI, 100). From the notes he wrote upon his first reading of *Principia*, it seems clear that he also had a clear under-standing of Newton's notion of inertia.[19] Hence, it is unlikely that he did not see the difference between Descartes's and Newton's view and Kepler's. Moreover, in the context of the correspondence, ap-pealing to Kepler's "lazy" inertia makes no sense: Clarke, not Leib-niz, held that inertia brings about loss of motion. If Leibniz thought that bodies have a natural tendency to rest, why would he find Clarke's claim objectionable?

One might insist that Leibniz's mention of Kepler and Descartes in the same breath indicates that he could not tell, or at least failed properly to appreciate, the difference between their views on inertia. However, more likely he was attracted by what was similar in their views, namely, that bodies offer resistance to being moved. His re-marks on inertia are often followed by the consideration of impact between bodies in which the effects of a body's *vis viva* is moderated by the other's mass. For example, in a note written in 1702, Leibniz associated Kepler's and Descartes's inertia as that by which a body receives new motion only through force and therefore resists the pressing body and diminishes its force. This would not happen if in bodies beside extension there were not gto δυναμικον, that is, the principle of the laws of motion, by which it comes about that the quantity of forces cannot increase and therefore a body cannot be impelled by another without a diminution of the latter's force. (GM VI, 100–101)[20]

This anti-Cartesian passage, with the standard critique that there is more in bodies than mere extension, in effect attempts a derivation of the aspect of inertia that interested Leibniz from the law of conservation of *vis viva*. This indicates that Leibniz tended to think of inertia in terms of resistance to impact more than in terms of rectilinear uniform motion.[21] But this should not surprise us, given the fundamental role played by *vis viva* in Leibniz's physics.

These differences should not obscure the fact that for both Clarke and Leibniz inertia is a manifestation of passivity. For Clarke, the *vis inertiae* is the "negative power" guaranteeing that matter is essentially inert, devoid of autokinesis, to borrow a term from Toland (W II, 697). For Leibniz, inertia is, with impenetrability, the phenomenal manifestation of what is passive in matter and ultimately of monadic primitive passive force, although the derivation of the former from the latter is obscure (GP III, 260; *Specimen Dynamicum*: GM VI, 236=L436–37). But while for Clarke inertia is the only power intrinsic to matter, for Leibniz it is not, since "every body is, by its form, continually acting and by its matter continually suffering and resisting" (*Specimen Dynamicum*: GM VI, 237=L 443).[22]

2.3 Gravity

Like Huygens, Leibniz never accepted Newtonian gravitation (To Leibniz, 18 November 1690: GM II, 57). Although he, like Huygens and others, understood Newton's revolutionary achievement in connecting mechanics and astronomy in the *Principia*, he tended to play down its physical significance: even if Newton had shown the exact mathematical relation between centripetal forces and Kepler's area law, he had not given any explanation of them. In this respect, Newton was a "mere" mathematician who had provided a clever mathematical model but not a physical explanation of the motions of the planets. Descartes's vortices, by contrast, provided a physical explanation of the motion of the planets, but a mathematically incorrect one, since, for example, Kepler's area law cannot be derived from it.

Leibniz saw himself as bringing together these two complementary methods by providing a vortical theory that is also mathematically correct.[23]

He did so in the *Tentamen*, published in 1689 and, contrary to his claims, composed after he had seen Newton's *Principia*. In it, he argued that since all bodies tend to move uniformly and to recede along the tangent when moving in a curve, planets must be constrained and moved by an ethereal matter because their motion is not uniform (they move faster when closer to the sun) and curved (GM VI, 149). He then supposed that this subtle matter moves around the sun with an harmonic motion, namely with a speed which is inversely proportional to the distances or radii from the sun. Each planet floats in this fluid and is endowed with two motions: a transradial one in which it is carried by and moves exactly like the fluid (harmonically), and a radial motion, which he called "paracentric," in which it moves along the radius from layer to layer of the fluid. The paracentric motion itself is the result of two radial impulses—a gravitational one, the mechanism of which Leibniz did not explain, and a centrifugal one arising from the planet's transradial motion and measured by the square of the transradial velocity divided by the distance from the center (GM VI, 152).[24] While the transradial harmonic motion provides Kepler's area law, the positing of orbits that are conic sections, for example, the ellipses of Kepler's first law, traversed with harmonic motion produces the inverse square law of gravitation (GM VI, 150, 156).

Although at the beginning of the *Tentamen* Leibniz praised Kepler's attempts at explaining gravity by means of a vortex, at the end of the tract he had to admit not having provided an explanation of gravity in spite of the fact that his mechanical model of planetary motion involves a centripetal impulse toward the sun (GM VI, 148, 161). Elsewhere, however, he considered various mechanical models, apparently favoring two. One involves a fluid propagating from the center in accordance with the inverse square law, in analogy with light. The fluid penetrates bodies through their pores, and since there is less receding fluid in them than elsewhere, they are pushed back toward the center in proportion to the number of their pores (*Tentamen*, Zweite Bearbeitung: GM VI, 164).[25] The other, developed in October 1690 in an unsent letter to Huygens, is a modification of Huygens's model for terrestrial gravity based on fluid matter moving in all directions on spherical surfaces around the earth.[26] Leibniz assumed the equality of *vis viva* in each circle of fluid, suggesting that it could explain the stability of the fluid system, and managed to infer Kepler's third law and the inverse square law (GM VI, 191–92).[27]

In 1693, before his relations with Newton had soured, Leibniz wrote to him praising the "astonishing discovery that Kepler's ellipses result simply from the conception of attraction or gravitation and trajection in a planet," while at the same time saying that gravitation must be caused by a fluid medium which, however, would not detract from the "importance and truth of [Newton's] discovery" (NC II, 258).[28] Newton replied that vortices would disturb the motion of planets and comets, and since "all phenomena of the heavens and of the sea" follow from "gravity acting in accordance with the laws described by me" and nature is "very simple, I have concluded myself that all other causes have to be rejected and that the heavens are to be stripped as far as may be of all matter, lest the motion of the planets and comets be hindered or rendered irregular." However, he continued, if someone were to explain gravity by the action of some ether, he would be far from objecting (NC III, 289). In effect, then, Newton challenged Leibniz to provide a mechanical model of gravity that would explain the phenomena of the heavens four years after Leibniz had allegedly done so.

Later, around 1713, in the middle of the priority dispute over the invention of the calculus, Newton went farther than challenging Leibniz: he claimed that the *Tentamen* bristled with errors and Keill, giving public voice to his master's views, called it "the most absurd piece of philosophy ever written."[29] Some of Newton's mathematical criticisms were ill taken, and some of the physical ones did not fare much better. For example, the claim that a vortical theory of attraction entails that bodies are pushed to the axis of the vortex and not to the center was based on Leibniz's mostly rhetorical praise of the alleged vortex theory of gravitation by Kepler, and not on Leibniz's actual unpublished models, which, like Huygens's, overcome the problem. Similarly, Aiton has argued that Newton's critique of Leibniz's notion of centrifugal force as not being equal and opposed to gravitational force missed the point that Leibniz was working within a framework that owed more to Huygens than to him.[30]

However, Leibniz's theory does have problems, some of which were pointed out early on. In spite of Leibniz's attempts, Huygens, whose rejection of nonmechanical gravitation was as firm as Leibniz's, could not see the need for the harmonic vortex. He asked Leibniz why the harmonic vortex is necessary given Newton's system, in which "the movement of the planets is explained by the heaviness towards the Sun and the *vis centrifuga* which are in a balance" (8 February 1690: GM II, 41; 24 August 1690: GM II, 46; 11 July 1692: GM II, 137). *Vis centrifuga* aside, Huygens's question was about the apparent redundancy of Leibniz's theory: why did Leibniz want the harmonic vortex in addition to that which produces gravity? Leibniz replied that one reason among others is that the harmonic vortex explains why all the planets move roughly in the same plane and in the same direction, while a theory like Newton's cannot (To Huygens, 26 September 1692: GM II, 144; VI, 190).

What other reasons Leibniz had in mind is unclear. Newton had not proved that a centripetal inverse-square force yields orbits that are one of the conics, but this seemed to be unnoticed by Leibniz, as his 1693 letter to Newton (quoted above) shows. One might suggest that Newton's derivation of elliptical orbits presupposes minimal or no resistance to the planet's motion, and, as we saw, such requirement was used to establish the existence of the void.[31] However, such un-Leibnizian consequence would be avoided by the presence of the gravity-producing fluid. It might be objected that since explaining how the gravity-producing fluid could both push the planet radially toward the center and at the same time offer no resistance to transradial motion would be very hard, Leibniz would have felt compelled to renounce the gravity-producing fluid. But that this is not so can be gathered by noting that, as we saw, the converse problem affects the harmonic vortex itself.

Huygens (privately) and Gregory (publicly) also noted that Leibniz's system fails to produce a satisfactory account of the motion of comets because they would be impeded by the Leibnizian vortices.[32] Leibniz answered that the vortex does not significantly impede the motion of comets passing through it, although it does conserve the motion of planets in it (To Huygens, 20 March, 1693: GM II, 155). But even if one were to accept Leibniz's answer, his theory suffers from other problems. For one thing, how the fluid in harmonic motion can offer no resistance to radial motion while pushing the planet transradially is unclear. Nor is it clear how the harmonic vortex and the gravitational vortex postulated in the unsent letter to Huygens can avoid interacting (GM VI, 191–92). More serious, the harmonic vortex transports the planet, which therefore moves according to Kepler's law of the areas, but it is the gravitational vortex that rotates in accordance with Kepler's third law; in the end, Leibniz could not account for Kepler's three laws together.[33]

An awareness of the problems besetting his theory was probably the reason that in the correspondence his criticisms of Newton's theory were essentially philosophical and did not address the physical adequacy of the two rival theories.[34] Newtonian gravitation, Leibniz told Conti, is not the result of natural material powers and therefore is either the effect of a miracle or a Scholastic occult quality, since there is a difference between a quality that is simply occult and a quality that is occult in the Scholastic fashion, "that is to say, which cannot be made clear, such as a primitive heaviness; for the occult qualities which are not chimerical are those whose cause we do not know but do not exclude" (To Conti, 6 December 1715: NC VI, 251=R 41; to Conti, 9 April 1716: NC VI, 307= R 64).[35]

When Leibniz's accusations made their way into the correspondence, Clarke rejected both. If God were regularly to make a body move about a fixed center, he claimed true to his views on miracles, then it would not be miraculous (Lz III, 17; Cl III, 17). Moreover, Clarke implied, Leibniz was wrong in thinking of universal gravitation as action at a distance. For action at a distance is contradictory, that is, metaphysically impossible, since something can act only where it is (Lz IV, 45; Cl IV, 45). One can sympathize with Clarke's retort. Certainly he was so adamant in holding that causation requires local presence, that not even God can act where he is not locally present, since he cannot do what is impossible. In this context, it was Leibniz who held that God can act where he is not locally (by situation), although, of course, Leibniz never dreamt of saying that God is in any spatial relation with creatures and therefore, strictly speaking, is neither distant nor in contact.

To Leibniz's charge that universal gravity is an occult Scholastic quality, that is, the very archetype of an unintelligible quality, Clarke explicitly replied that one should not characterize it as occult just because its cause is unknown, especially when gravitation through empty space is a "matter of fact discovered by experience" (Lz V, 118–23; Cl V, 118–23). Here Clarke was towing the party line. Answering the charges against gravitation in a draft letter to Conti, Newton complained that Leibniz had surreptitiously changed the meaning of 'miracle' and 'occult quality' in order to use them "in railing at universal gravity." What is wrong with Scholastic occult qualities, he claimed, is not that their causes are considered unknown but that they are considered unknowable.[36]

In query 23 of the 1706 *Optice*, Newton had stated his justification for the use of (non-Scholastic) occult qualities:

> To say that every species of things is endow'd with occult specific qualities by which it acts, is to say nothing. But to derive from

natural phenomena two or three general principles of motion, and afterwards to explain how the properties and actions of all corporeal things follow from these principles, would be a very great step in philosophy, though the causes of these principles be not yet discovered. (NO 344–45).[37]

Newton's basic point, then, is that the cause of gravitation is knowable in principle and that his appeal to occult properties is ultimately justified by the success of the theory in which they are embedded. In retrospect, one can hardly disagree with the broad features of his reply, especially since his cosmology, in which the elliptical orbits of the planets are obtained from inertia and the inverse square law, requires that interplanetary space be void or nearly so, and therefore unable to support vortices, which cannot account for the Keplerian motions of the planets anyway.

As the correspondence progressed, Leibniz realized that his charge that Newtonian gravitation is uncaused was unjustified and his criticism shifted, in effect amounting to the charge that according to the Newtonians gravity is a primitive property of matter, that is, a property not further explainable in material terms. As such, his point was reasonably well taken. Some of Newton's followers seem to have been ready to think of universal gravitation as primitive in the sense of being essential to matter.[38] Newton disagreed; already in 1693 he had told Bentley that the view that "gravity should be innate, inherent, and essential to matter" is so absurd that no competent philosopher would accept it (Februray 25 1693: NC III, 253–54). However, even he was not immune from toying with the idea that gravity could be an intrinsic property of matter, as when in a draft of an answer to Leibniz's letter to Hartsoeker he compared it to hardness, which he did take to be originally endowed in various degrees by God to all matter (NC V, 300; NO *quaestio* 23, 335). Nevertheless, whatever his private views, at least publicly he professed agnosticism on whether gravity is primitive to matter or not. For example, in query 23 of the 1706 *Optice* he stated that "what I call Attraction may be performed by impulse, or by some other means unknown to us" (NO *quaestio* 23, 322); similarly, he had told Bentley that he had left to the consideration of his readers whether the cause of gravitation be "material or immaterial."[39]

By contrast, even in his public utterances Clarke did not seem to have doubts that gravitation is a primitive feature of matter. For example, in the notes appended to his 1702 edition and translation into Latin of Rohault's *Physics*, he criticized the Cartesian physicist for not allowing that "gravity does not depend upon the air or the aether, but is an original connate and immutable affection of all matter."[40] He expanded on the point by claiming that gravity is "an original and general law of all matter impressed on it by God, and maintained in it perpetually by some efficient power, which penetrates the solid substance of it . . . wherefore we ought no more to enquire how bodies gravitate, than how bodies began first to be moved."[41] In 1710, Clarke added more notes, in one of which he discussed the cause of gravity. He concluded, as he had done a few years before in the *Discourse*, that since universal gravitation cannot be produced by impulse because it is in proportion to the masses and not the "surfaces" of the bodies involved, it must be the result of the action of an immaterial cause.[42] The point was the same he made in *A Demonstration* and to Collins: the cause of gravity must penetrate the very center of every particle of matter, something that no appeal to any sort of subtle matter can possibly explain (WB 555–56; W III, 847–48, 904). In this Clarke was in agreement with Huygens, who had rejected the idea that all the small parts in various bodies attract each other on the basis of its apparent mechanical inexplicability.[43] Indeed, so convinced was Clarke that the cause of gravitation is immaterial that in his 1710 edition of Rohault's *Physics*, after quoting from Newton's query 23 of the 1706 *Optice*, he added the gloss "not bodily impulse" to Newton's more modest statement on page 322, that "What I call attraction may be performed by impulse."[44] Ultimately then, his rejection of Leibniz's views on gravitation was even more extreme than Newton's, who left open the possibility of a mechanical, or perhaps quasi-mechanical (through a non-Cartesian ether), explanation of gravity.

One might be tempted to read Clarke as claiming that gravitation requires an immaterial cause in the sense that God originally superadded to matter a gravitational power, which now operates without further divine intervention. The suggestion is not unreasonable, since Locke seems to have understood gravitation in this way. Indeed, this is how Collins, and perhaps Cheyne, understood it.[45] However, Clarke's position was quite different. He replied to Collins: "You find fault with me for asserting that Gravitation is the Effect of the continued and regular Operation of some other Being on Matter: whereas, you think, it does not appear but that Matter gravitates by virtue of Powers originally placed in it by God, and is now left to itself to act by those original Powers" (W III, 792). Since only substances can act, no material impulse can cause gravitation, and since matter can operate only by impulse, only spiritual substances can cause gravitation (W III, 848). In sum, bluntly put, all matter has gravity because God, or angels acting on divine orders, do the pulling, a view reminiscent of the medieval one according to which angels move the orbs of the planets.[46] Clarke's *Deus Pantokrator* is, then, the constant mover and overseer of the world, not the do-nothing god of the deists.

Leibniz, who believed that, divine miraculous activity aside, only matter can act on matter and that even angelic action is material, felt justified in giving a rather curt answer to Clarke's claims that the cause of gravitation is immaterial:

> are perhaps some immaterial substances, or some spiritual rays, or some accident without a substance, or some kind of *species intentionalis*, or some other I know not what, the means by which [gravitation] is pretended to be performed? Of which sort of things, the author seems to have still a good stock in his head, without explaining himself sufficiently. (Lz V, 119)[47]

According to Clarke, Leibniz continued, the means of causation of universal gravitation are "invisible, intangible, not mechanical. He might as well have added, inexplicable, unintelligible, precarious, and unexampled" (Lz V, 120). It would be, then, a divine miracle unworthy of the divine wisdom.

The confrontation between Leibniz and Clarke on universal gravity was one between two different methodological outlooks. Leibniz was still enough of a Cartesian mechanist to deny that gravity could be a primitive property of matter, while Clarke flatly stated that it is, with Newton publicly uncommitted on the issue. One might deprecate Newton's lack of decisiveness, but one must also recognize that the cause of gravity, although significant, was not a central concern of his. Following much of the English mechanist tradition, he wisely settled for a science that could, although it need not, be causally incomplete, and therefore felt justified in adopting occult qualities such as gravitation.[48]

It did not escape Leibniz that these different methodological outlooks were linked to different theological views. As we saw in the chapter on miracles, Leibniz emphasized the role of secondary causes in the course of nature, and consequently the possibility of a causally complete natural science. By contrast, Clarke's God is the extrinsic and continually acting cause of the operations of an otherwise totally passive and inert matter endowed only with the *vis inertiae*. The course of nature is but God acting in accordance with his good pleasure. Certainly, God follows rules of order and proportion, but this does not change the fact that such a view makes it appealing to pursue a causally incomplete science: if God is the direct cause of gravity, then gravity becomes a primary quality of matter and its cause is effectively removed from natural science. To be sure, Newton did not always fully agree with this view and periodically tried to provide a material explanation of gravity. But he certainly took Clarke's view seriously enough to consider it an acceptable account.[49]

In Leibniz's eyes, however, the theological price was unacceptable. Given Clarke's view that matter is inert and action requires substantial presence, his account of the cause of gravitation demands the substantial presence of God in the world, a view which is entailed by the degradation of God into the world-soul, and which was confirmed by Clarke's denial that universal gravity is miraculous. At the end, the rejection of mechanism, which in More was limited to the queer "hylarchic principles," in Clarke had degenerated into a dangerous theological position.[50]

For Leibniz, in spite of its undeniable success, Newton's physics was at best a mere mathematical model. It was replete with attractive and repulsive powers, and populated by atoms the solidity of which was either unexplainable or reduced to attractive powers among their parts. Motive force was identified with quantity of motion, thus requiring constant divine recharging of the system of the world at the physical level, and atoms moved in an infinite void space, indeed literally in God himself. This was bad physics leading to worse theology, with a God operating either by miracles or as a part of nature.

In Leibniz's physical views, Clarke saw confirmation of his suspicions about his interlocutor's philosophy and theology. The rejection of a libertarian view of the divine will, coupled with the belief that more matter is better than less, led to the inevitable, indeed necessary, existence of an infinite amount of matter. Leibniz's views on motive force was based on the attribution to matter of a living principle, thus leading to a form of hylozoism. Worse, Leibniz's insistence that natural phenomena be explained in terms of properties conceived as modifications of the essence of matter led to the removal of God from nature and ultimately could degenerate into atheism.

Leibniz never saw Clarke's fifth letter; he died on 4 November 1716. On 29 November, Conti wrote Newton from Hanover: "Mr. Leibniz is dead; the dispute is over" (NC VI, 376–77). He was wrong. Not only did the disputes about the invention of calculus and nature of force continue unabated, but even the Leibniz-Clarke controversy had a posthumous spasm, as it were. For in 1720, as an addition to the first German edition of the correpondence, Thümming, a young follower of Wolff, took it upon himself to provide a "Leibnizian" answer to Clarke's fifth reply. The letter, although touching on all of the main topics of the correspondence and periodically referring to Wolff's work, failed to add anything significant. It did, however, repeat the charge that by making space and time divine attributes Clarke had destroyed divine simplicity.[51] Thümming continued by claiming that a source of Clarke's shallow views lay in the confusion between the understanding and the imagination, the same error besetting Locke's philosophy.[52] Clarke had the good sense not to answer. However, in 1744, long after the principals had died (indeed, even Thümming had died six years earlier), Gregory Sharpe, an English theologian, anonymously published a long answer to Thümming's letter, which added nothing of importance to the issues.[53] That was really the end.

Although Leibniz entertained amicable relations with some British intellectuals (e.g., Thomas Burnett), his relations with Locke and Clarke turned out to be less than warm, to put it mildly. His muddled, and failed, attempt to engage Locke ultimately prompted Locke's withering comment that "even great parts will not master any subject without great thinking, and even the largest minds have but narrow swallows."[54] Leibniz remarked to Caroline, who had been critical of Locke's *Essay*, that Locke's remark sprang in part from the wide disagreement between them on great issues (To Caroline, 10 May 1715: KLC 39–40).[55] To some extent, Leibniz's comment could be applied to Clarke as well. To be sure, Clarke and Leibniz shared the goal of defeating naturalism, and certainly, in contrast to Locke's ambiguous position, Clarke was as strong a supporter of the natural immortality of the soul as Leibniz. However, they disagreed on so many metaphysical and theological issues (such as divine immensity and eternity, the relation of God to the world, the soul and its relation to the body, free will, space and time, the nature of miracles), and on so many scientific issues (such as the nature of matter, the existence of atoms and the void, the size of the universe, the nature of motive force), which they perceived as having theological implications, that they failed to reach any significant agreement. The exchange ended as pointedly as it had started.

The correspondence was more than an academic exchange between two philosophers motivated by intellectual curiosity. Of

course, the acrimonius background against which it developed set
its tone. But more than that, it was a confrontation in which the two
participants thought that the stake was the defense of natural religion, and ultimately the possibility of giving a foundation to morality, which was under attack by atheists and libertines. The exchange
between Leibniz and Clarke, then, was an internecine fight within
the antinaturalist camp, between supporters of natural religion who
ended up by accusing each other of crypto-naturalism. At bottom, I
think, their suspicions about each other's theories sprang from two
distinct but related sources, one theological and one metaphysical.
First, they disagreed on the nature of God. Leibniz by and large remained faithful to the Thomistic view proposing an unextended, operationally but not substantially present God, whose mental life is
not successive, and whose mode of cognition of the world is radically
different from ours. Clarke, however, found this view of God unintelligible at best (e.g., what could nonsuccessive duration be?) and
contradictory at worst (e.g., how could God operate in the world
without being substantially there?). He replaced it with a picture of
a God who, like our souls, is extended, has successive thoughts, and
whose mode of cognition of the world is analogous to ours. Leibniz
found this view demeaning of the divine nature and ultimately leading to the debasement of God into the soul of the world (the problem
was compounded by Clarke's attribution of extension to the soul).
Ultimately, then, the disagreement was on how strictly to take the
Biblical claim that we humans are made in God's image.

Second, Leibniz and Clarke were at odds on the metaphysical
requirements of free will. Leibniz was a determinist compatibilist
who thought that, barring mental confusion (impossible in God), the
will is causally determined by the judgment about the good. By contrast, Clarke was an incompatibilist libertarian who claimed that the
judgment about the good is a reason, but not a cause, of the will's
action. Leibniz found an essentially uncaused will to be an obscurantist fiction destructive of any science of the mind, and conducive
to an irrational God whose motivations are essentially independent
of his evaluations. Clarke thought that determinism destroyed free
will and rendered the world the inevitable outcome of the divine
nature because even Leibniz agreed that the divine judgment cannot
but be what it is. The disagreement, then, was on the relation of the
understanding and the will between two philosophers who had rejected Descartes's extreme voluntarist view that truth depends on
the divine will.

NOTES

Introduction

1. For a book length biography of Leibniz, see E. J. Aiton, *Leibniz: A Biography* (Bristol: Adam Hilger, 1985); for much shorter but still helpful ones, see B. Mates, *The Philosophy of Leibniz: Metaphysics and Language* (Oxford: Oxford University Press, 1986), chap. 1 and R. Ariew, "G. W. Leibniz, Life and Works," in *The Cambridge Companion to Leibniz*, ed. N. Jolley (Cambridge: Cambridge University Press, 1995), pp. 18–42; for both Clarke and Caroline, see *Dictionary of National Biography*, ed. L. Stephen and S. Lee (1882; reprint, London: Oxford University Press, 1949–50), s.v. An interesting contemporary biography of Clarke centered on the Trinitarian controversy is W. Whiston, *Historical Memoirs of the Life of Dr. Samuel Clarke* (London, 1730).

2. See H. G. Alexander, ed., *The Leibniz-Clarke Correspondence: With Extracts from Newton's "Principia" and "Opticks"* (Manchester: Manchester University Press, 1956), pp. xlii–xlix; C. Maclaurin, *An Account of Sir Isaac Newton's Philosophical Discoveries* (London, 1748), especially pp. 64–90; L. Euler, "Reflexions sur l'espace et le tems," *Mémoires de l'académie des sciences de Berlin* (1748): 324–33, reprinted in *Leonhardi Euleri Opera Omnia* (Leipzig and Berlin: Teubner, 1911–), third series, vol. 2, pp. 376–83; M. A. Voltaire, *The Elements of Sir Isaac Newton's Philosophy*, trans. J. Hanna (1738; reprint, London: Cass, 1967); S. Al Azm, *The Origins of Kant's Arguments in the Antinomies* (Oxford: Clarendon Press, 1972).

3. See, for example, J. Earman, *World Enough and Space-Time* (Cambridge, Mass.: MIT Press, 1989), introduction and chaps. 1, 4, 6.

4. R. Westfall, *Never at Rest. A Biography of Isaac Newton* (Cambridge: Cambridge University Press, 1980), p. 778; R. Hall, *Philosophers at War. The Quarrel between Leibniz and Newton* (Cambridge: Cambridge University Press, 1980), p. 219.

5. On Newton's manuscript, see Westfall, *Never at Rest*, p. 778–79. Hall, *Philosophers at War*, p. 220.

6. A. Koyré and I. B. Cohen, "Newton & the Leibniz-Clarke Correspondence," *Archives Internationales d'Histoire des Sciences* 15 (1962): 63–126, have probably overemphasized Newton's role; for a more judicious view, see NC VI, xxix–xxx; Hall, *Philosophers at War*, pp. 219–20; *Der Leibniz-Clarke Briefwechsel* ed. and trans. V. Schüller (Berlin: Akademie Verlag, 1991), pp. 477–80. See also Westfall, *Never at Rest*, p. 778, and Hall's new biography of Newton, *Issac Newton. Adventurer in Thought* (Cambridge: Cambridge University Press, 1996), pp. 319–21.

7. See J. P. Ferguson, *The Philosophy of Dr. Samuel Clarke and Its Critics* (New York: Vantage Press, 1974), pp. 249.

8. See *Voltaire's Philosophical Letters*, ed. and trans. E. Dilworth (Indianapolis: Bobs Merrill, 1961), letter 7, p. 28.

9. Hall, *Philosophers at War*, p. 145; see also chap. 8.

10. On this, see N. Jolley, *Leibniz and Locke: A Study of the "New Essays on Human Understanding"* (Oxford: Clarendon Press, 1984), chap. 4; Hall, *Philosophers at War*, chap. 8.

11. E. J. Aiton, *The Vortex Theory of Planetary Motions* (London: MacDonald, 1972), chap. 6, and E. J. Aiton, "The Mathematical Basis of Leibniz's Theory of Planetary Motion," in *Leibniz's Dynamica*, ed. A. Heinekamp, Studia Leibnitiana Supplementa 13, (Wiesbaden: F. Steiner 1984), pp. 209–25. For Leibniz's knowledge of *Principia* before the composition of the *Tentamen*, see D. Bertoloni Meli, *Equivalence and Priority: Newton versus Leibniz* (Oxford: Clarendon Press, 1993).

12. Wolff to Leibniz, 22 September 1714, February 1715: NC VI, 179–80, 206–7; Leibniz to Wolff, 22 March 1715: NC VI, 211; Caroline to Leibniz, 10 January 1716: KLC 71–72; Newton to Conti, 26 February 1716: NC VI, 285–8; Leibniz to Conti, 29 March 1716: NC VI, 304–11.

13. Aiton, *Leibniz*, pp. 321–22.

14. Leibniz was not off the mark here with respect to Cheyne's rather xenophobic remarks in 1703: see Hall, *Philosophers at War*, pp. 131–32.

15. Leibniz's attack against Newton and his circle might have confirmed Caroline in her support for Leibniz, but for all this his hopes were dashed by George I, who was not well disposed toward Leibniz and was not ready to let him go anywhere, much less to London, as long as he did not produce the long-delayed history, which never saw the light of day (KLC 46). Furthermore, Leibniz's effort at securing an official position at the British

court may have become known to the Newtonians; if so, it probably acted as a further irritant because they had every reason to fear a loss of influence at a court that was in fact a German one in which German was spoken (George I never bothered to learn English). On George's court, see V. H. H. Green, *The Hanoverians:1714–1815* (London: Edward Arnold,1948), pp. 33–34, 77–86.

16. *Acta Eruditorum* (October 1717): 440–47; on the plausible attribution of the review (which starts with a quotation from a letter of Leibniz to Wolff about the Leibniz-Clarke correspondence) to Wolff, see *Der Leibniz-Clarke Briefwechsel*, pp. 552.

Chapter 1: God

1. For Clarke's distinction among four types of deism and their errors, see WN 600–608. For a discussion of Clarke's views in the context of the Newtonian movement, see J. E. Force, "The Newtonians and Deism," in *Essays on the Context, Nature, and Influence of Isaac Newton's Theology*, ed. J. E. Force and R. H. Popkin (Dordrecht: Kluwer Academic Publishers, 1990), pp. 43–74.

2. See WB 524, 530; NE IV,10,7. Clarke's basic critique of the Ontological Argument was that the modal principle, which says that the possibility of a necessity entails that necessity, is uncertain, a view Leibniz disagreed with. The whole of *A Demonstration* is, in effect, a long version of the Cosmological Argument capped with a version of the argument from design. Clarke's proof was very well known throughout the eighteenth century, and it is generally assumed that Demea in Hume's *Dialogues on Natural Religion* represents Clarke. A history of Clarke's argument is given by J. P. Ferguson, *The Philosophy of Dr. Samuel Clarke and Its Critics* (New York: Vantage Press, 1974), chap. 3, and W. L. Rowe, *The Cosmological Argument* (Princeton: Princeton University Press, 1975). For Leibniz's version of the Cosmological Argument, see, for example, *De Rerum Originatione Radicali*: GP 7, 302–8 = L 486–92; *Monadology*, §§ 36–38: GP 6, 612 = L 646. On this, see D. Blumenfeld, "Leibniz's Ontological and Cosmological Arguments," in *The Cambridge Companion to Leibniz*, ed. N. Jolley (Cambridge: Cambridge University Press, 1995), pp. 353–81.

3. For for the first view, see S. Boethius, *The Consolation of Philosophy*, trans. R. Green (Indianapolis: Bobs Merrill, 1962), chap. 5; Anselm, *Monologion* (Bonn: Hanstein, 1929), chaps. 20–23; T. Aquinas, *Summa Theologiae* (New York: Mc Graw-Hill, 1970), 1st part, question 10. The second view has traditionally been in the minority, but (relatively) recently it has become widespread; for an account, A. Kenny, *The God of the Philosophers* (Oxford: Clarendon Press, 1979); R. Sorabji, *Time, Creation and the Continuum* (Ithaca: Cornell University Press, 1983), chap. 16. For a brief historical survey of the notions of duration and eternity, see H. A. Wolfson,

The Philosophy of Spinoza (New York: Meridian Books, 1960), chap. 10; for an exhaustive account, see F. Suarez, *Disputationes Metaphysicae* (1597; reprint, Hildesheim: G. Olms, 1965), disputation 50, section 3.

4. See, e.g., Aquinas, *Summa Theologiae*, 1st part, question 8, article 2.

5. The standard Scholastic formula is: *Totus in toto and totus in qualibet sui parte.* For examples of holenmerism, see Augustine, *Liber de Praesentia Dei* (Letter 187), chap. 4, §11, *Patrologia Latina*, ed. J. P. Migne (Paris, 1845), vol. 33, pp. 831–47, especially p. 836; Anselm, *Monologion*, chap. 22; F. Suarez, *Disputationes Metaphysicae*, disputation 30, section 7, § 51. For a modern example, see N. Malebranche, *Dialogues on Metaphysics*, trans. W. Doney (New York: Abaris Books, 1980), dialogue 8, sect. 4.

6. B. Spinoza *Ethica*, I, definition 8, in *Opera*, ed. C. Gebhardt, (Heidelberg: C. Winters, 1925), vol. 2, p. 46; for Leibniz's approving comment, *Ad Ethicam B. d. Sp.* (GP I, 140=L 197).

7. On this, see J. Jalabert, *Le Dieu de Leibniz* (Paris: Presses Universitaires de France, 1960), pp. 146–48.

8. See also Jalabert, *Le Dieu de Leibniz*, p. 148. This requires distinguishing the divine essence from its operations, the former being eternal, the latter in time and space (NE II, 15, 2). The whole issue bristles with difficulties. The topic of the prerequisites for causal activity already had a distinguished history, which, as far as I know, has not been studied in any detail; see E. Grant, *Much Ado about Nothing: Theories of Space and Vacuum from the Middle Ages to the Scientific Revolution* (Cambridge: Cambridge University Press,1981), pp.146, 157.

9. The Socinians were the followers of Fausto Sozzini (1539–1604) and the forerunners of modern day Unitarians. Their main theological views included the denials of the Trinity, the divinity of Christ, the natural immortality of the soul, divine foreknowledge and, most mercifully, the existence of hell. For a brief account, see *Encyclopedia of Philosophy*, ed. P. Edwards (New York: Macmillan, 1967), s.v. For a useful philosophical discussion of Leibniz's critique of Socinian theological metaphysics, see N. Jolley, *Leibniz and Locke: A Study of the "New Essays on Human Understanding"* (Oxford: Clarendon Press, 1984), chap. 2 and appendix.

10. In this, Clarke was in agreement with Newton. See J. E. McGuire, "Existence, Actuality and Necessity: Newton on Space and Time," *Annals of Science* 35 (1978): 463–508, especially 495, and A. Koyré and I. B. Cohen, "Newton & the Leibniz-Clarke Correspondence," *Archives Internationales d'Histoire des Sciences* 15 (1962): 63–126, especially 97. He was, alas, also in agreement with the hated Hobbes, although, of course, he did not mention it. See T. Hobbes, *Leviathan*, ed. C. B. Macpherson (New York: Penguin Books, 1968), chap. 46. For an opposing view, see R. Cudworth, *The True Intellectual System of the Universe* (1678; reprint, New York: Garland Publishing, 1978), pp. 644–45. For Clarke's reading of Boethius's dictum, see WB 539. F. Suarez, *Disputationes Metaphysicae*, disputation 50, section 3, notes

that Aureolus denied the possibility of nonsuccessive duration, and therefore concluded that duration is not attributable to God.

11. For this argument, which Kenny attributes to Suarez, see Kenny, *The God of the Philosophers*, pp. 38–39. Clarke often used the blanket term "Scholastic" to refer to a set of views about divine duration, presence, and knowledge, which he considered unintelligible at best. Providing detailed information on the Scholastics who adopted these views would be beyond the scope of this book. However, for a high Scholastic, see Aquinas. *Summa Theologiae*, 1st part, question 8 (omnipresence); question 9, 10 (eternity); question 14, article 5 (God's knowledge of things other than himself). For a late Scholastic, see Suarez, *Disputationes Metaphysicae*, disputation 30, section 7 (immensity); disputation 30, section 8, and disputation 50, section 4 (eternity); disputation 30, section 15 (God's knowledge of things other than himself).

12. So, things are eternally present to God only as objects of divine knowledge. For similar view, see J. Locke, *An Essay Concerning Human Understanding*, ed. P. H. Nidditch (Oxford: Clarendon Press, 1979), bk. 2, chap. 15, sec. 12. Kenny, *The God of the Philosophers*, pp. 38–39, attributes this view to Suarez.

13. For Newton, see "De gravitatione," in *Unpublished Scientific Papers of Isaac Newton*, ed. and trans. A. R. Hall and M. B. Hall (Cambridge: Cambridge University Press,1962), p. 137; J. E. McGuire, "Existence, Actuality and Necessity: Newton on Space and Time," *Annals of Science* 35 (1978): 506; E. Grant, *Much Ado about Nothing*, p. 244, 416 n. 420. Actually, Grant seems to argue that holenmerism is both unintelligible and contradictory; but, I assume, it cannot be both. For a defense of holenmerism, see Cudworth, *The True Intellectual System of the Universe*, pp. 781–83. Leibniz read Newton as Grant does: to Johann Bernoulli, December 1715: GM III, 951–52.

14. See Gregory's remarks in a memorandum of December 1705, quoted in Grant, *Much Ado about Nothing*, pp. 245–46: "the plain truth is that he [Newton] believes God to be omnipresent in the literal sense." R. S. Westfall, *Never at Rest: A Biography of Isaac Newton* (Cambridge: Cambridge University Press,1980), p. 647, notes that Whiston gave an identical account of Newton's view. The view that God is actually extended was not wildly uncommon; Collins wrote: "Most of the modern Priests contend that God is *Immaterial*, but they differ in their Notion of *Immateriality*; some by *Immaterial Being* understanding *extended Substance without Solidity*; others by *Immaterial Being* understanding *unextended Being*." Collins continued by mentioning More, Turner, and Clarke among the supporters of the first view; see A. Collins, *A Discourse of Free Thinking* (London, 1713), pp. 47–48. For a defense of divine simplicity as compatible with the claim that God is substantially present (but neither circumscriptive nor definitive) in the world, see Suarez, *Disputationes Metaphysicae*, disputation 30, section 7 §§ 49–51; disputation 51, section 6, § 7.

15. In spite of Clarke's obvious distaste for Scholasticism, there are similarities between his and some scholastic views on divine immensity and infinite space. See Grant, *Much Ado about Nothing*, especially chaps. 6–7; see also P. Bayle, *Dictionnaire historique et critique* (Paris: Editions sociales,1974), s.v. Leucippe n. G.

16. See W II, 753; III, 896; NP III, general scholium, 762; see also Malebranche, *Dialogues on Metaphysics*, dialogue 8, secs. 5–8.

17. See More's third letter to Descartes: H. More, *Opera Omnia* (1674–79; reprint, Hildesheim: G. Olms, 1966), vol. 2, tome 2, p. 255; for a similar argument, see Suarez, *Disputationes Metaphysicae*, disputation 30, section 7, §§ 3–4.

18. See N. Pike, *God and Timelessness* (London: Routledge and Paul, 1970), p. 105; for a criticism, see P. Helm, *Eternal God: A Study of God Without Time* (Oxford: Clarendon Press, 1988), pp. 68–72.

19. For Leibniz toying with a similar view, see NE II,15, 2.

20. A similar thought found its way into the third edition of *Principia*: NP III, general scholium, 763–64. For a sympathetic analysis of Clarke's argument, see W. L. Rowe, *The Cosmological Argument* (Princeton: Princeton University Press, 1975), pp. 231–33.

21. Leibniz had made a similar point in NE II, 15, 2. For Berkeley's related misgivings, see *A Treatise Concerning the Principle of Human Knowledge* § 117, in G. Berkeley, *Berkeley's Philosophical Writings*, ed. D. M. Armstrong (New York: Collier Books, 1965), p. 110.

22. Koyré and Cohen claim that Clarke was attacking Raphson; see their "Newton & the Leibniz-Clarke Correspondence," 86 n. 54.

23. In 1676, Leibniz had held a position similar to Clarke's and claimed that there is something "eternal" in space that consists in the "immeasurability of God" (A VI, 3, 391, also in G. W. Leibniz, *G. W. Leibniz: De Summa Rerum*, ed. and trans. H. R. Parkinson [New Haven: Yale University Press, 1992], p. 43). This passage is briefly discussed in R. M. Adams, *Leibniz: Determinist, Theist, Idealist* (Oxford: Oxford University Press, 1994), pp. 123–24.

24. This is the same position Clarke took in answering an anonymous critic of his *A Demonstration* (W II, 753, undated). I take Clarke's statement to Leibniz to be his gloss on Newton's claim that "by existing always and everywhere, [God] constitutes [constituit] duration and space" (NP III, general scholium, 761). I disagree with R. Hall's suggestion that we should read *constituit* as "established, created, ordered," so that space and time become "elements of the divine creation." See R. Hall, "Newton and the Absolutes: Sources," in *The Investigation of Difficult Things*, ed. P. M. Harmann and A. E. Shapiro (Cambridge: Cambridge University Press, 1992), pp. 261–85, especially p. 270. Certainly, if Hall is right, Clarke's and Newton's views were at odds, since for the former, space and time are necessary existents. McGuire, in "Predicates of Pure Existence: Newton on God's Space and Time," in *Philosophical Perspectives on Newtonian Science*, ed. P. Bricker

and R. I. G. Hughes (Cambridge, Mass: MIT Press, 1990), pp. 92–108, especially pp.105–6, notes that perhaps Newton held that God causes space and time in the same way in which Augustine's foot eternally embedded in sand causes the eternally present footprint. But even assuming that Clarke adopted this view, the objection stands.

25. See also Clarke's last letter to Butler: W II, 750.

26. For the reply to Butler, see W II, 745.

27. J. E. McGuire believes that for Newton, God is in space and time: "Existence, Actuality and Necessity," 463–508, especially 470; if he is right, Clarke and Newton disagreed on this issue.

28. This is a point Leibniz made also to Conti: R 42.

29. See Grant, *Much Ado about Nothing*, pp. 227, 231, 244 for supporters of this view; see also A. Koyré, *From the Closed World to the Infinite Universe* (Baltimore: Johns Hopkins University Press, 1957), pp. 195–96.

30. Paul's *dictum* is in *Acts* 17, 28. Spinoza too claimed that his own view was in agreement with it; see his letter to Oldenburg, end of 1675: Spinoza, *Opera*, vol. 4, pp. 306–9, especially p. 307. A reference to the same passage was made by Locke as well in a point of the *Essay* where he seemed ready to allow that a relational theory of space was as reasonable as the absolute theory; see Locke, *An Essay Concerning Human Understanding*, bk. 2, chap. 13, sec. 26. For Leibniz's own reading of Paul's saying, see G. W. Leibniz, *Philosophical Essays*, ed. and trans. R. Ariew and D. Garber (Indianapolis: Hackett Publishing, 1989), pp. 275–76. According to Grant, Paul's statement was often employed to support the view that infinite space is God's immensity: Grant, *Much Ado about Nothing*, pp. 406 n. 329.

31. The point is clearly made in Grant, *Much Ado about Nothing*, pp. 240–42. Grant (p. 410 n. 373) also notes that in *quaestio* 23 of the 1706 *Optice* (NO 346), Newton claimed, against his considered judgment, that space is "divisible in infinitum."

32. Bayle, *Dictionnaire historique et critique*, s.v. Leucippus, n. G; s.v. Zeno of Elea, n. I. N. Malebranche, *Oeuvres complètes*, ed. A. Robinet (Paris: J. Vrin, 1958–60), vol. 6, pp. 204, 219, 223; *Dialogues on Metaphysics*, dialogue 8, sec. 8; on this see D. Radner, *Malebranche* (Assen: Van Gorcum, 1978), pp. 113–16.

33. B. Spinoza, *Ethica* I, Propositions 12, 13, in *Opera*, vol. 2, p. 55. However, in *Ethica* I, proposition 15, scholium (*Opera*, vol. 2, 57–60), he had also noted that since nothing acts on God, even if extension were to entail divisibility, one could not claim that "the extended substance is unworthy of the divine nature."

34. For his analogous reply to Collins, see W III, 794.

35. On 3 November 1715, before the controversy started, Caroline told Leibniz that Clarke was the right man to translate the *Theodicy* into English. To show to Leibniz Clarke's merits, she sent him a few books by Clarke. Among them was an edition of the letters Clarke had written to Dodwell and Collins on the issue of thinking matter. Leibniz read and an-

notated them. In his third letter, Clarke claimed that space is "an extension whose Parts (improperly so called) depend on each other for their existence . . . because of the contradiction which a Separation of them manifestly would imply" (W III, 794). On the side of the word "Separation," Leibniz wrote "an Deus unam partem spatii destruere nequit." Leibniz's own copy of Clarke's letters is at the Niedersächsische Landesbibliothek in Hanover.

36. GP III, 622; VII, 562; this issues will be taken up in the chapter on space and time.

37. "Every part of space is *always,* and every indivisible moment of duration is *everywhere"* (NP III, general scholium, 761).

38. See J. Toland, *Letters to Serena* (1704; reprint, Stuttgart-Bad Cannstatt: F. Fromann, 1964), letter 5, sec.12; for Clarke's attack on Toland, see W II, 531; T. Hobbes, *De Corpore* II, 7, in *Opera Philosophica quae Latine scripsit omnia,* ed. W. Molesworth (1845; reprint, Aalen: Scientia Verlag, 1966), vol. 1; for More, see Koyré and Cohen, "Newton & the Leibniz-Clarke Correspondence," especially 87 n. 55, who give the following quotation from More's *An Antidote against Atheism*: "For if after the removal of *corporeal Matter* out of the world, there will be still *Space* and *Distance* in which this very Matter, while it was there, was also conceived to lye, and this *distant Space* cannot but be something, and yet not corporeal, because neither impenetrable nor tangible; it must of necessity be a Substance Incorporeal necessarily and eternally existent of itself: which the clearer *Idea* of a *Being absolutely perfect* will more fully and punctually inform us to be the *Self-subsisting God.*"

39. See Ferguson, *The Philosophy of Dr. Samuel Clarke and Its Critics,* pp. 52, 102. P. Gassendi, *Opera Omnia in sex tomos* (1658; reprint, Stuttgart-Bad Canstatt: F. Fromann, 1964), vol. 1, p. 182a; Newton. "De gravitatione," pp.132, 137; however, on p. 136 space and time are considered attributes.

40. In one of the drafts for the *Avertissement au Lecteur* printed in the Des Maizeaux French preface to the 1720 edition of the Leibniz-Clarke correspondence, he wrote that when the terms "Quality" or "Property" are applied to God, they must not be taken "in that sense wherein they are vulgarly, by the writers of Logick & Metaphysics applied to finite & created beings; for those writers consider space & duration as quantities & not as qualities." See the texts of the various drafts in Koyré and Cohen, "Newton & the Leibniz-Clarke Correspondence"; the one just quoted, draft E, is at p. 101. J. Carriero, in "Newton on Space and Time: Comments on J. E. McGuire," in *Philosophical Perspectives on Newtonian Science,* pp.109–33, especially pp.122–28, reasonably holds that Newton was unhappy with Clarke's use of the word "property," which intimated that space and time are divine *propria,* that is, necessary but nonessential accidents of God.

41. Des Maizeaux, *Recueil de diverses pièces . . . par Mrs. Leibniz, Clarke, Newton, & autre autheurs celèbres* (Amsterdam, 1720), tome 1, p. v. Koyré and Cohen, by publishing the several drafts written in Newton's hand, have shown that the *Avertissement* was composed by him. However,

as they themselves point out, there is no reason to doubt that Clarke contributed to it. See their "Newton & the Leibniz-Clarke Correspondence," especially p. 95.

42. A similar point was made by Newton in one of the drafts for the *Avertissement*: immensity and eternity should be considered divine qualities in the same sense in which "the Predicaments of *Ubi & Quando* should be called qualities or properties when applied to the existence of a Being wch is omnipresent & eternal." See Koyré and Cohen, "Newton & the Leibniz-Clarke Correspondence," especially p. 96.

43. Probably, as Clarke pointed out in a note to Leibniz's first letter in his edition of the correspondence, what Leibniz had in mind was a passage in *quaestio* 23 of the 1706 *Optice*: "For while comets move in very eccentric orbits in all manner of positions, blind fate could never make all the planets move one and the same way in orbs concentric, some inconsiderable irregularities excepted which may have arisen from the mutual actions of comets and planets upon one another, and which will be apt to increase, till this system wants a reformation" (NO 345–46).

44. On Newton's millenarism and its relation to his cosmological views both before and after the *Opticks*, see D. Kubrin, "Newton and the Cyclical Cosmos: Providence and the Mechanical Philosophy," *Journal of the History of Ideas* 28 (1967): 325–46, especially 332–33; M. C. Jacob, *The Newtonians and the English Revolution 1689–1720*, (Ithaca: Cornell University Press, 1976), chap. 3, especially pp. 134–42.

45. In a similar vein, on 6 December 1715, he told Conti that the Newtonians had a narrow notion of divine wisdom and power (NC VI, 251–52=R 42).

46. He made the same point to Conti in the letter of 6 December 1715 (NC VI, 251–52=R 42).

47. On this, see F. E. Manuel, *The Religion of Isaac Newton* (Oxford: Clarendon Press, 1974), especially pp. 57–63; J. E. Force "Sir Isaac Newton, 'Gentleman of Wide Swallow'?" in *Essays on the Context, Nature and Influence of Isaac Newton's Theology*, ed. J. E. Force and R. H. Popkin (Dordrecht: Kluwer Academic Publishers, 1990), pp. 119–41.

48. See M. I. J. Griffin, *Latitudinarianism in the Seventeenth-Century Church of England* (Leiden: E. J. Brill, 1992), p. 106.

49. Or so Whiston claimed; see Westfall, *Never at Rest*, pp. 651–53; P. Casini, *L'universo-macchina: Origini della filosofia newtoniana* (Bari: Laterza, 1969), pp. 85–88. On Whiston's religious views, see J. E. Force, *William Whiston: Honest Newtonian* (Cambridge: Cambridge University Press, 1985).

50. See Edwards's comments on Newton in Ferguson, *The Philosophy of Dr. Samuel Clarke and Its Critics*, p. 252.

51. The full title was: *The Scripture-Doctrine of the Trinity: wherein every text in the New Testament relating to that doctrine is distinctly considered, and the Divinity of our blessed Saviour, according to the Scriptures,*

proved and explained (London, 1712). The book had three editions: 1712, 1719, 1732. On Clarke's views, including his opinion about the Holy Ghost, see J. P. Ferguson, *An Eighteenth Century Heretic: Dr. Samuel Clarke* (Kineton: Roundwood Press, 1976), p. 54. More generally, see chaps. 5–8, 10–11; and L. Stewart, "Samuel Clarke, Newtonianism and the Factions of post-revolutionary England," *Journal of the History of Ideas* 42 (1981): 53–71.

52. See Ferguson, *An Eighteenth Century Heretic*, pp. 83–84. Manuel, *The Religion of Isaac Newton*, p. 61, points out that in Clarke's own copy of *The Book of Common Prayer* (London, 1724), all the trinitarian passages were "slashed through with violent penstrokes." In W I, 21–22, Clarke attributed eternity to the Father only. For Voltaire's almost contemporary and flippant evaluation, see M. A. Voltaire, *Voltaire's Philosophical Letters*, ed. and trans. E. Dilworth (Indianapolis: Bobs Merrill, 1961), letter 7, pp. 27–29.

53. These references were correctly given by Clarke, who also gave Lz V, 29, a misinterpretation.

54. For the view that a necessary agent is no agent at all, see WB 548. We shall consider this issue in detail in the chapter on free will.

55. Johann Bernoulli made a similar point with respect to Newton's criticism of Cartesian vortices: since Newton thought that God has to rewind the machine of the world, why could not Descartes claim that the friction among his vortices does not cause them grind to a halt because God intervenes by refurnishing each particle with the lost force? (Johann Bernoulli to Leibniz, 3 July 1716: GM III, 966).

56. See W I, 55. On the issue of "fitness" in Clarke's moral philosophy, see H. Ducharme, *The Moral Self, Moral Knowledge and God: An Analysis of the Theory of Samuel Clarke* (Ph.D. Diss., Oriel College, Oxford, 1974); Ferguson, *The Philosophy of Dr. Samuel Clarke and Its Critics*, chap. 5.

57. See NP, Editor's Preface, 33. In "De gravitatione," Newton had claimed that the view that bodies have "as it were, a complete, absolute and independent reality in themselves" is the modern highroad to atheism: *Unpublished Scientific Papers of Isaac Newton*, p. 144.

58. See his 1702 *Reflections on the Doctrine of a Single Universal Spirit*: in GP VI, 529–38=L 554–60. Of course, here we are not interested in the adequacy of Leibniz's historical analysis. However, for a similar view regarding Spinoza, see Bayle, *Dictionnaire historique et critique*, s.v. Spinoza, n. A.

59. Two days before Leibniz had sent his fourth letter, where he clearly intimated that Clarke viewed the relation force-God-world on the basis of that force-soul-body; see Lz IV, 32–34. Generally, Leibniz thought that Clarke's views of the relation between God and the world was badly anthropomorphic; see his letter to Wolff of 23 December 1715: R 45.

60. For Leibniz, being the world-soul and being the creator and preserver of the world are incompatible notions. See GP VII, 134, 148, 151, 152;

Theodicy, preliminary discourse, §§ 8; 195; 217: GP VI, 54, 232, 247–48; Grua 558.

61. See also Cl III, 11–12.

62. Leibniz made the same point to Conti on 25 November 1715 (NC VI, 253=R 43); to Caroline, 14 April 1716 (R 65); and to Bernoulli, 7 June 1716 (R 117). The fact that for Clarke, as for Newton, the soul has a *sensorium*, probably also contributed to reinforce Leibniz's suspicions; see Cl IV, 37; for Newton, see the 1706 *Optice, quaestio* 20 (NO 315).

63. See the different texts, both coming from the 1706 *Optice, quaestio* 20 (NO 315), in A. Koyré and I. B. Cohen, "The Case of the Missing *Tanquam*: Leibniz, Newton & Clarke," *Isis* 52 (1961): 555–66. For a different evaluation of Koyré's and Cohen's discovery, see F. E. L. Priestley, "The Clarke-Leibniz Controversy," in *The Methodological Heritage of Newton*, ed. R. E. Butts and J. W. Davis (Toronto: University of Toronto Press, 1970), pp. 34–56.

64. See the full definition in G. W. Leibniz and S. Clarke, *The Leibniz-Clarke Correspondence: With Extracts from Newton's "Principia" and "Opticks,"* ed. H. G. Alexander (Manchester: Manchester University Press, 1956), p. 33.

65. Koyré and Cohen, "The Case of the Missing *Tanquam*," find Clarke's reply satisfactory; Priestley, in "The Clarke-Leibniz Controversy," in my opinion correctly, does not.

66. Locke, *An Essay concerning Human Understanding*, bk. 4, chap.18, sec. 19; NE IV, 18, 19; WN 673.

67. For a brief account of the interpretation of the biblical *dictum* in the early modern period, see E. Craig, *The Mind of God and the Works of Man* (Oxford: Clarendon Press, 1987), chap. 1.

68. For Leibniz, see *Principles of Nature and Grace*, § 14; Grua II, 495–96; *Theodicy*, preface, § 4; *Monadology* §§ 47–48. GP VI 614–15=L 647; for a discussion, see Jalabert, *Le Dieu de Leibniz*, pp. 139–40; G. Grua, *Jurisprudence universelle et Theodicée selon Leibniz* (Paris: Presses Universitaires de France, 1953), pp. 32–42, 92–98, 246–51. For Clarke, see W IV, 732; *On the Goodness of God*: W I, 91; *On imitating the Holiness of God*: W I, 157; *On the Justice of God*: W I, 101. This view, especially regarding the moral attributes, was common among Latitudinarian theologians; in particular, Tillotson, whom Clarke admired and often quoted, held it and for the same reasons: if God's moral perfections were different from ours in nature, then we could not imitate them: see A. Collins, *A Discourse on Free Thinking* (London, 1713), p. 51.

Chapter 2: The Soul

1. H. Dodwell, *An Epistolary Discourse, proving, from the Scriptures and the First Fathers, that the Soul is a Principle naturally mortal; but*

immortalized actually by the Pleasure of God, to Punishment; or, to Reward, by its union with the Divine Baptismal Spirit: Wherein is proved, that none may have the power of giving this divine immortalizing Spirit, since the Apostles, but only the Bishops (London, 1706).

2. For example, Leibniz knew, and probably read, Dodwell's book. He wrote Smith, an English divine, that he was surprised that a scholar like Dodwell could write such paradoxes on the nature of the soul: Leibniz to Smith, 2 September 1707, in *Leibniz-Briefwechsel* 872, fol. 102, in Leibniz Archiv, Niedersächsische Landesbibliothek, Hanover.

3. See also WB 562. This sort of argument was quite old. Its history has been documented by B. L. Mijuskovic, *The Achilles of Rationalist Arguments* (The Hague: M. Nijhoff, 1974). It is also the argument that Kant, after accepting it in the precritical period, allegedly destroyed in the Second Paralogism. See K. Ameriks, *Kant's Theory of Mind* (Oxford: Clarendon Press, 1982), chap. 2. To my knowledge, there is neither a satisfactory nor even a full-scale analysis of Clarke's version (or versions) of the argument from the unity of consciousness. In addition to Mijuskovic, see H. Ducharme, "Personal Identity in Samuel Clarke," *Journal of the History of Philosophy* 24 (1986): 359–83, especially 378–82; J. W. Yolton, *Thinking Matter: Materialism in Eighteenth-Century Britain* (Minneapolis: University of Minnesota Press, 1983), pp. 39–41; R. Attfield, "Clarke, Collins and Compounds," *Journal of the History of Philosophy* 15 (1977): 45–54.

4. J. Locke, *An Essay concerning Human Understanding*, ed. P. H. Nidditch (Oxford: Clarendon Press, 1979), bk. 4, chap. 10, sec. 16. See also J. L. Mackie, *The Miracle of Theism* (Oxford: Clarendon Press, 1982), chap. 7; M. R. Ayers "Mechanism, Superaddition, and the Proof of God's Existence in Locke's *Essay*," *Philosophical Review* 90 (1981): 210–51.

5. Locke, *An Essay concerning Human Understanding*, bk. 4, chap. 3, sec. 6.

6. The point was repeated with respect to the brain at W III, 790–91.

7. Clarke claimed that all powers and qualities fall into three mutually exclusive classes. They inhere in the subjects to which they are ascribed— for example, size inheres in the particle of matter to which it is ascribed; they do not inhere in the subject to which they are usually ascribed, but they inhere in another subject—for example, color does not inhere in the rose, but in the soul; or they are not powers or qualities at all, but effects of systems of matter—for example, ". . . *Magnetism,* and *Electrical Attractions,* are not *real Qualities* at all, residing in any subject, but *merely Abstract Names* to express the *Effects* of some determinate motions of certain Streams of Matter" (W III, 760). Since consciousness cannot inhere in a composite like the brain, and the materialist does not want to claim that the motions in the brain produce thought in something else, the materialist is left with what Clarke considered the obviously unacceptable conclusion that consciousness is not a mode of the brain, but merely the effect of the motions of the brain.

8. See also WB 554; the point was similar to Descartes's in the *Second Replies*, in *Oeuvres de Descartes*, ed. C. Adam and P. Tannery (1897–1913; reprint, Paris: J. Vrin, 1964–76), vol. 7, p. 135.

9. To my knowledge, Clarke's views on the mind-body relation, especially in connection with Occasionalism, have not been satisfactorily studied. On this, see J. E. Le Rossignol, *The Ethical Philosophy of Samuel Clarke* (Leipzig, 1892), especially pp. 29–30; J. P. Ferguson, *The Philosophy of Dr. Samuel Clarke and Its Critics* (New York: Vantage Press, 1974), especially pp. 244–45; H. M. Ducharme, *The Moral Self, Moral Knowledge and God: An Analysis of the Theory of Samuel Clarke* (Ph.D. diss., Oriel College, 1984), especially pp. 49–50, where Ducharme takes the view that Clarke is a one-way interactionist.

10. Descartes, *Oeuvres de Descartes*, vol. 8B, p. 359. Descartes made a somewhat similar point in the *Traité de l'Homme*, in *Oeuvres de Descartes*, vol. 11, p. 144.

11. See More's third letter to Descartes, in H. More, *Opera Omnia* (1674–79; reprint, Hildesheim: G. Olms, 1966), vol. 2, tome 2, p. 255. The same point is repeated, for example, in "Enchiridium Metaphysicum," chap. 27, secs. 2–5, in *Opera Omnia*, vol. 2, tome 1, pp. 307–9, in the middle of a sustained attack against nullibilism, the position that the soul is not in space and which More associated most closely with Descartes, whom he called "nullibistarum princeps." On Descartes's reception in England, see A. Pacchi, *Cartesio in Inghilterra da More a Boyle* (Bari: Laterza, 1973).

12. H. More, *Immortalitas Animae*, bk. 1, chap. 2, sec. 12, in More, *Opera Omnia*, vol. 2, tome 2, pp. 294–95.

13. H. More, *Immortalitas Animae*, bk. 1, chap. 6, sec. 1, in More, *Opera Omnia*, vol. 2, tome 2, p. 302. For his views on emanation, see secs. 2–3, in More, *Opera Omnia*, vol. 2, tome 2, pp. 302–3.

14. H. More *Immortalitas Animae*, bk. 1, chap. 6, sec. 3, in More, *Opera Omnia*, vol. 2, tome 2, p. 303, where he also explains that the soul enjoys "perfect *indivisibility* of the parts, although not an intellectual *indivisibility*." One might infer that for More, God could split a soul, but such a conclusion would be wrong. He held that even material atoms, although intellectually divisible because extended, cannot be divided by God because of their "real infinite littleness," even if, of course, God could annihilate them. See his scholium to sec. 3 of the Preface to *Immortalitas Animae*, in More, *Opera Omnia*, vol. 2, tome 2, p. 288. T. Hobbes argued that since the soul is not extended, it is nowhere, and therefore does not exist; see his "De Homine," 11, 4, in *Opera Philosophica quae Latine scripsit omnia*, ed. W. Molesworth (1845; reprint, Aalen: Scientia Verlag, 1966); Cudworth took no position on the extension of the soul: see his *The True Intellectual System of the Universe* 1678; reprint, New York: Garland Publishing, 1978), p. 833.

15. For a discussion of the point, see J. Hostler, *Leibniz's Moral Philosophy* (New York: Harper and Row, 1975), p. 59.

16. Unpublished letter to Hugony, undated, quoted in N. Jolley, *Leibniz*

and Locke: A Study of the "New Essays on Human Understanding" (Oxford: Clarendon Press, 1984), pp. 64–65.

17. On this, see R. C. Sleigh, "Leibniz on Malebranche on Causality," in *Central Themes in Early Modern Philosophy*, ed. J. A. Cover and M. Kulstad (Indianapolis: Hackett Publishing Company, 1990), pp. 161–93.

18. On this see D. Radner, "Is There a Problem of Cartesian Interaction?" *Journal of the History of Philosophy* 23 (1985): 35–49, and Richardson's and Loeb's replies and Radner's rejoinder at pp. 221–36.

19. See also *Monadology*, § 80: GP VI, 620–21=L 651. The issue is discussed by R. S. Woolhouse, "Leibniz's Reaction to Cartesian Interactionism," *Proceedings of the Aristotelian Society* 86 (1985–86): 69–82, especially 71.

20. The controversy between Clarke and Collins went through four editions by 1711, was amply discussed in England, and had some following on the Continent as well. For Le Clerc, who warmly approved of Clarke's arguments, see his *Bibliotheque Choisie* 26 (1713): 375–411.

21. That this point was on Leibniz's mind is clearly indicated by the fact that he commented on Clarke's claim to Collins that "the Consciousness of a Man, is not a Multitude of Consciousnesses, but One" (W III, 790) by writing under the word "Consciousness" "etendue" and "durete."

22. See E. O'Neill "Influxus Physicus," in *Causation in Early Modern Philosophy*, ed. S. Nadler (University Park: Pennsylvania State University Press, 1993), pp. 27–56, especially pp. 52–53.

23. Locke, *An Essay concerning Human Understanding*, bk. 2, chap. 21, sec. 4.

24. Newton had made a similar point: Newton to Conti, 26 February 1716, R 62–63.

25. N. Malebranche, *The Search after Truth*, trans. T. M. Lennon and J. Olscamp (Columbus: Ohio State University Press, 1980), Clarification 15, p. 670.

26. Descartes as well argued that God gave us the power to move our body. See *Descartes: Philosophical Letters*, ed. and trans. A. Kenny (Oxford: Clarendon Press, 1970), pp. 252, 257.

27. See Locke. *An Essay concerning Human Understanding*, bk. 2, chap. 21, sec. 4; G. W. Leibniz, *De Ipsa Natura* §10: GP IV, 509–10=L 502–3.

28. N. Malebranche, *The Search after Truth*, clarifications 1 and 11, pp. 552, 633–38. See also D. Radner, *Malebranche*. (Assen: Van Gorcum, 1978), pp. 70–72; Locke, *An Essay concerning Human Understanding*, bk. 2, chap. 23, secs. 4-5; bk. 2, chap. 27, sec. 27; bk. 4, ch. 6, sec. 14.

29. P. Bayle, *Dictionnaire historique et critique* (Paris: Editions sociales, 1974), s.v. Rorarius n. L.

30. A. Vartanian, *Diderot and Descartes: A Study of Scientific Naturalism in the Enlightenment* (Princeton: Princeton University Press, 1953), especially chap. 4.

31. A. Koyré & I. B. Cohen, "Newton & the Leibniz-Clarke Correspon-

dence," *Archives Internationales d'Histoire des Sciences* 15 (1962): 63–126, especially 113.

Chapter 3: Free Will

1. The exchange with Bulkeley took place at the beginning of 1716, in the midst of the controversy with Leibniz. Clarke published it immediately, as one can gather from R 103.

2. See also WB 559; W IV, 734; on this, see J. E. Le Rossignol, *The Ethical Philosophy of Samuel Clarke* (Leipzig, 1892), pp. 67–68.

3. Clarke did not mention names, but almost certainly he had in mind some of the early English deists like Blount, Gildon, Tindal, Toland, and, possibly, Collins. On the influence of Spinoza on the English deists, see R. L. Colie, "Spinoza and the Early English Deists," *Journal of the History of Ideas* 20 (1959): 23–46.

4. See also WB 560.

5. B. Spinoza, *Ethica*, part 1, proposition 17, corollary 2, and proposition 34, in *Opera*, ed. C. Gebhardt (Heidelberg: C. Winters, 1925), vol. 2, pp. 61, 77.

6. On the possible connection between the acceptance of the Principle of Sufficient Reason and that of the existence of necessary links between events, see J. Bennett, *A Study of Spinoza's Ethics* (Indianapolis: Hackett Publishing, 1985), pp. 31–32.

7. B. Spinoza, *Ethica*, part 2, proposition 49, corollary in *Opera*, vol. 2, p. 131; R. J. Delahunty, *Spinoza* (London: Routledge and Paul,1985), p. 229.

8. T. Hobbes, *Of Liberty and Necessity*, in *English Works*, ed. W. Molesworth (1839; reprint, Aalen: Scientia Verlag, 1966), vol. 4, p. 247; see also p. 268. The same point was made to Clarke by Bulkeley (W IV, 713). For Hobbes's definition of volition, see *Leviathan*, ed. C. B. Macpherson (New York: Penguin Books, 1968), part 1, chap. 6.

9. The same point was made to Hobbes by Bramhall; see Hobbes, *English Works*, vol. 5, p. 73. On the Hobbes-Bramhall controversy, see G. Hunter, "The Fate of Thomas Hobbes," *Studia Leibnitiana* 21[1] (1989): 5–20.

10. See, for example, W IV, 728, where Clarke states that if we have in us the principle of action, then our "*active Substance*, in which the Principle of Self-Motion resides, is itself the only proper, physical, and immediate CAUSE of the Motion or Action." Clarke's views, then, were more radical than those held nowadays by some contemporary supporters of agent causation, who merely require that the agent is a concause, albeit a fundamental one, of action. See, for example, R. M. Chisholm, "Human Freedom and the Self," in *Free Will*, ed. G. Watson (Oxford: Oxford University Press, 1982), p. 28.

11. So eager was Clarke to show that we can be assured of the propriety of God's behavior that at times he sounded as if he held that God is neces-

sarily good. For example, he claimed that the moral attributes are "as essential" to the divine nature as the metaphysical ones, or that God can no more choose immorally than destroy its own being (WB 565, 573). In fact, Collins took him to hold that God acts necessarily for the good and consequently has no power of self-determination, no ability to do otherwise, that is, no Clarkean free will (W III, 874). Clarke replied by restating his distinction between natural or metaphysical necessity and moral necessity, which is grounded in the fact that motives, be they rational or not, have no causal power on the will (WB 906). But it is unclear whether Clarke's answer is satisfactory even on his own terms, for even if God's understanding does not causally affect the divine will, the link between the two could perhaps be unbreakable even by God, who then would not be able to do otherwise even if the will is causally self-determining. The issue deserves further study.

12. See also WB 558. For an explicit attempt to link the allegedly introspective evidence of Clarkeian freedom to the experimental (i.e., Newtonian) as opposed to the metaphysical (i.e., Leibnizian) method, see C. Maclaurin, *An Account of Sir Isaac Newton's Philosophical Discoveries* (London, 1748), p. 83.

13. See, for example, R. Descartes, *The Principles of Philosophy*, part 1, proposition 41 in R. Descartes, *Oeuvres de Descartes*, ed. C. Adam and P. Tannery (1897–1913: reprint Paris: J. Vrin, 1964–76), vol. 8a, p. 20.

14. See also WB 561. For a philosopher ready to argue that thought might stem from powers in matter different from figure and motion, see Collins's letter to Clarke in W III, 803. In *A Demostration*, Clarke also tried to show that divine foreknowledge is compatible with free will. Briefly put, his argument was that knowledge does not impose any necessity on the thing known. Since this issue did not arise in the exchange with Leibniz, it can be left aside. However, Collins took it up in *A Philosophical Inquiry Concerning Human Liberty*, and Clarke replied at W IV, 732–33.

15. On Locke's argument and related topics, see V. Chappell, "Locke on Freedom of the Will," in *Locke's Philosophy: Content and Context*, ed. G. A. J. Rogers (Oxford: Oxford University Press, 1994), pp. 101–21.

16. Grua, sec. 5.

17. See Leibniz's comment to proposition 28 of the *Ethics* part I: GP I, 148=L 203. See also *Theodicy* § 173: GP VI, 217.

18. On this, see also Grua 384: "Really all the actions of creatures are contingent, since they follow from the previous state of the thing not necessarily, but because of a decree of the divine will."

19. On this, see R. Adams, "Leibniz's Theories of Contingency," in *Leibniz: Critical and Interpretive Essays*, ed. M. Hooker (Minneapolis: Minnesota University Press, 1982), pp. 243–83; R. Adams, *Leibniz, Determinist, Theist, Idealist* (Oxford: Oxford University Press, 1993), pp. 36–42.

20. R. Adams, "Leibniz's Theories of Contingency," in *Leibniz: Critical and Interpretive Essays*, p. 51; see also B. Mates, *The Philosophy of Leib-*

niz: *Metaphysics and Language* (Oxford: Oxford University Press, 1986), p.120 n. 61.

21. On Leibniz's rejection of the "third realm," see N. Jolley, *The Light of the Soul* (Oxford: Clarendon Press, 1990), pp.135–39, and Mates, *The Philosophy of Leibniz*, p. 246.

22. A necessary condition because choice in a state of equilibrium could not be brought about merely by antecedent mental states; not a sufficient condition because freedom of indifference is compatible with the denial that relevantly identical options can be given.

23. Descartes, *The Principles of Philosophy*, part 1, proposition 41 in *Oeuvres*, vol. 8a, p. 20.

24. B. Spinoza, *Ethica*, part 3, proposition 2, scholium, in *Opera*, vol. 2, pp. 141–44; see also Letter 58 in *Opera*, vol. 4, pp. 265–68.

25. On this, see M. Kulstad, "Two Arguments on *Petites* Perceptions," in *Essays in the Philosophy of Leibniz*, ed. M. Kulstad, Rice University Studies in Philosophy 63 (Houston, Tex.: Rice University, 1977), pp. 58–59.

26. See also W 730.

27. See also *Theodicy* §§ 303–4: GP VI, 296–97; NE II, 21,13.

28. On this, see W. L. Rowe, "Causality and Free Will in the Controversy Between Collins and Clarke," *The Journal of the History of Philosophy* 25 (1987): 51–67, especially 60–61; for the idea of the agent as an unmoved mover, see R. Chisholm, "Human Freedom and the Self," in *Free Will*, p. 32.

29. See also *On King* 20: GP VI, 421–22; *Theodicy* § 48: GP VI, 129; NE II, 21, 47.

30. For a contemporary admission that agent causation destroys the possibility of a science of the mind, see R. Chisholm, "Human Freedom and the Self," in *Free Will*, p. 33.

31. On this, see E. Vailati, "Leibniz on Locke on Weakness of the Will," *Journal of the History of Philosophy* 28 (1990): 213–28.

32. Leibniz was also convinced that careful introspection reveals not only that we do not have liberty of indifference, but also that even when we think we choose in a state of equilibrium we are moved by perception, which at the moment we fail to apperceive (*Theodicy* § 35: GP VI, 122–23). However, Leibniz did not make this point in the correspondence, and if Clarke saw it in the *Theodicy*, he did not comment on it.

33. At one point, Clarke actually seemed ready to argue that the temporal location of the world is not indifferent because our world is one of a series (Cl IV,15). On this complex issue, see the last chapter in the book.

34. P. Bayle, *Dictionnaire historique et critique* (Paris: Editiones sociales, 1974), s.v. Buridan, n. C. For Bayle, a person could act in a state of equilibrium by tossing a coin or by mere will, that is, by choosing one alternative just "because [one] will have it so." N. Rescher, in "Choice without Preference: A Study of the History and the Logic of the Problem of

Buridan's Ass," in N. Rescher, *Essays in Philosophical Analysis* (Pittsburg: University of Pittsburgh Press, 1969), pp. 111–57, especially p. 141, points out that since associating alternative A with heads and alternative B with tails is equivalent with associating A with tails and B with heads, one must have a random process that does the selection and the association.

35. See N. Rescher, "Choice Without Preference," p. 156.

36. Of course, at times Leibniz claimed that the Identity of Indiscernibles follows from the Principle of Sufficient Reason (Lz V, 26). However, he was also ready to claim that it follows from the very nature of truth (C 8–10).

37. G. H. R. Parkinson, *Leibniz on Human Freedom*, in Studia Leibnitiana Supplementa 2 (Wiesbaden: F. Steiner, 1970), p. 49.

38. Bayle, *Dictionnaire historique et critique*, s.v. Buridan, n. C.

39. J. Locke, *An Essay Concerning Human Understanding*, ed. P. H. Nidditch (Oxford: Clarendon Press, 1979), bk. 2, chap. 21, sec. 47; NE II, 21, 47. Locke was not always consistent on this issue: see Locke, *An Essay concerning Human Understanding*, bk. 2, chap. 21, sec. 56. For a discussion, see J. Colman, *John Locke's Moral Philosophy* (Edinburgh: Edinburgh University Press, 1983), pp. 219–20.

40. Spinoza, *Ethica*, part 2, proposition 49, scholium, in *Opera*, vol. 2, pp. 131–36.

41. For Leibniz, motives include not only reasons, but also dispositions, passions, feelings, and so on (Lz V, 15).

Chapter 4: Space and Time

1. "I do not define time, space, place, and motion as being well known to all" (NP I, definition 8, scholium, 46).

2. Cf. NP I, definition 8, scholium, 48; see also Newton's early "De gravitatione" for the claim that space cannot be thought of as nonexistent, in *Unpublished Scientific Papers of Isaac Newton*, ed. and trans. A. R. Hall and M. B. Hall (Cambridge: Cambridge University Press, 1962), p. 104. E. Grant, in *Much Ado about Nothing: Theories of Space and Vacuum from the Middle Ages to the Scientific Revolution* (Cambridge: Cambridge University Press, 1981), p. 408, notes that Hobbes and More claimed that the idea of space cannot be thought away.

3. Cf. J. E. McGuire, "Newton on Place, Time, and God: An Unpublished Source," *British Journal for the History of Science* 11 (1978): 114–29, 116; Newton, "De gravitatione," in *Unpublished Scientific Papers*, p. 104. For later developments of the issue with relation to Clarke's critics, see J. P. Ferguson, *The Philosophy of Dr. Samuel Clarke and Its Critics* (New York: Vantage Press, 1974). See also Voltaire's *The Elements of Sir Isaac Newton's Philosophy*, trans. J. Hanna (1738; reprint, London: Cass, 1967), pp. 180–81.

4. Cf. Newton, "De gravitatione," in *Unpublished Scientific Papers*, pp. 100–105.

5. See G.S. Kirk and J.E. Raven, *The Presocratic Philosophers* (Cambridge: Cambridge University Press, 1983), p. 408.

6. G. Berkeley, *De Motu* § 53, in *Berkeley's Philosophical Writings*, ed. D. M. Armstrong (New York: Collier Books, 1965), p. 266. Leibniz implied that the void is a mere nothingness because its proportion of perfection to that of matter is like that of nothing to something; see Lz IV, *post scriptum*.

7. Newton also points out less controversial positive qualities such as tridimensionality; moreover, and to the extent it is identified with the space of geometry, space also has the properties discovered by geometrical theorems. See Newton. "De gravitatione," in *Unpublished Scientific Papers*, pp.101–2.

8. McGuire. "Newton on Place, Time, and God," 116.

9. Cf. Newton, "De gravitatione," in *Unpublished Scientific Papers*, p. 101.

10. J. Locke, *An Essay Concerning Human Understanding*, ed. P. H. Nidditch (Oxford: Clarendon Press, 1979), bk. 2, chap. 13, sec. 21; see also Newton. "De gravitatione," in *Unpublished Scientific Papers*, pp. 101–2, where Newton uses geometrical figures instead of hands or sticks. For a general discussion, see R. Sorabji, *Matter, Space, and Motion: Theories in Antiquity and Their Sequel* (Ithaca: Cornell University Press, 1988), pp. 125–41, 160–63. The objection was Alexander of Aphrodisia's: see Sorabji, ibid., pp. 126–28.

11. Newton, "De gravitatione," in *Unpublished Scientific Papers*, p. 105; NP I, definition 8, scholium, 47.

12. Grant, *Much Ado about Nothing*, pp. 227, 231. See also A. Koyré, *From the Closed World to the Infinite Universe* (Baltimore: Johns Hopkins University Press, 1957), chap. 8.

13. NP I, definition 8, scholium, passim; in "De gravitatione," in *Unpublished Scientific Papers*, p. 137, the invariability of space is deduced from God's immutability.

14. See P. Bayle, *Dictionnaire historique et critique* (Paris: Editions sociales, 1974), s.v. Leucippus, n. G; C. Maclaurin, *An Account of Sir Isaac Newton's Philosophical Discoveries* (London, 1748), p. 77.

15. To Caroline, 12 May 1716, R 76; Lz IV, *post scriptum*; C. I. Gerhardt, "Zu Leibniz's Dynamik," *Archiv für Geschichte der Philosophie* I (1888): 566–81, 580, quoted in D. Bertoloni Meli, "Leibniz on the Censorship of the Copernican System," *Studia Leibniziana* 20 (1988): 19–42, 25.

16. See G. A. Hartz and J. A. Cover, "Space and Time in the Leibnizian Metaphysic," *Nous* 22 (1988): 493–519.

17. Presumably, the numerical analogue of points and instants in the unity/proper fraction example would be infinitesimal.

18. This issue will be developed shortly. On continuity, see F. Schmidt, "Ganzes und Teil bei Leibniz," *Archiv für Geschichte der Philosophie* 53 (1971): 267–78, especially 273–75; E. Giusti, "Immagini del Continuo," in *L'Infinito in Leibniz: Problemi e Terminologia,* ed. A. Lamarra (Roma: Edizioni dell'Ateneo, 1986), pp. 3–32; H. Breger, "Das Kontinuum bei Leibniz," ibid., 53–67; A. Lamarra, "Leibniz on Locke on Infinity," ibid., 173–92; B. Russell, *A Critical Exposition of the Philosophy of Leibniz* (London: Allen & Unwin, 1937), chap. 9.

19. At GM VI, 99, however, motion is taken to be a continuum.

20. As Leibniz pointed out earlier in the paragraph, there is no need to assume that bodies preserve their distance relations as long as we can determine some law governing their movements. See also NE II, 14, 16.

21. On Leibniz's construction of the notion of space, see C. D. Broad, "Leibniz's Last Controversy with the Newtonians," in *Leibniz: Metaphysics and Philosophy of Science,* ed. R. S. Woolhouse (Oxford: Oxford University Press 1981), pp.157–74; A. T. Winterbourne, "On the Metaphysics of Leibnizian Space and Time," *Studies in History and Philosophy of Science* 13 (1982): 201–14; E. J. Khamara, "Leibniz's Theory of Space: A Reconstruction," *The Philosophical Quarterly* 43 (1993): 472–88; R. T. W. Arthur, "Space and Relativity in Newton and Leibniz," *British Journal for the Philosophy of Science,* 45 (1994): 220–40, especially 235–38, where Arthur correctly notices that Leibniz's construction of space involves the use of counterfactuals.

22. I get the first notion from Rescher's "Leibniz and the Plurality of Space-Time Frameworks," in N. Rescher, *Leibniz's Metaphysics of Nature* (Dordrecht: D. Reidel Publishing, 1981), pp. 85–100. Rescher, however, does not consider the second and with Clarke takes the third to embody the notion of space in any particular world (Cl III, 2). The difference between the second and third notion did not escape the anonymous *Acta Eruditorum* reviewer (probably Wolff) of the 1717 Clarke edition of the correspondence: see the October issue for the year 1717, pp. 442, 443.

23. In the *New Essays,* Leibniz pointed out that a temporal vacuum, in contrast to a spatial one, is unobservable in principle (NE II, 15, 11). Although this provides an extra reason for holding that a temporal vacuum does not exist, it is not sufficient to support the conclusion that it cannot possibly exist.

24. Cf.: "Two are the requisites for the continuum: first that any two of its parts which together are equipollent [aequantes] with it have something in common which, however, is not a part; second, that there be *partes extra partes,* as it is commonly said, that is, that one can take two of its parts (which together are not equipollent with it) which have nothing in common, not even a minimum" (*Prota,* GM V, 184). One can argue that for Leibniz a continuous interval is what we consider a closed connected interval: see E. Giusti, "Immagini del Continuo," in *L'Infinito in Leibniz: Problemi e Terminologia,* pp. 25–26.

25. "Things are continuous . . . if their limits are one; contiguous if their limits are together; successive if they have nothing of the same nature as themselves between them" (*Physics* bk. 6, chap. 1, 231a); see also bk. 5, chap. 3, 227a, both in *Aristotle: The Basic Works*, ed. R. McKeon (New York: Random House, 1970), pp. 307–8.

26. See Giusti, "Immagini del Continuo," in *L'Infinito in Leibniz*, especially pp. 28–30.

27. On the issue of Leibnizian infinitesimals, H. J. Bos. "Differentials, Higher Order Differentials and the Derivative in the Leibnizian Calculus," *Archive for History of Exact Sciences* 14 (1974):1–90; M. Horvath, "On the Attempts Made by Leibniz to Justify his Calculus," *Studia Leibnitiana* 28 (1986): 60–71.

28. On this, see G. Mc Donald Ross, "Are There Real Infinitesimals in Leibniz's Metaphysics?" in *L'Infinito in Leibniz: Problemi e Terminologia*, pp.125–41.

29. See B. Mates, *The Philosophy of Leibniz: Metaphysics and Language* (Oxford: Oxford University Press, 1986), pp. 230–31, for some of the problems involved in Leibniz's extension of the notion of simultaneity to the states of different substances; R. McRae, "Time and the Monad," *Nature and System* 1 (1979): 103–9; R. T. W. Arthur. "Leibniz's Theory of Time," in *The Natural Philosophy of Leibniz*, ed. K. Okruhlik and J.M. Brown (Dordrecht: Reidel Publishing, 1985), pp. 263–313. For Leibniz's handling, such as it is, of the direction of time see his letter to Bourguet, 5 August 1715: GP III, 582.

30. See, for example, B. Russell, *The Principles of Mathematics*, (1903; reprint, New York: Norton, 1938), sec. 442; R. Swinburne, "Tensed Facts," *American Philosophical Quarterly* 27 (1990): 117–30.

31. See R. Le Poidevin and M. MacBeath, eds., *The Philosophy of Time* (Oxford: Oxford University Press, 1993), p. 6. For a quasi-Leibnizian construction of time, see G. Forbes, "Time, Events and Modality," ibid., pp. 80–95, and R. Le Poidevin, "Relationism and Temporal Topology: Physics or Metaphysics?" ibid., pp. 149–67. Both Forbes and Le Poidevin incorrectly take Leibniz to construct time out of actual events only.

32. On the obscure issue of continual preservation and its relationship to duration and the monad, see J. Jalabert, *La theorie leibnizienne de la substance* (Paris: Presses Universitaires de France, 1947), pp. 126–78; J. E. McGuire, "Labirinthus Continui: Leibniz on Substance, Activity, and Matter," in *Motion and Time, Space and Matter*, ed. P. K. Machamer and R. G. Turnbull (Columbus: Ohio State University Press, 1976), pp. 290–326.

33. On historical antecedents, see J. Jalabert, *La theorie leibnizienne*, p. 120, and R. Sorabji, *Time, Creation and the Continuum*, (Ithaca: Cornell University Press, 1983) pp. 79–80; 236–8.

34. Perhaps Clarke became suspicious of Leibniz's views on the issue when he read in the *Theodicy* § 195: GP VI, 232, that "the universe must extend through all future eternity."

35. McGuire, "Newton on Place, Time, and God,"114–29, especially 118. One might think that Newton's millenarist views and his beliefs about the periodical renovation of the solar system would clearly support the idea of an infinite succession of worlds. But the solar system is not the world. On these issues, see D. Kubrin. "Newton and the Cyclical Cosmos: Providence and the Mechanical Philosophy," *Journal of the History of Ideas* 28 (1967): 325–46; P. Kerzsberg, "The Cosmological Question in Newton's Science," *Osiris* 2 (1986): 69–106.

36. See also the letter to Bourguet of 5 August 1715: GP III, 582–83.

37. Here Leibniz was perhaps influenced by Saint Augustine's *Confessions*, bk. 2, chap. 11 in *Confessions*, trans. R. S. Pine-Coffin (Harmondsworth: Penguin Books, 1961), pp. 261–62. The original source might be Aristotle's *Physics*, bk. 4, chap. 11 in *Aristotle: The Basic Works*, pp. 290–93.

38. On this, see Sorabji. *Time, Creation and the Continuum*, pp. 1–63.

39. Aristotle, *Physics*, bk. 4, chap. 11 in *Aristotle: The Basic Works*, pp. 290–93. On this, see G. E. L. Owen. "Aristotle on Time," in *Logic, Science and Dialectic*, ed. M. Nussbaum (Ithaca: Cornell University Press, 1986), pp. 295–314, especially 309–10.

40. See R. Laymon, "Newton's Bucket Experiment," *Journal of the History of Philosophy* 16 (1978): 399–413; H. Stein, "Some Philosophical Prehistory of General Relativity," in *Foundations of Space-Time Theories*, ed. J. Earman, C. Glymour, J. J. Stachel (Minneapolis: Minnesota University Press, 1977), pp. 3–49; in particular, J. Earman, *World Enough and Space-Time* (Cambridge, Mass.: MIT Press, 1989), chap. 4 contains an account of reactions to the bucket experiment, and J. B. Babour, *Absolute or Relative Motion?* (Cambridge: Cambridge University Press, 1989), vol. 1, develops a long historical account of the issues surrounding the topic.

41. Earman, *World Enough and Space-Time*, p. 13, points out that the participants in the classical debates on absolute rotation assumed reasonably but wrongly that absolute motion presupposes absolute space.

42. Newton. "De gravitatione," in *Unpublished Scientific Papers*, p. 96. J. B. Babour, in *Absolute or Relative Motion?* vol. 1, pp. 399 ff., notes Galileo's use of the term "absolute motion" in his (faulty) explanation of the tides as caused by the composition of the rotation and revolution of the earth in the fourth day of the *Dialogo*.

43. On this complex issue, in addition to Stein, "Some Philosophical Prehistory of General Relativity," and Earman, *World Enough and Space-Time*, see H. R. Bernstein, "Leibniz and Huygens on the 'Relativity' of Motion," in *Leibniz Dynamica*, ed. A. Heinekamp, Studia Leibnitiana Supplementa 13, (Wiesbaden: F. Steiner, 1984), pp. 85–102, and Babour, *Absolute or Relative Motion?* vol. 1, pp. 672–75 .

44. See D. Bertoloni Meli, *Equivalence and Priority: Newton versus Leibniz* (Oxford: Clarendon Press, 1993) p. 224, notes.

45. The same point can be made with respect to bodies hitting each other with any sort of motion (*Specimen Dynamicum*: GM VI, 248).

46. From this he inferred the need of force as the cause of change of position.

47. On this, see I. Hacking. "Why Motion is only a well-founded Phenomenon," in *The Natural Philosophy of Leibniz*, pp. 131–50. For such use of PSR in Leibniz, see Mates, *The Philosophy of Leibniz: Metaphysics and Language*, p. 156; for Clarke's, see W II, 531.

48. See also *Dynamica de Potentia*: GM VI, 341–45. The idea of the primacy of rectilinear uniform motion can be found in Descartes's *Le Monde*, in *Oeuvres de Descartes*, ed. C. Adam and P. Tannery (1897–1913; reprint, Paris: J. Vrin, 1964–76), vol. 11, pp. 43, 49. For a discussion, see A. Koyré, *Newtonian Studies* (Cambridge, Mass: MIT Press, 1965), pp. 74 ff.

49. The point is made by Bertoloni Meli, *Equivalence and Priority*, pp. 78–83.

50. The point is made in ibid., pp. 83–4.

51. See ibid., p. 83.

52. See, for example, Russell, *A Critical Exposition of the Philosophy of Leibniz*, § 41; Stein, "Some Philosophical Prehistory of General Relativity," p. 31.

53. Lz V, 47; GP IV, 369; Gerhardt, "Zu Leibniz's Dynamik," 580; *Discourse on Metaphysics* §18: GP IV, 444=L 315; to Huygens 12/22 June 1694, in C. I. Gerhardt, ed., *Der Briefwechsel von G. W. Leibniz mit Mathematikern* (Berlin, 1899), p. 738. On this, see G. H. R. Parkinson, "Science and Metaphysics in the Leibniz-Newton Controversy," in Studia Leibnitiana Supplementa 2 (Wiesbaden: F. Steiner, 1969), pp. 79–112, especially pp. 105–7.

54. This is the theological version of Cleomedes's argument: see R. Sorabji, *Matter, Space, and Motion*, pp. 129–31; for a discussion of its medieval versions and its importance after the condemnation in 1277 in emphasizing the *potentia Dei absoluta*, see Grant, *Much Ado about Nothing*.

55. See NP, Laws of Motion, corollary 6, 64. See Ferguson, *The Philosophy of Dr. Samuel Clarke*, pp. 45–46; Arthur, "Space and Relativity in Newton and Leibniz," 220–40, especially 225.

56. The reference to logarithms is probably based on the fact that $\log a/b = \log a - \log b$.

57. For a discussion of the issues, see E. Sylla, "Compounding Ratios: Bradwardine, Oresme, and the First Edition of Newton's *Principia*," in *Transformation and Tradition in the Sciences*, ed. E. Mendelson (Cambridge: Cambridge University Press, 1984), pp. 11–43, especially pp. 28–35.

58. See also Cl IV, 41. A similar point was made by L. Euler in a 1748 paper, "Reflexions sur l'espace et le tems," *Mémoires de l'académie des sciences de Berlin* (1748): 324–33; reprinted in *Leonhardi Euleri Opera Omnia* (Leipzig and Berlin: Teubner, 1911), third series, vol. 2, pp. 376–83, especially pp. 382–83.

Chapter 5: Miracles and Nature

1. B. Spinoza, *Tractatus Theologico-Politicus*, chap. 6, in *Opera*, ed. C. Gebhardt (Heidelberg: C. Winters, 1925), vol. 3, pp. 82 ff.

2. On the English scene, see R. M. Burns, *The Great Debate on Miracles: from Joseph Glanville to David Hume* (Lewisburg, Penn.: Bucknell University Press, 1980), chap. 2. Burns convincingly argues that the epistemological view that lay great stress on probable judgments as the only ones attainable by humans in the investigation of the natural world, and which was held by many prominent thinkers associated with the Royal Society, favored the acceptance of miracles and their evidential role in the establishment of Christianity. It would be interesting, but beyond the scope of this chapter, to compare Clarke's views with Hobbes's and Locke's; see T. Hobbes's *Leviathan*, ed. C. B. Macpherson (New York: Penguin Books, 1968), chap. 37 and J. Locke's *Discourse on Miracles*, in *The Works of John Locke* (1823; reprint, Aarlen: Scientia Verlag, 1963), vol. 9, pp. 256–66. On the Continent, during the period 1684–87, there was an acrimonious exchange on the nature of miracles between Malebranche and Arnauld.

3. On the issue of theological voluntarism and the laws of nature, see F. Oakley, *Omnipotence, Covenant and Order* (Ithaca: Cornell University Press, 1984), especially chaps. 3 and 4, the latter of which also deals with related political theories; A. Funkenstein, *Theology and the Scientific Imagination* (Princeton: Princeton University Press, 1986), chap. 3. If the laws of nature are but divine volitions causally independent of the divine understanding, and space is infinite while the world is finite, then the hypothesis that God has created different worlds with different laws of nature in different parts of space is, to put it with Newton, neither "incoherent" nor "in conflict with reason" (NO *quaestio* 23, 347). In fairness, however, one should point out that the context does not clarify whether Newton is talking about *potentia ordinata* or *potentia absoluta*.

4. For Suarez's contribution, see C. Wilson, "*De Ipsa Natura*: Sources of Leibniz's Doctrines of Force, Activity and Natural Law," *Studia Leibnitiana* 19 (1987): 148–72, and E. Zilsel, "The Genesis of the Concept of Physical Law," *The Philosophical Review* 51 (1942): 245–79.

5. See Boyle: "But to speak strictly, to say, that the nature of this or that body is but the law of God prescribed to it, is but an improper and figurative expression: for, . . . a law being but a notional rule of acting according to the declared will of a superior, it is plain that nothing but an intellectual Being can be properly capable of receiving and acting by a law. For it does not understand, it cannot know what the will of the legislator is; nor can it act with regard to it, or know when it does in acting either conform to it or deviate from it." *A Free Enquiry into the Vulgarly Received Notion of Nature*, in *Works of the Honourable Robert Boyle*, ed. T. Birch (1744; reprint, Hildesheim: Georg Olms, 1965), vol. 4, p. 367. On Boyle's attempt to refute hylozoism, see J. R. Jacob, "Boyle's Atomism and the Restoration

Assault on Pagan Naturalism," *Social Studies of Science* 8 (1978): 211–33. For Clarke, matter is a "solid substance capable of division, figure and motion, and whatever properties can arise from the modification of these" (WB 561).

6. Clarke's wording at W II, 697–98, quoted above, is strongly reminiscent of Malebranche's account in *Traité de la Nature et de la Grace*, first elucidation, sec. 3: "properly speaking, what we call 'Nature' is nothing else but the general laws which God has established to construct and conserve his work." See N. Malebranche, *Oeuvres complètes*, ed. A. Robinet (Paris: J. Vrin, 1958–60), vol. 5, p. 148. The view that matter is inactive and all its alleged activities are nothing but God's ordinary operations is to be found in Augustine, who may have inspired Malebranche. For Augustine's views on the issue, see *The Essential Augustine*, ed. and trans. V. J. Bourke (Indianapolis: Hackett Publishing, 1981), pp. 115–16. Augustine, like Clarke, also believed that miracles must be unusual events (ibid., p.116).

7. Clarke's critique of Malebranche and LeClerc is briefly considered by P. Casini, who in *L'universo macchina: Origini della filosofia newtoniana* (Bari: Laterza, 1969), pp. 189–90 gives a quotation from Clarke's 1697 edition of Rohault's *Physics*. Casini points out that Clarke's note was incorporated into a longer one in the 1702 edition. However, in the 1710 edition the note was eliminated, possibly a signal of Clarke's changing ideas on the issue. In the first *Enquiry*, Hume attributed to Clarke the view that matter has "real though subordinate and derived power." See D. Hume, *Enquiries Concerning Human Understanding and Concerning the Principles of Morals*, ed. L. A. Selby-Bigge and P. H. Nidditch (Oxford: Clarendon Press, 1978), p. 73 n. 1. The topic of the relationship between Clarke and Occasionalism has been neglected; C. J. McCracken's *Malebranche and British Philosophy* (Oxford: Oxford University Press, 1983) devotes almost no attention to it.

8. For Boyle: *Works of the Honourable Robert Boyle*, vol. 5, p. 46; for Locke: *An Essay Concerning Human Understanding* ed. P. H. Nidditch (Oxford: Clarendon Press, 1979) bk. 4, chap. 10, sec. 10; for Descartes: *Principia Philosophiae*, part 2, proposition 36, in *Oeuvres de Descartes*, ed. C. Adam and P. Tannery (1897–1913; reprint, Paris: J. Vrin, 1964–76), vol. 9B, p. 61; for Gassendi: *Opera Omnia in sex tomos* (1658; reprint, Stuttgart-Bad Canstatt: F. Fromann, 1964), vol. 1, pp. 336–37; on this, see O. R. Bloch, *La Philosophie de Gassendi: nominalisme, materialisme, et metaphysique* (La Haye: M. Nijhoff, 1971), pp. 210–20.

9. On the general issue of the reduction of nature from a living thing to a conglomerate of lifeless particles, see C. Merchant, *The Death of Nature* (San Francisco: Harper and Row, 1980); on the difficulties of mechanism and the introduction of active powers, see A. Gabbey, "The Mechanical Philosophy and its Problems: Mechanical Explanations, Impenetrability, and Perpetual Motion," in *Change and Progress in Modern Science*, ed. J. C. Pitt (Dordrecht: D. Reidel Publishing, 1985), pp. 9–84, and J. Henry, "Occult

Qualities and the Experimental Philosophy: Active Principles in Pre-Newtonian Matter Theory," *History of Science* 24 (1986): 335–81. For Newton, see, for example, NO *quaestio* 23, passim; E. Mc Mullin, *Newton on Matter and Activity* (Notre Dame, Ind.: University of Notre Dame Press, 1978); J. E. McGuire, "Force, Active Principles, and Newton's Invisible Realm," *Ambix* 15 (1968): 154–208. The related issue of gravitation will be discussed in the last chapter.

10. J. Toland, *Letters to Serena* (1704; reprint, Stuttgart-Bad Cannstatt: F. Fromann, 1964), letter 5. Serena was Sophie Charlotte, Leibniz's patron pupil and friend who was to die only a year later, in 1705. Clarke was right in singling out Toland; P. H. D'Holbach, in *Systeme de la nature, ou des lois du monde physique et du monde moral* (1821; reprint, Hildsheim: Georg Olms, 1966), book 1, chap. 2, referred to "the celebrated Toland" as having "conclusively established" that "the essence of matter is to act." On Toland, see C. Giuntini, *Panteismo e Ideologia Repubblicana: John Toland (1670–1722)* (Bologna: Il Mulino, 1979). On the issue of the inertness of matter in eighteenth century English thought, see J. W. Yolton, *Thinking Matter: Materialism in Eighteenth Century Britain* (Minneapolis: University of Minnesota Press, 1983), chaps. 5 and 6.

11. William Wotton, in *A Letter to Eusebia: Occasioned by Mr. Toland's Letters to Serena*, published in 1704, claimed that "the only reason why Mr. Toland finds fault with Spinoza, is, for asserting that there is only one substance in the universe, and at the same time not allowing it to be self-moving. . . . What Mr. Toland therefore superadds to Spinoza's scheme is this. He makes motion to be essential to matter; i.e., he makes matter to be self-moving; whereby we may suppose that he intends to supply all the defects of Spinoza's thesis: i.e., make the world without God." On this, see R. L. Colie, "Spinoza and the Early English Deists," *Journal of the History of Ideas* 20 (1959): 23–46, from which I have taken Wotton's quotation.

12. For the Lord God, NP III, general scholium, 760; on this, J. E. Force, "Newton's God of Dominion: The Unity of Newton's Theological, Scientific, and Political Thought," in *Essays on the Context, Nature and Influence of Isaac Newton's Theology*, ed. J. E. Force and R. H. Popkin (Dordrecht: Kluwer Academic Publishers, 1990), pp. 75–102, especially pp. 84–85.

13. See also, *A New System of the Nature and Communication of Substances* § 13: GP IV, 483–84=L 457; *Theodicy* § 207: GP VI, 240–41.

14. For a brief account, see D. Radner, *Malebranche* (Assen: Van Gorcum, 1978), pp. 36–39.

15. N. Malebranche, *Oeuvres complètes*, vol. 8, p. 696. On this, see M. Gueroult, *Malebranche* (Paris: Aubier, 1955–59), vol. 2, p. 243, and R. C. Sleigh, *Leibniz and Arnauld: A Commentary on their Correspondence* (New Haven: Yale University Press, 1990), p. 154.

16. See also letter to Arnauld, 30 April 1687: GP II, 93; GP IV, 587.

17. Less successful is Leibniz's attempt to marshal the data of inner experience against Malebranche's view, since it is open to Malebranche to

reply, as Hume was to do, that we do not experience the power whereby we produce our thoughts any more than we perceive the power whereby we move our body. See N. Malebranche, *Oeuvres complètes*, vol. 3, pp. 227–28, and *The Search after Truth*, trans. T. M. Lennon and J. Olscamp (Columbus: Ohio State University Press, 1980), elucidation 15, p. 670.

18. *Theodicy* § 393. GP VI, 350–51; *Reponse aux reflexions . . . de M. Bayle . . .* GP IV, 568=L 583; *Entretien de Philarete et d'Ariste*: GP VI, 579=L 554. Sleigh, *Leibniz and Arnauld*, p.134, correctly argues that for Leibniz the diachronic identity condition for a substance is that at any moment some of its states be caused by some of its previous states. Since for Malebranche creatures have no real causal history, they do not persist through time and end up by looking very much like accidents. See also R. C. Sleigh's "Leibniz on Malebranche on Causality," in *Central Themes in Early Modern Philosophy*, ed. J. Cover and M. Kulstad (Indianapolis: Hackett Publishing, 1990), p. 161–93. For an analysis of some of Leibniz's other criticisms of Malebranche's views on miracles, see Sleigh, *Leibniz and Arnauld*, p. 162–64; R. S. Woolhouse, "Leibniz and Occasionalism," in *Metaphysics and Philosophy of Science in the Seventeenth and Eighteenth Centuries*, ed. R. Woolhouse (Dordrecht: Kluwer Academic Press, 1988), pp. 165–83, especially pp. 165–71; R. S. Woolhouse, *Descartes, Spinoza and Leibniz: The Concept of Substance in Seventeenth Century Metaphysics* (London: Routledge, 1993), chap. 7; D. Rutherford, "Natures, Laws and Miracles: the Roots of Leibniz's Critique of Occasionalism," in *Causation in Early Modern Philosophy*, ed. S. Nadler (University Park: Pennsylvania State University Press, 1993), pp. 135–58.

19. For this criticism, see R. Mc Rae, "Miracles and Laws," in *The Natural Philosophy of Leibniz*, ed. K. Okruhlik and J. B. Brown (Dordrecht: D. Reidel Publishing, 1985), pp. 171–81, especially p. 178.

20. *Discourse on Metaphysics* § 7: GP 427–63=L 303–31. See also *Eclaircissement des difficultés que M. Bayle . . .* :GP IV, 520=L 494. I do not claim that Leibniz always and clearly adopted this view, but I think that he adopted it frequently enough to allow one to consider it a significant component of his thought. For a related point, see D. Rutherford, *Leibniz and the Rational Order of Nature* (Cambridge: Cambridge University Press, 1995), pp. 243–44.

21. See N. Malebranche, *Dialogues on Metaphysics*, trans. W. Doney (New York: Abaris Book, 1980), chap. 7, §§ 11–12; M. Gueroult, *Malebranche*, vol. 2, pp. 247–48.

22. There is a serious complication. The essence E determines more than the class of modifications. It also determines the class C of predicates that are compatible with it, and among which God can choose those that are involved in miracles. One may wonder whether natures could be grounded in C rather than in its subset S, whose elements are modifications. Leibniz's answer seems to have been negative, as the final part of his draft for a reply to Lamy (quoted above) intimates. However, it is dubious that

this answer is compatible with divine omnipotence together with the fact
that God creates the natures of things. In other words, God could create a
world in which what is within the powers of creatures is a subset of what
is miraculous in the actual world. If this analysis is correct, Leibniz's point
that Occasionalism is unable to distinguish between proper and arbitrary
laws of nature can be turned against him. Leibniz, I believe, would have
replied that ultimately it is God's benevolence that leads to the creation of
natures grounded in modifications, which are consequently tied with intelligible laws of nature. But an analogous reply, based on God's attributes and
criteria of order and proportion, had been provided by Malebranche as well.
On this issue, as on many others, Malebranche's system seems to have been
much more resilient than Leibniz thought or pretended to think.

23. *Discourse on Metaphysics* § 6: GP IV, 431–32=L 306; see also *Theodicy* § 242: GP VI, 261–62.

24. G. Berkeley, *A Treatise Concerning the Principles of Human
Knowledge*, part 1, sec. 16, in *Berkeley's Philosophical Writings*, ed. D. M.
Armstrong (New York: Collier Books, 1965), p. 67.

25. J. Locke, *An Essay concerning Human Understanding*, bk. 4, chap.
3, sec. 6.

26. Locke, second reply to Stillingfleet, in *The Works of John Locke*,
vol. 4, pp. 467–68. For Leibniz's comments, see NE preface, 60–68. See also
N. Jolley, *Leibniz and Locke: A Study of the "New Essays on Human Understanding"* (Oxford: Clarendon Press, 1984), chap. 4.

27. See also NE IV, 3, 6 for a forceful statement of the same point.

28. Bayle too read Locke's theory of substance as Leibniz did: J. S. Whitmore, "Bayle's Criticism of Locke," in *Pierre Bayle: Le Philosophe de Rotterdam*, ed. Dibon (Amsterdam: Elsevier, 1959), pp. 81–97, especially pp.
84–86.

29. Of course, it is possible that Leibniz did not do full justice to Locke's
position on substance. On this, see Jolley, *Leibniz and Locke*, chap. 5.

30. Of course, had Locke known Leibniz's criticism, he would probably
have been less than impressed. For one thing, he, like Clarke, considered
rarity an essential characteristic of miracles. See Locke, *The Works*, vol. 9,
pp. 256–65. It may be worth noticing that Locke criticized the view that
miracles are to be defined as operations beyond the powers of creatures; see
especially pp. 263–64. Leibniz's two accounts of miracles can be linked
through the idea that a miracle does not agree with the order of nature. For
the order of nature is given by the laws of nature, that is, by God's general
volitions. But as Leibniz claimed in his criticism of Occasionalism, God's
volitions impart the force that constitutes the substance of things. It follows,
then, that what can in principle be accomplished through the force of creatures is determined by God's general volitions, namely, it is what can be
covered by the laws of nature, that is, what pertains to the order of nature,
and consequently, because of God's benevolence, is intelligible.

31. We know now that the anonymous account was by Newton him-

self. It is now in the appendix of R. Hall, *Philosophers at War: The Quarrel between Leibniz and Newton* (Cambridge: Cambridge University Press, 1980). For Newton's comments on Leibniz's and his own methods, see pp. 312–14.

32. Leibniz viewed excessive appeal to miracles, or what in his mind amounted to the same thing, to God's arbitrary decisions as a refuge of ignorance (NE preface, 66).

33. The point was also made at WN 697. For Newton as well, rarity is a necessary condition for miracles: see his letter to Conti of 26 February 1716 (R 63).

34. This was Newton's view as well (Newton to Conti, 16 February 1716: NC VI, 285–86=R 63).

35. See also WN 698.

36. Leibniz's view of miracles was quite similar to Aquinas's: *Summa Theologiae* (New York: Mc Graw-Hill, 1970), part 1, question 110, article 4, body; *Summa Contra Gentiles* (Turin: Marietti, 1961), bk. 3, chap. 102. The stone example is from Aquinas, but can be found in Clarke as well.

37. It is clear from Leibniz's letter to Caroline of the end of November 1715 that he had read Clarke's letter to Dodwell and his replies to Collins's defense of Dodwell (KLC 60–1=R 32). In the same letter he also said he read another book by Clarke, almost certainly one, or possibly both, of Clarke's Boyle Lectures.

38. The beginning of this passage was mistranslated by Clarke; whereas Leibniz spoke of an "infinite [*infinie*] difference" between the natural and the supernatural, Clarke's translation reads "vast difference."

39. See also WB 562. The point is made by J. P. Ferguson, *The Philosophy of Dr. Samuel Clarke and Its Critics* (New York: Vantage Press, 1974), p. 249. On the issue of substance, Newton shared at least some of Clarke's views; for example, in NP III, General Scholium, 763, in a passage perhaps showing Clarke's influence, he claimed that we do not know the substance of anything.

40. Caroll's book was, *Remarks upon Mr. Clarke's Sermons, Preached at St. Paul's against Hobbes, Spinoza and other Atheists* (London, 1704).

41. The two passages are from *Specimen Dynamicum*: GM VI, 234–54-L 434–52.

42. The passage is from the *Theodicy* § 291: GP VI, 189–90.

43. We shall address the topic of the nature and conservation of quantity of motion in the last chapter.

44. The importance of the issue of the activity of matter in the Correspondence has been clearly pointed out by S. Shapin in "Of Gods and Kings: Natural Philosophy and Politics in the Leibniz-Clarke Disputes," *Isis* 72 (1981):187–215, who, however, is not aware of Clarke's remarks in *A Demonstration* or in *The Philosophical Transactions*. Moreover, like Clarke he seems to think that Leibniz did hold that matter is "ultimately active and sentient" (196). The view that for Leibniz each part of matter is ensouled

was repeated in C. MacLaurin's *An Account of Sir Isaac Newton's Philosophical Discoveries* (London, 1748), p. 82. Apparently, Locke too had expressed interest in Leibniz's alleged view that all matter is animate; see Jolley, *Leibniz and Locke*, p. 38.

Chapter 6: Matter and Force

1. For a similar argument, see M. A. Voltaire, *The Elements of Sir Isaac Newton's Philosophy*, trans. J. Hanna (1738; reprint, London: Cass, 1967), chap. 17; Craig, in a memorandum composed after Newton's death, noted that Newton considered Cartesianism a vehicle deliberately constructed for atheism: R. S. Westfall, "The Problem of Force: Huygens, Newton, Leibniz," in *Leibniz's Dynamica*, ed. A. Heinekamp, Studia Leibnitiana Supplementa 13 (Wiesbaden: F. Steiner 1984), pp. 71–84, especially p. 79. For the claim that Cartesianism led to Spinozism, a view Leibniz shared, see C. Maclaurin's *An Account of Sir Isaac Newton's Philosophical Discoveries* (London, 1748), pp. 74–78.

2. Augustine, *The City of God*. trans. J. Healey (London: Dutton, 1973), bk. 10, chap. 31; Aquinas. *Summa Theologiae*. (New York: Mc Graw-Hill Book Company, 1970), 1st part, question 46, article 2. The issue of the eternity of the world was a source of intense controversy in the thirteenth century.

3. On the link between atomism and Newton's third rule of philosophizing, see J. E. McGuire, "Atoms and the Analogy of Nature: Newton's Third Rule of Philosophizing," *Studies in History and Philosophy of Science* 1 (1970): 3–58.

4. On Leibniz and atomism, see R. Bregman, "Leibniz and Atomism," *Nature and System* 6 (1984): 237–48; C. Wilson, "Leibniz and Atomism," *Studies in History and Philosophy of Science* 13 (1982): 175–99.

5. The same argument shows that there is no undifferentiated plenum.

6. Aristotle, *De Generatione et Corruptione* bk. 1, chap. 8, 325b6–12 in *Aristotle: The Basic Works*, ed. R. McKeon (New York: Random House, 1970), p. 499.

7. Voltaire, *The Elements of Sir Isaac Newton's Philosophy*, chap. 10, pp. 110–11. Voltaire rather rashly was ready to talk, like Bernoulli a generation earlier, of the infinitieth term of the infinite progression, but his argument does not rest on this mistake.

8. On this, see H. Guerlac, "Newton's Optical Aether: His Draft of a Proposed Addition to His Opticks," in *Essays and Papers in the History of Modern Science*, ed. H. Guerlac (Baltimore: Johns Hopkins University Press, 1977), pp. 120–30.

9. For some references available to both Leibniz and Clarke, see P. Bayle, *Dictionnaire historique et critique* (Paris: Editions sociales, 1974), s.v. Leucippus n. G.

10. In the 1687 edition, this was at the end of section 7.

11. See Leibniz's comment in D. Bertoloni Meli, *Equivalence and Priority: Newton versus Leibniz* (Oxford: Clarendon Press, 1993), pp. 98–99, where Leibniz remarks on Newton's claim (eliminated in the second and third edition) in book 3, proposition 6, corollary 3, that "Therefore the vacuum is necessarily given." For other Newtonian reasons for the vacuum based on the motion of planets and comets, which an all-pervasive fluid would impede, see query 20, NO 309–10; for one based on the fall of bodies, see NP III, 6, corollary 3. In the seventh edition of *A Demonstration*, the last published during his lifetime, Clarke added a postscript containing the argument from fluid resistance and that from the equal falling velocity of bodies of unequal mass. The postscript was added to the text of later editions and to that contained in the 1738 edition of his collected works. See WB 532.

12. On this, see E. J. Aiton, "Leibniz on Motion in a Resisting Medium," *Archive for History of Exact Sciences* 9 (1972): 257–76.

13. On this, see W. Scott, *The Conflict between Atomism and Conservation Theory 1644–1860* (London: Macdonald & Co., 1970), chap. 1.

14. On this, see E. McMullin, *Newton on Matter and Activity* (Notre Dame, Ind.: University of Notre Dame Press, 1978).

15. On the different judgments about the physical importance of the controversy, see D. Papineau, "The *Vis Viva* Controversy," in *Leibniz: Metaphysics and Philosophy of Science*, ed. R. S. Woolhouse (Oxford: Oxford University Press, 1981), pp. 139–56, especially pp. 139–41.

16. See M. Gueroult, *Leibniz. Dynamique et Métaphysique* (Paris: Aubier-Montaigne, 1967), pp. 199–200; G. Buchdal, *Metaphysics and the Philosophy of Science: The Classical Origins Descartes to Kant* (Oxford: Basil Blackwell, 1969), p. 416; R. M. Adams, *Leibniz: Determinist, Theist, Idealist* (New York: Oxford University Press, 1994), chap. 13. The issue of the relation between *vis mortua* and *vis viva* is far from settled. For an account, see Bertoloni Meli, *Equivalence and Priority*, pp. 87–90. For a useful account of Leibniz's physics and its relation to philosophy, see D. Garber, "Leibniz: Physics and Philosophy," in *The Cambridge Companion to Leibniz*, ed. N. Jolley (Cambridge: Cambridge University Press, 1995), pp. 270–352, especially pp. 289–90.

17. For Newton, see I. B. Cohen, "Newton's Copy of Leibniz's *Theodicée*: With Some Remarks on the Turned-Down Pages of Books in Newton's Library," *Isis* 73 (1982): 410–14.

18. Some commentators have been convinced, for example A. Koyré. *Newtonian Studies* (Cambridge, Mass.: MIT Press, 1965), pp. 76–77; C. Wilson, *Leibniz's Metaphysics: A Historical and Comparative Study* (Princeton: Princeton University Press, 1989), p. 140; Adams, *Leibniz*, p. 393. For a forcefully argued opposing view, see H. R. Bernstein, "Passivity and Inertia in Leibniz's Dynamics," *Studia Leibnitiana* 13 (1981): 97–113.

19. They can be found in Bertoloni Meli, *Equivalence and Priority*, appendix 1, p. 220.

20. For a similar statement, see also *Theodicy* § 380: GP VI, 341; to De Volder, 3 April 1699: GP II, 169=L 517.

21. On this, see Bertoloni Meli, *Equivalence and Priority*, p. 30–31.

22. For a discussion of the very obscure issue of how Leibniz tried to derive inertia from the characteristics of monads, see Adams, *Leibniz*, pp. 393–95.

23. For a brief analysis of Newton's basic steps, see I. B. Cohen, "Newton's Third Law and Universal Gravity," in *Newton's Scientific and Philosophical Legacy*, ed. P. B. Schurer and G. Debrock (Dordrecht: Kluwer Academic Publishers, 1988), pp. 25–53. On Leibniz's view of his own role, see Bertoloni Meli, *Equivalence and Priority*, p. 32.

24. Leibniz made a mistake in the calculation of the centrifugal force, which he later corrected. On this, see E. J. Aiton, *The Vortex Theory of Planetary Motions* (London: MacDonald, 1972), pp. 138–39; E. J. Aiton, "The Mathematical Basis of Leibniz's Theory of Planetary Motion," in *Leibniz's Dynamica*, Studia Leibnitiana Supplementa 13 (Weisbaden: F. Steiner, 1984) pp. 209–25.

25. For other models, *De Causa Gravitatis*: GM VI, 193–203.

26. For Huygens's model, see Aiton, *The Vortex Theory of Planetary Motions*, pp. 75–78.

27. On this see Aiton, *The Vortex Theory of Planetary Motions*, pp. 133–34; Bertoloni Meli, *Equivalence and Priority*, pp.165–66.

28. Leibniz was being very polite, or more likely, like Huygens had not noticed that Newton had merely stated, but not proved, that in the presence of a centripetal inverse-square force the orbit will be a conic (NP I, 13, corollary, 125). The lack of proof was criticized by Johann Bernoulli in 1710, and the second edition (1713) of *Principia* contained an inchoate outline of the proof, which, however, Newton never provided. On this, see D. T. Whiteside's remarks in *The Mathematical Papers of Isaac Newton*, ed. D. T Whiteside (Cambridge: Cambridge University Press, 1974), vol. 6, pp. 146–49.

29. *Correspondence of Sir Isaac Newton and Professor Cotes*, ed. J. Edleston (1850; reprint, London: F. Cass, 1969), pp. 307–14; NC VI, 116–22. J. Keill's attack was published in the *Journal literaire de la Haye* in 1714. Leibniz chose not to reply and told Wolff that he did not want to deal with people like Keill, whom they considered a rude country bumpkin. For an analysis, see Aiton, "The Mathematical Basis of Leibniz's Theory of Planetary Motion," pp. 209–25.

30. *Correspondence of Sir Isaac Newton and Professor Cotes*, p. 311; NC VI, 116; Aiton, *The Vortex Theory*, p. 138.

31. This is Koyré's view, A. Koyré, *Newtonian Studies*, pp. 137–38.

32. For Huygens, see GM II, 150. For Gregory, see R. Hall, *Philosophers at War: The Quarrel between Leibniz and Newton* (Cambridge: Cambridge University Press, 1980) pp. 160–61.

33. Aiton, *The Vortex Theory*, p. 134. For more critical remarks, see C.

Maclaurin's, *An Account of Sir Isaac Newton's Philosophical Discoveries*, pp. 79–80.

34. As Bertoloni Meli dramatically puts it, "in the eighteenth century Leibniz had left Newton master of celestial mechanics" (Bertoloni Meli, *Equivalence and Priority*, p. 216).

35. The letter was for Newton, who did not take up the issue. The same point is also made in *Antibarbarus Physicus* (GP VII, 338). For the Leibniz-Newton exchange via Conti, see A. Koyré and I. B. Cohen, "Newton & the Leibniz-Clarke Correspondence," *Archives Internationales d'histoire des sciences* 15 (1962): 63–126. Leibniz had made the same point to Hartsoeker on 6 February 1711 (GP III, 518). The letter was published in the *Memoires de Trévoux* and was, of course, badly received by the Newtonians. For Newton's draft of a direct reply, see NC V, 298–300. For an account of Leibniz's critique of Newton's philosophy of science, see G. H. R. Parkinson, "Science and Metaphysics in the Leibniz-Newton Controversy," in Studia Leibnitiana Supplementa 2 (Wiesbaden: F. Steiner, 1969), pp. 79–112, especially pp. 93–96 on gravitation. See also Koyré, *Newtonian Studies*, especially the appendices to chaps. 3 and 7.

36. Newton's draft is in Koyré and Cohen, "Newton and the Leibniz-Clarke Correspondence," 70.

37. In a draft for a direct reply to Leibniz's letter to Hartsoeker, Newton expanded the point by noting that understanding how gravity determines the motions of the heavens "without knowing the cause of gravity, is as good a progress in philosophy as to understand the frame of a clock & the dependance of ye wheels upon one another without knowing the cause of the gravity of the weight whc moves the machine is in the philosophy of clockwork, or the understanding the frame of the bones & muscles & their connection in the body of an animal & how the bones are moved by the contracting or dilating of the muscles without knowing how the muscles are contracted or dilated by the power of ye mind, is [in] the philosophy of animal motion" (NC V, 300).

38. On this, see Koyré's claim that Cotes held such a view: Koyré, *Newtonian Studies*, pp.158–59. However, whether Cotes really meant what he seems to have said in the draft of the preface to the second edition of the *Principia* that he sent to Clarke is far from clear. Certainly, in a later letter to Clarke he denied ever claiming that gravity is essential to matter. See his letter of 25 June 1713 (NC V, 412–13).

39. 25 February 1693: NC III, 253–54. See also P. Casini, *L'universo-macchina: Origini della filosofia newtoniana* (Bari: Laterza, 1969), especially chaps. 2 and 4. On this and related issues, see also R. S. Westfall, *Force in Newton's Physics* (London: MacDonald and Co., 1971), p. 396. Newton at times toyed with the idea that gravity could be explained by appealing to a very subtle ether; however, R. Hall, in "Newton and the Absolutes: Sources," in *The Investigation of Difficult Things*. ed. P. M. Harman and A. E. Shapiro (Cambridge: Cambridge University Press, 1992), pp. 261–85, es-

pecially p. 282, notes that Newton's ether is not mechanistic because it must be exceedingly rare so as not to offer effective resistance to the tails of comets; hence, there must be interactive forces among its (relatively distant) particles: in short, Newtonian ether is not a Cartesian or Leibnizian one.

40. On Clarke's notes and their substantive changes in the course of the various editions, see M. A. Hoskin, "Mining All Within: Clarke's Notes to Rohault's *Traité de Physique*," *The Thomist* 24 (1961): 253–63.

41. *Jacobi Rohaulti Physica; latine vertit, recensuit et uberioribus iam Annotationibus, ex illustrissimi Isaaci Newtoni Philosophia maximam partem haustis, amplificavit et oravit S. Clarke, S. T. P.* (London, 1702), pp. 81–83: quoted in Hoskin. "Mining All Within," 359.

42. Ibid., book 1, chap. 11, sec. 15, n. 6, pp. 50–51; quoted in Hoskin, "Mining All Within," 362. The same point is also made at W III, 760, 792, 847; W II, 601. In the general scholium in the second edition of *Principia* (1713), p. 484, Newton made a similar point, which was noted by the anonymous reviewer of *Acta Eruditorum* (March 1714), p. 142, and repeated by Wolff to Leibniz (Wolff to Leibniz, 4 March 1716: NC VI, 297–98). See also Voltaire's remarks in *The Elements of Sir Isaac Newton's Philosophy*, pp. 163–64: a fluid can operate on a body only in proportion to the surface of that body, like the wind on a sail; but gravity is proportional to the mass, not the surface, of bodies. Hence, it cannot be caused by a fluid.

43. C. Huygens, *Discours sur la cause de la pesanteour*, in *Oeuvres Complétes* (La Haye: M. Nijoff, 1888–1950), vol. 21, p. 471; on this, see Koyré, *Newtonian Studies*, pp.118 ff.

44. "non utique corporeo" said Clarke. See *Jacobi Rohaulti Physica; latine vertit, recensuit et uberioribus iam Annotationibus, ex illustrissimi Isaaci Newtoni Philosophia maximam partem haustis, amplificavit et oravit S. Clarke, S. T. P.*, book I, chap. 11, sec. 15, n. 6, pp. 50–51; quoted in Hoskin, "Mining All Within," 362. One might object that at Cl V, 118–23 and 124–30, Clarke told Leibniz that philosophers may try to find the cause of gravitation, "be it *mechanical* or *not mechanical*." However, the point was merely rhetorical, since Clarke was only arguing that whatever the cause of gravitation, its existence among bodies separated by empty space is certain. Indeed, in a note appended at Cl V, 110–16, he again repeated his contention that since gravity is proportional to masses and not to surfaces it is not produced by mechanical forces.

45. For Locke, see his Second Reply to Stillingfleet, in *The Works of John Locke* (1823; reprint, Aarlen: Scientia Verlag, 1936), vol. 4, pp. 467–68; for Collins, W III, 771; for Cheyne, *Philosophical Principles of Natural Religion* (London, 1705), p. 41, quoted in Koyré, *Newtonian Studies*, p. 156.

46. Whiston, in *A New Theory of the Earth* (London, 1708), p. 284, agreed with Clarke: see J. E. Force, "Newton's God of Dominion: The Unity of Newton's Theological, Scientific, and Political Thought," in *Essays on the Context, Nature and Influence of Isaac Newton's Theology*, ed. J. E.

Force and R. H. Popkin (Dordrecht: Kluwer Academic Publishers, 1990), pp. 75–102, especially p. 85.

47. According to Leibniz, angels have bodies. The only being without a body is God. See Lz V, 61; NE preface, 58.

48. That Newton settled for a causally incomplete science in which the mathematical definition of forces and not the explanation of their causes is central is noted by R. S. Westfall, for example, in "The Problem of Force in Huygens, Newton, and Leibniz," in *Leibniz's Dynamica*, Studia Leibnitiana Supplementa 13 (Weisbaden: F. Steiner, 1984), pp. 71–84. On Newton's methodological precursors, see J. Henry, "Occult Qualities and the Experimental Philosophy: Active Principles in Pre-Newtonian Matter Theory," *History of Science* 24 (1986): 335–81, especially 358–59.

49. On Newton's belief between 1684 and 1710 that God is the direct cause of gravity and its relation to "Ancient Wisdom," especially with Platonizing Stoicism in which *pneuma* is dematerialized (a sort of world-soul), see B. J. T. Dobbs, "Newton's Alchemy and his 'Active Principle' of Gravitation," in *Newton's Scientific and Philosophical Legacy*, ed. P. B. Scheurer and G. Dobrock (Dordrecht: Kluwer Academic Publishers, 1988), pp. 55–80.

50. For Leibniz's judgment on More, see NE III, 10, 14; *De Ipsa Natura* § 2: GP IV, 504=L 498.

51. *Merckwürdige Schriften*, ed. H. Köhlern (Jena, 1720), pp. 243–65, reprinted in G. W. Leibniz and S. Clarke, *Der Leibniz-Clarke Briefwechsel*, ed. and trans. V. Schüller (Berlin: Akademie Verlag, 1991), pp. 322–38, especially p. 329.

52. Leibniz and Clarke, *Der Leibniz-Clarke Briefwechsel*, p. 329.

53. *A Defence of the late Dr. Samuel Clarke against the Reply of Sieur Lewis-Philip Thumming, in favour of Mr. Leibniz* (London, 1744). There is a German translation of his long reply in Leibniz and Clarke, *Der Leibniz-Clarke Briefwechsel*, pp. 385–429.

54. Locke to Molineux, 10 April 1697, in J. Locke, *The Works of John Locke* (1823; reprint, Aarlen: Scientia Verlag, 1963), vol. 9, p. 407.

55. Leibniz also told Caroline that Locke "seemed to think that everything is corporeal, matter can think, and similar things which hiddenly destroy religion" (KLC 40). See also Leibniz's letter to Remond, 14 March 1714: GP III, 612. For the muddle surrounding Leibniz's abortive attemps at engaging Locke, see N. Jolley, *Leibniz and Locke: A Study of the "New Essays on Human Understanding"* (Oxford: Clarendon Press, 1984), chap. 3.

REFERENCES

Excludes works cited under "Abbreviations"

Adams, R. M. "Leibniz's Theories of Contingency." In *Leibniz: Critical and Interpretive Essays*, edited by M. Hooker, pp. 243–83. Minneapolis: University of Minnesota Press,1982.

———. *Leibniz: Determinist, Theist, Idealist*. New York: Oxford University Press, 1994.

Aiton, E. J. "Leibniz on Motion in a Resisting Medium." *Archive for History of Exact Sciences* 9 (1972): 257–76.

———. *The Vortex Theory of Planetary Motions*. London: MacDonald, 1972.

———. "The Mathematical Basis of Leibniz's Theory of Planetary Motion." In *Leibniz's Dynamica*, edited by A. Heinekamp, pp. 209–25. Studia Leibnitiana Supplementa 13. Wiesbaden: F. Steiner 1984.

———. *Leibniz: A Biography*. Bristol: Adam Hilger, 1985.

Al-Azm, S. *The Origins of Kant's Arguments in the Antinomies*. Oxford: Clarendon Press, 1972.

Allison, A. *Kant's Transcendental Idealism. An Interpretation and Defense*. New Haven: Yale University Press, 1983.

Ameriks, K. *Kant's Theory of Mind*. Oxford: Clarendon Press, 1982.

Anselm. *Monologion*. Bonn: Hanstein, 1929.

Aquinas, T. *Summa Contra Gentiles*. Turin: Marietti, 1961.

———. *Summa Theologiae*. New York: Mc Graw-Hill, 1970.

Ariew, R. "G. W. Leibniz, Life and Works." In *The Cambridge Companion to Leibniz*, edited by N. Jolley, pp. 18–42. Cambridge: Cambridge University Press, 1995.

Aristotle. *Aristotle: The Basic Works*. Edited by R. McKeon. New York: Random House, 1970.

Arnauld, A. *Oeuvres*. 1775–83. Reprint, Brussels: Culture et Civilization, 1967.

Arthur, R. T. W. "Leibniz's Theory of Time." In *The Natural Philosophy of Leibniz*, edited by K. Okruhlik and J.M. Brown, pp. 263–313. Dordrecht: Reidel Publishing, 1985.

———. "Space and Relativity in Newton and Leibniz." *British Journal for the Philosophy of Science* 45 (1994): 220–40.

Attfield, R. "Clarke, Collins and Compounds." *Journal of the History of Philosophy* 15 (1977): 45–54.

Augustine. *Liber de Praesentia Dei*. Vol. 33 of *Patrologia Latina*. Edited by J. P. Migne, letter 187. Paris, 1845.

———. *Confessions*. Translated by R. S. Pine-Coffin. Harmondsworth: Penguin Books, 1961.

———. *The City of God*. Translated by J. Healey. London: Dutton, 1973.

———. *The Essential Augustine*. Edited and translated by V. J. Bourke. Indianapolis: Hackett Publishing, 1981.

Ayers, M. R. "Mechanism, Superaddition, and the Proof of God's Existence in Locke's *Essay*." *Philosophical Review* 90 (1981): 210–51.

Babour, J. B. *Absolute or Relative Motion?* Cambridge: Cambridge University Press, 1989.

Barrow, I. *The Usefulness of Mathematical Learning explained and demonstrated*. 1734. Reprint, London: Cass, 1970.

Bayle, P. *Dictionnaire historique et critique*. Paris: Editions sociales, 1974.

Bennett, J. *A Study of Spinoza's Ethics*. Indianapolis: Hackett Publishing, 1985.

Berkeley, G. *Berkeley's Philosophical Writings*. Edited by D. M. Armstrong. New York: Collier Books, 1965.

Bernstein, H. R. "Passivity and Inertia in Leibniz's Dynamics." *Studia Leibnitiana* 13, no. 1 (1981): 97–113.

———. "Leibniz and Huygens on the 'Relativity' of Motion." In *Leibniz's Dynamica*, edited by A. Heinekamp, pp. 85–102. Studia Leibnitiana Supplementa 13. Wiesbaden: F. Steiner, 1984.

Bertoloni Meli, D. "Leibniz on the Censorship of the Copernican System." *Studia Leibniziana* 20, no. 1 (1988): 19–42.

———. *Equivalence and Priority: Newton versus Leibniz*. Oxford: Clarendon Press, 1993.

Bloch, O. R. *La Philosophie de Gassendi: nominalisme, materialisme, et metaphysique*. La Haye: M. Nijhoff, 1971.

Boethius, S. *The Consolation of Philosophy*. Translated by R. Green. Indianapolis: Bobs Merrill, 1962.

Bos, H. J. "Differentials, Higher Order Differentials and the Derivative in the Leibnizian Calculus." *Archive for History of Exact Sciences* 14 (1974): 1–90.

Boyle, R. *Works of the Honourable Robert Boyle.* Edited by T. Birch. 1744. Reprint, Hildesheim: Georg Olms, 1965.

Breger, H. "Das Kontinuum bei Leibniz." In *L'Infinito in Leibniz. Problemi e Terminologia.* Edited by A. Lamarra, pp. 53–67. Roma: Edizioni dell'Ateneo, 1986.

Bregman, R. "Leibniz and Atomism." *Nature and System* 6 (1984): 237–48.

Bricker, P., and R. I. G. Hughes, eds. *Philosophical Perspectives on Newtonian Science.* Cambridge, Mass.: MIT Press, 1990.

Broad, C. D. "Leibniz's Last Controversy with the Newtonians." In *Leibniz: Metaphysics and Philosophy of Science.* Edited by R. S. Woolhouse, pp. 157–74. Oxford: Oxford University Press, 1981.

Buchdal, G. *Metaphysics and the Philosophy of Science: The Classical Origins Descartes to Kant.* Oxford: Basil Blackwell, 1969.

Burns, R. M. *The Great Debate on Miracles: from Joseph Glanville to David Hume.* Lewisburg: Bucknell University Press, 1980.

Burtt, E. A. *Metaphysical Foundations of Modern Physical Science.* London: Routledge & Paul, 1972.

Butts, R. E., and J. W., Davis. eds. *The Methodological Heritage of Newton.* Toronto: University of Toronto Press, 1970.

Carriero, J. "Newton on Space and Time: Comments on J. E. Mc Guire." In *Philosophical Perspectives on Newtonian Science*, edited by P. Bricker and R. I. G. Hughes, pp.109–33. Cambridge, Mass: MIT Press, 1990.

Casini P. *L'universo-macchina: Origini della filosofia newtoniana.* Bari: Laterza, 1969.

Chisholm, R. M. "Human Freedom and the Self." In *Free Will*, edited by G. Watson, pp. 24–35. Oxford: Oxford University Press, 1982.

Clarke, S., trans. and ed. *Jacobi Rohaulti Physica; latine vertit, recensuit et uberioribus iam Annotationibus, ex illustrissimi Isaaci Newtoni Philosophia maximam partem haustis, amplificavit et oravit S. Clarke, S. T. P.* London, 1702.

Cohen, I. B. "Newton's Copy of Leibniz's *Theodicée*: With Some Remarks on the Turned-Down Pages of Books in Newton's Library." *Isis* 73 (1982): 410–14.

———. "Newton's Third Law and Universal Gravity." In *Newton's Scientific and Philosophical Legacy*, edited by P. B. Schurer and G. Debrock. Dordrecht: Kluwer Academic Publishers, 1988.

Colie, R. L. "Spinoza and the Early English Deists." *Journal of the History of Ideas* 20 (1959): 23–46.

Collins, A. *A Discourse on Free Thinking.* London, 1713.

———. *A Philosophical Inquiry concerning Human Liberty.* in *Determinism and Freewill: Anthony Collins' "A Philosophical Inquiry concerning Human Liberty".* Edited by J. O'Higgins. The Hague: M. Nijhoff, 1976.

Colman, J. *John Locke's Moral Philosophy.* Edinburgh: Edinburgh University Press, 1983.

Cover, J. A., and M. Kulstad, eds. *Central Themes in Early Modern Philosophy.* Indianapolis: Hackett Publishing, 1990.

Craig, E. *The Mind of God and the Works of Man.* Oxford: Clarendon Press, 1987.

Cudworth, R. *The True Intellectual System of the Universe.* 1678. Reprint, New York: Garland Publishing, 1978.

Delahunty, R. J. *Spinoza.* London: Routledge and Paul, 1985.

Descartes, R. *Oeuvres de Descartes.* Edited by C. Adam and P. Tannery. 1897–1913. Reprint, Paris: J. Vrin, 1964–76.

———. *Descartes: Philosophical Letters.* Edited and translated by A. Kenny. Oxford: Clarendon Press, 1970.

Des Maizeaux, *Recueil de diverses pièces . . . par Mrs. Leibniz, Clarke, Newton, & autre autheurs celèbres.* Amsterdam, 1720.

D'Holbach, P. H. *Systeme de la nature, ou des lois du monde physique et du monde moral.* 1821. Reprint, Hildsheim: Georg Olms, 1966.

Dibon, P., ed. *Pierre Bayle. Le Philosophe de Rotterdam.* Amsterdam: Elsevier, 1959.

Dobbs, B. J. T. "Newton's Alchemy and his 'Active Principle' of Gravitation." In *Newton's Scientific and Philosophical Legacy,* edited by P. B. Scheurer and G. Dobrock, pp. 55–80. Dordrecht: Kluwer Academic Publishers, 1988.

Ducharme, H. *The Moral Self, Moral Knowledge and God: An Analysis of the Theory of Samuel Clarke.* Ph.D. diss., Oriel College, Oxford, 1974.

———. "Personal Identity in Samuel Clarke." *Journal of the History of Philosophy.* 24 (1986): 359–83.

Earman, J., C. Glymour, and J. J. Stachel, eds. *Foundations of Space-Time Theories.* Minneapolis: University of Minnesota Press, 1977.

Earman, J. *World Enough and Space-Time.* Cambridge, Mass.: MIT Press, 1989.

Edwards, P. ed. *The Encyclopedia of Philosophy.* New York: Macmillan, 1967.

Euler, L. "Reflexions sur l'espace at le tems." *Mémoires de l'académie des sciences de Berlin* (1748): 324–33; reprinted in *Leonhardi Euleri Opera Omnia.* Leipzig and Berlin: Teubner, 1911, third series, vol. 2, pp. 376–83.

Ferguson, J. P. *The Philosophy of Dr. Samuel Clarke and Its Critics.* New York: Vantage Press, 1974.

———. *An Eighteenth Century Heretic. Dr. Samuel Clarke.* Kineton: Roundwood Press, 1976.

Forbes, G. "Time, Events and Modality." In *The Philosophy of Time,* edited by R. Le Poidevin and M. MacBeath, pp. 80–95. Oxford: Oxford University Press, 1993.

Force, J. E. *William Whiston: Honest Newtonian*. Cambridge: Cambridge University Press, 1985.

———. "Newton's God of Dominion: The Unity of Newton's Theological, Scientific, and Political Thought." In *Essays on the Context, Nature and Influence of Isaac Newton's Theology*, edited by J. E. Force and R. H. Popkin, pp. 75–102. Dordrecht: Kluwer Academic Publishers, 1990.

———. "Sir Isaac Newton, 'Gentleman of Wide Swallow'?" *Essays on the Context, Nature and Influence of Isaac Newton's Theology*, edited by J. E. Force and R. H. Popkin, pp. 119–41. Dordrecht: Kluwer Academic Publishers, 1990.

Force, J. E., and R. H. Popkin, eds. *Essays on the Context, Nature, and Influence of Isaac Newton's Theology*. Dordrecht: Kluwer Academic Publishers, 1990.

Funkenstein, A. *Theology and the Scientific Imagination*. Princeton: Princeton University Press, 1986.

Gabbey, A. "The Mechanical Philosophy and its Problems: Mechanical Explanations, Impenetrability, and Perpetual Motion." In *Change and Progress in Modern Science*, edited by J. C. Pitt, pp. 9–84. Dordrecht: D. Rerdel Publishing, 1985.

Garber, D. "Leibniz: Physics and Philosophy." In *The Cambridge Companion to Leibniz*, edited by N. Jolley, pp. 270–352. Cambridge: Cambridge University Press, 1995.

Gascoigne, J. *Cambridge in the Age of the Enlightenment*. Cambridge: Cambridge University Press, 1989.

Gassendi, P. *Opera Omnia in sex tomos*. 1658. Reprint, Stuttgart-Bad Canstatt: F. Fromann, 1964.

Gerhardt, C. I., ed. *Der Briefwechsel von G. W. Leibniz mit Mathematikern*. Berlin, 1899.

Giuntini, C. *Panteismo e Ideologia Repubblicana: John Toland (1670–1722)*. Bologna: Il Mulino, 1979.

Giusti, E. "Immagini del Continuo." In *L'Infinito in Leibniz. Problemi e Terminologia*, edited by A. Lamarra, pp. 3–32. Roma: Edizioni dell' Ateneo, 1986.

Grant, E. *Much Ado about Nothing: Theories of Space and Vacuum from the Middle Ages to the Scientific Revolution*. Cambridge: Cambridge University Press, 1981.

Green, V. H. H. *The Hanoverians: 1714–1815*. London: Edward Arnold, 1948.

Griffin, M. I. J. *Latitudinarianism in the Seventeenth-Century Church of England*. Leiden: E. J. Brill, 1992.

Grua, G. *Jurisprudence universelle et Theodicée selon Leibniz*. Paris: Presses Universitaires de France, 1953.

Guerlac, H. *Essays and Papers in the History of Modern Science*. Baltimore: John Hopkins University Press, 1977.

Gueroult, M. *Malebranche*. Paris: Aubier, 1955–59.

———. *Leibniz. Dynamique et Métaphysique*. Paris: Aubier-Montaigne, 1967.

Hacking, I. "Why Motion is only a well-founded Phenomenon." In *The Natural Philosophy of Leibniz*, edited by K. Okruhlik and J. R. Brown, pp. 131–50. Dordrecht: Kluwer Academic Presses, 1985.

Hall, R. *Philosophers at War: The Quarrel between Leibniz and Newton*. Cambridge: Cambridge University Press, 1980.

———. "Newton and the Absolutes: Sources." In *The Investigation of Difficult Things*, edited by P. M. Harman and A. E. Shapiro. Cambridge: Cambridge University Press, 1992.

———. *Issac Newton. Adventurer in Thought*. Cambridge: Cambridge University Press, 1996.

Harman, P. M. and A. E. Shapiro, eds. *The Investigation of Difficult Things*. Cambridge: Cambridge University Press, 1992.

Hartz, G. A. and J. A. Cover. "Space and Time in the Leibnizian Metaphysics." *Nous* 22 (1988): 493–519.

Hazard, P. *La Crise de la Conscience Européenne 1680–1715*. Paris: Gallimard, 1961.

Heinekamp, A., ed. *Leibniz's Dynamica*. Studia Leibnitiana Supplementa 13. Wiesbaden: F. Steiner, 1984.

Helm, P. *Eternal God: A Study of God Without Time*. Oxford: Clarendon Press, 1988.

Henry, J. "Occult Qualities and the Experimental Philosophy: Active Principles in Pre-Newtonian Matter Theory." *History of Science* 24 (1986): 335–81.

Hobbes, T. *English Works*. Edited by W. Molesworth. 1839. Reprint, Aalen: Scientia Verlag, 1966.

———. *Opera Philosophica quae Latine scripsit omnia*. Edited by W. Molesworth. 1845. Reprint, Aalen: Scientia Verlag, 1966.

———. *Leviathan*. Edited by C. B. Macpherson. New York: Penguin Books, 1968.

Horvath, M. "On the Attempts Made by Leibniz to Justify his Calculus." *Studia Leibnitiana* 18, no. 1 (1986): 60–71.

Hoskin, M. A. "Mining All Within: Clarke's Notes to Rohault's *Traité de Physique*." *The Thomist* 24 (1961): 253–63.

Hostler, J. *Leibniz's Moral Philosophy*. New York: Harper and Row, 1975.

Hume, D. *Enquiries Concerning Human Understanding and Concerning the Principles of Morals*. Edited by L. A. Selby-Bigge and P. H. Nidditch. Oxford: Clarendon Press, 1978.

Hunt, J. *Religious Thought in England from the Reformation to the End of last Century*. 1871. Reprint, New York: AMS Press, 1983.

Hunter, G. "The Fate of Thomas Hobbes." *Studia Leibnitiana* 21, no. 1 (1989): 5–20.

Huygens, C. *Oeuvres Complétes*. La Haye: M. Nijoff, 1888–1950.

Jacob, J. R. "Boyle's Atomism and the Restoration Assault on Pagan Naturalism." *Social Studies of Science* 8 (1978): 211–33.

Jacob, M. C. *The Newtonians and the English Revolution 1689–1720*. Ithaca: Cornell University Press, 1976.

Jalabert, J. *La theorie leibnizienne de la substance*. Paris: Presses Universitaires de France, 1947.

———. *Le Dieu de Leibniz*. Paris: Presses Universitaires de France, 1960.

Jolley, N. *Leibniz and Locke: A Study of the "New Essays on Human Understanding"*. Oxford: Clarendon Press, 1984.

———. *The Light of the Soul*. Oxford: Clarendon Press, 1990.

———, ed. *The Cambridge Companion to Leibniz*. Cambridge: Cambridge University Press, 1995.

Kenny, A. *The God of the Philosophers*. Oxford: Clarendon Press, 1979.

Kerzberg, P. "The Cosmological Question in Newton's Science." *Osiris* 2 (1986): 69–106.

Khamara, E. J. "Leibniz's Theory of Space: A Reconstruction." *The Philosophical Quarterly* 43 (1993): 472–88.

Kirk, G. S., and J. E. Raven. *The Presocratic Philosophers*. Cambridge: Cambridge University Press, 1983.

Koyré, A. *From the Closed World to the Infinite Universe*. Baltimore: Johns Hopkins University Press, 1957.

———. *Newtonian Studies*. Cambridge, Mass.: MIT Press, 1965.

Koyré, A., and I. B. Cohen. "The Case of the Missing *Tanquam*: Leibniz, Newton & Clarke." *Isis* 52 (1961): 555–66.

———. "Newton & the Leibniz-Clarke Correspondence." *Archives Internationales d'Histoire des Sciences* 15 (1962): 63–126.

Kubrin, D. "Newton and the Cyclical Cosmos: Providence and the Mechanical Philosophy." *Journal of the History of Ideas* 28 (1967): 325–46.

Kulstad, M. "Two Arguments on *Petites* Perceptions." In *Essays in the Philosophy of Leibniz*, edited by M. Kulstad. Rice University Studies in Philosophy, 63. Houston, Tex.: Rice University, 1977.

Lamarra, A., ed. *L'Infinito in Leibniz: Problemi e Terminologia*. Roma: Edizioni dell' Ateneo, 1986.

———. "Leibniz on Locke on Infinity." In *L'Infinito in Leibniz. Problemi e Terminologia*, edited by A. Lamarra, pp. 173–92. Roma: Edizioni dell' Ateneo, 1986.

Laymon, R. "Newton's Bucket Experiment." *Journal of the History of Philosophy* 16 (1978): 399–413.

Le Clerc, J., ed. *Bibliotheque Choisie*. Amsterdam, 1687–.

Leibniz, G. W. *Philosophical Essays*. Edited and translated by G. W. Ariew and D. Garber. Indianapolis: Hackett Publishing Company, 1989.

———. *G. W. Leibniz: De Summa Rerum*. Edited and translated by H. R. Parkinson. New Haven: Yale University Press, 1992.

Leibniz, G. W. and S. Clarke. *The Leibniz-Clarke Correspondence: With Extracts from Newton's "Principia" and "Opticks."* Edited by H. G. Alexander. Manchester: Manchester University Press, 1956.

———. *Der Leibniz-Clarke Briefwechsel.* Edited and translated by V. Schüller. Berlin: Akademie Verlag, 1991.

Le Poidevin R. "Relationism and Temporal Topology: Physics or Metaphysics?" In *The Philosophy of Time*, edited by R. Le Poidevin and M. MacBeath, pp. 149–67. Oxford: Oxford University Press, 1993.

Le Poidevin, R., and M. MacBeath, eds. *The Philosophy of Time.* Oxford: Oxford University Press, 1993.

Le Rossignol, J. E. *The Ethical Philosophy of Samuel Clarke.* Leipzig, 1892.

Locke, J. *The Works of John Locke.* 1823. Reprint, Aarlen: Scientia Verlag, 1963.

———. *An Essay concerning Human Understanding.* Edited by P. H. Nidditch. Oxford: Clarendon Press, 1979.

Loemker, L. E. *Struggle for Synthesis: The Seventeenth Century Background of Leibniz's Synthesis of Order and Freedom.* Cambridge, Mass: Harvard University Press, 1972.

Machamer, P. K., and R. G. Turnbull, eds. *Motion and Time, Space and Matter.* Columbus: Ohio State University Press, 1976.

Mackie, J. L. *The Miracle of Theism.* Oxford: Clarendon Press, 1982.

Maclaurin, C. *An Account of Sir Isaac Newton's Philosophical Discoveries.* London, 1748.

Malebranche, N. *Oeuvres complètes.* Edited by A. Robinet. Paris: J. Vrin, 1958–60.

———. *Dialogues on Metaphysics.* Translated by W. Doney. New York: Abaris Books, 1980.

———. *The Search after Truth.* Translated by T. M. Lennon and J. Olscamp. Columbus: Ohio State University Press, 1980.

Mancosu, P. *Philosophy of Mathematics and Mathematical Practice in the Seventeenth Century.* New York: Oxford University Press, 1996.

Manuel, F. E. *The Religion of Isaac Newton.* Oxford: Clarendon Press, 1974.

Mates, B. *The Philosophy of Leibniz: Metaphysics and Language.* Oxford: Oxford University Press, 1986.

McCracken, C. J. *Malebranche and British Philosophy.* Oxford: Oxford University Press, 1983.

McDonald Ross, G. "Are There Real Infinitesimals in Leibniz's Metaphysics?" In *L'Infinito in Leibniz. Problemi e Terminologia.* edited by A. Lamarra, pp.125–41. Roma: Edizioni dell'Ateneo, 1986.

McGuire, J. E. "Force, Active Principles, and Newton's Invisible Realm." *Ambix* 15 (1968): 154–208.

———. "Atoms and the Analogy of Nature: Newton's Third Rule of Philosophizing." *Studies in History and Philosophy of Science* 1 (1970): 3–58.

———. "Labirinthus Continui: Leibniz on Substance, Activity, and Matter."

In *Motion and Time, Space and Matter*, edited by P. K. Machamer and R. G. Turnbull, pp. 290–326. Columbus: Ohio State University Press, 1976.

———. "Existence, Actuality and Necessity: Newton on Space and Time." *Annals of Science* 35 (1978): 463–508.

———. "Newton on Place, Time, and God: An Unpublished Source." *British Journal for the History of Science* 11 (1978): 114–29.

———. "Predicates of Pure Existence: Newton on God's Space and Time." In *Philosophical Perspectives on Newtonian Science*, edited by P. Bricker and R. I. G. Hughes, pp. 92–108. Cambridge, Mass: MIT Press, 1990.

McMullin, E. *Newton on Matter and Activity*. Notre Dame: University of Notre Dame Press, 1978.

McRae, R. "Time and the Monad." *Nature and System* 1 (1979): 103–9.

———. "Miracles and Laws." In *The Natural Philosophy of Leibniz*, edited by K. Okruhlik and J. B. Brown, pp. 171–81. Dordrecht: Reidel Publishing, 1985.

Mendelsohn, E. *Transformation and Tradition in the Sciences*. Cambridge: Cambridge University Press, 1984.

Merchant, C. *The Death of Nature*. San Francisco: Harper and Row, 1980.

Mijuskovic, B. L. *The Achilles of Rationalist Arguments*. The Hague: M. Nijhoff, 1974.

More, H. *Opera Omnia*. 1674–79. Reprint, Hildesheim: G. Olms, 1966.

Nadler, S., ed. *Causation in Early Modern Philosophy*. University Park: Pennsylvania State University Press, 1993.

Newton, I. *Unpublished Scientific Papers of Isaac Newton*. Edited and translated by A. R. Hall and M. B. Hall. Cambridge: Cambridge University Press, 1962.

———. *Correspondence of Sir Isaac Newton and Professor Cotes*. Edited by J. Edleston. 1850. Reprint, London: F. Cass, 1969.

———. *The Mathematical Papers of Isaac Newton*. Edited by D. T. Whiteside. Cambridge: Cambridge University Press, 1974.

Nussbaum, M., ed. *Logic, Science and Dialectic*. Ithaca: Cornell University Press, 1986.

Oakley, F. *Omnipotence, Covenant and Order*. Ithaca: Cornell University Press, 1984.

Okruhlik, K., and J. R. Brown, eds. *The Natural Philosophy of Leibniz*. Dordrecht: D. Reidel Publishing, 1985.

O'Neill, E. "Influxus Physicus." In *Causation in Early Modern Philosophy*, edited by S. Nadler, pp. 27–56. University Park: Pennsylvania State University Press, 1993.

Owen, G. E. L. "Aristotle on Time." In *Logic, Science and Dialectic*. Edited by M. Nussbaum, pp. 295–314. Ithaca: Cornell University Press, 1986.

Pacchi, A. *Cartesio in Inghilterra da More a Boyle*. Bari: Laterza, 1973.

Papineau, D. "The *Vis Viva* Controversy." In *Leibniz: Metaphysics and Philosophy of Science*, edited by R. S. Woolhouse, pp. 139–56. Oxford: Oxford University Press, 1981.

Parkinson, G.H.R. "Science and Metaphysics in the Leibniz-Newton Controversy." In Studia Leibnitiana Supplementa 2 pp. 79–112. Wiesbaden: F. Steiner, 1969.

———. *Leibniz on Human Freedom*. Studia Leibnitiana Supplementa. 2. Wiesbaden: F. Steiner, 1970.

Pike, N. *God and Timelessness*. London: Routledge and Paul, 1970.

Pitt, J. C., ed. *Change and Progress in Modern Science*. Dordrecht: D. Reidel Publishing, 1985.

Radner, D. *Malebranche*. Assen: Van Gorcum, 1978.

———. "Is There a Problem of Cartesian Interaction?" *Journal of the History of Philosophy* 23 (1985): 35–49.

Rescher, N. "Choice without Preference: A Study of the History and the Logic of the Problem of Buridan's Ass." In *Essays in Philosophical Analysis*, edited by N. Rescher, pp. 111–57. Pittsburg: University of Pittsburgh Press, 1969.

———. *Leibniz's Metaphysics of Nature*. Dordrecht: D. Reidel Publishing, 1981.

Rogers, G.A.J., ed. *Locke's Philosophy: Content and Context*. Oxford: Oxford University Press, 1994.

Rowe, W. L. *The Cosmological Argument*. Princeton: Princeton University Press, 1975.

———. "Causality and Free Will in the Controversy Between Collins and Clarke." *The Journal of the History of Philosophy* 25 (1987): 51–67.

Russell, B. *A Critical Exposition of the Philosophy of Leibniz*. London: Allen & Unwin, 1937.

———. *The Principles of Mathematics*. 1903. Reprint, New York: Norton, 1938.

Rutherford, D. "Natures, Laws and Miracles: the Roots of Leibniz's Critique of Occasionalism." In *Causation in Early Modern Philosophy*, edited by S. Nadler, pp. 135–58. University Park: Pennsylvania State University Press, 1993.

———. *Leibniz and the Rational Order of Nature*. Cambridge: Cambridge University Press, 1995.

Scheurer, P. B., and G. Dobrock, eds. *Newton's Scientific and Philosophical Legacy*. Dordrecht: D. Reidel Publishing, 1988.

Schmidt, F. "Ganzes und Teil bei Leibniz." *Archiv für Geschichte der Philosophie* 53 (1971): 267–78.

Scott, W. *The Conflict between Atomism and Conservation Theory 1644–1860*. London: MacDonald and Co., 1970.

Shapin, S. "Of Gods and Kings: Natural Philosophy and Politics in the Leibniz-Clarke Disputes." *Isis* 72 (1981): 187–215.

Sleigh, R. C. "Leibniz on Malebranche on Causality." In *Central Themes in*

Early Modern Philosophy, edited by J. A. Cover and M. Kulstad, pp. 161–93. Indianapolis: Hackett Publishing, 1990.

———. *Leibniz and Arnauld: A Commentary on their Correspondence.* New Haven: Yale University Press, 1990.

Sorabji, R. *Time, Creation and the Continuum.* Ithaca: Cornell University Press, 1983.

———. *Matter, Space, and Motion: Theories in Antiquity and Their Sequel.* Ithaca: Cornell University Press, 1988.

Spinoza, B. *Opera.* Edited by C. Gebhardt. Heidelberg: C. Winters, 1925.

Stein, H. "Some Philosophical Prehistory of General Relativity." In *Foundations of Space-Time Theories,* edited by J. Earman, C. Glymour, and J. J. Stachel, pp. 3–49. Minneapolis: University Of Minnesota Press, 1977.

Stephen L. *History of English Thought in the Eighteenth Century.* 3d ed. 1902. Reprint, Bristol: Thoemmes, 1991.

Stephen, L., and S. Lee, eds. *Dictionary of National Biography.* 1882. Reprint, London: Oxford University Press, 1949–50.

Stewart, L. "Samuel Clarke, Newtonianism and the Factions of post-revolutionary England." *Journal of the History of Ideas* 42 (1981): 53–71.

Suarez, F. *Disputationes Metaphysicae.* 1597. Reprint, Hildesheim: G. Olms, 1965.

Swinburne, R. *The Coherence of Theism.* Oxford: Clarendon Press, 1977.

———. "Tensed Facts." *American Philosophical Quarterly* 27 (1990): 117–30.

Sylla, E. "Compounding Ratios. Bradwardine, Oresme, and the First Edition of Newton's *Principia.*" In *Transformation and Tradition in the Sciences,* edited by E. Mendelsohn, pp. 11–43. Cambridge: Cambridge University Press, 1984.

Teeter Dobbs, B. J. and M. C. Jacob. *Newton and the Culture of Newtonianism.* Atlantic Highlands: Humanities Press International, 1995.

Toland, J. *Letters to Serena.* 1704. Reprint, Stuttgart-Bad Cannstatt: F. Fromann, 1964.

Vailati E. "Leibniz on Locke on Weakness of the Will." *Journal of the History of Philosophy* 28 (1990): 213–28.

Vartanian, A. *Diderot and Descartes: A Study of Scientific Naturalism in the Enlightenment.* Princeton: Princeton University Press, 1953.

Voltaire, M. A. *Voltaire's Philosophical Letters.* Edited and translated by E. Dilworth. Indianapolis: Bobs Merrill, 1961.

———. *The Elements of Sir Isaac Newton's Philosophy.* Translated by J. Hanna. 1738. Reprint, London: Cass, 1967.

Westfall, R. S. *Force in Newton's Physics.* London: MacDonald and Co., 1971.

———. *Never at Rest: A Biography of Isaac Newton.* Cambridge: Cambridge University Press, 1980.

————. "The Problem of Force: Huygens, Newton, Leibniz." In *Leibniz's Dynamica*, edited by A. Heinekamp. Studia Leibnitiana Supplementa 13. Wiesbaden: F. Steiner, 1984.

Whiston, W. *Historical Memoirs of the Life of Dr. Samuel Clarke*. London, 1730.

Whitmore, J. S. "Bayle's Criticism of Locke." In *Pierre Bayle: Le Philosophe de Rotterdam*, edited by A. Dibon, pp. 81–97. Amsterdam: Elsevier, 1959.

Wilson, C. "Leibniz and Atomism." *Studies in History and Philosophy of Science* 13 (1982): 175–99.

————. "*De Ipsa Natura*. Sources of Leibniz's Doctrines of Force, Activity and Natural Law." *Studia Leibnitiana* 19, no. 2 (1987): 148–72.

————. *Leibniz's Metaphysiscs: A Historical and Comparative Study*. Princeton: Princeton Univeristy Press, 1989.

Winterbourne, A. T. "On the Metaphysics of Leibnizian Space and Time." *Studies in History and Philosophy of Science* 13 (1982): 201–14.

Wolfson, H. A. *The Philosophy of Spinoza*. New York: Meridian Books, 1960.

Woolhouse R. S., ed. *Leibniz: Metaphysics and Philosophy of Science*. Oxford: Oxford University Press, 1981.

————. "Leibniz's Reaction to Cartesian Interactionism." *Proceedings of the Aristotelian Society* 86 (1985–86): 69–82.

————, ed. *Metaphysics and Philosophy of Science in the Seventeenth and Eighteenth Centuries*. Dordrecht: Kluwer Academic Press, 1988.

————. "Leibniz and Occasionalism." In *Metaphysics and Philosophy of Science in the Seventeenth and Eighteenth Centuries*. Edited by R. Woolhouse, pp. 165–83. Dordrecht: Kluwer Academic Press, 1988.

————. *Descartes, Spinoza and Leibniz: The Concept of Substance in Seventeenth Century Metaphysics*. London: Routledge, 1993.

Yolton, J. W. *Thinking Matter: Materialism in Eigtheenth Century Britain*. Minneapolis: University of Minnesota Press, 1983.

Zilsel, E. "The Genesis of the Concept of Physical Law." *The Philosophical Review*. 51 (1942): 245–79.

INDEX